Advance Praise for *Winning the Story Wars*

"You may think you know how important stories are to the success of your enterprise—but *Winning the Story Wars* will take your understanding to a whole new level. A crucial book in our media-saturated world."

— Robert Hanson, CEO, American Eagle Outfitters;
former Global President, Levi's

"If the idea of a marketing book based on the mythological explorations of Joseph Campbell strikes you as an oxymoron, welcome to the club. Yet *Winning the Story Wars* proves to be a provocative look at the power of marketing to help us all along the hero's journey toward a better world."

— Tim O'Reilly, founder and CEO, O'Reilly Media

"Jonah Sachs powerfully illustrates just how broken and dysfunctional our current model of storytelling has become. We need to reconnect the vital link between higher purpose and effective story, and *Winning the Story Wars* shows us how."

— John Gerzema, Executive Chairman, BrandAsset Consulting;
coauthor, *The Brand Bubble*

"Using stories as his medium, Sachs demystifies the art of storytelling. He illuminates the transformational social change that is possible if we, as individuals and marketers, tell stories that engage and empower everyone to design a better future."

— Lynelle Cameron, Director of Sustainability, Autodesk

"Jonah Sachs has a gift for telling positive stories that go viral. He sat down to figure out why his best work has such resonance, then broke the answers into simple, inspiring steps. The result is a how-to book for communicators who want to change the world."

— Fred Krupp, President, Environmental Defense Fund

WINNING THE

STORY
WARS

WINNING THE

STORY
WARS

Why Those Who Tell—and Live—
the Best Stories Will Rule the Future

JONAH SACHS

HARVARD BUSINESS REVIEW PRESS
Boston, Massachusetts

Library of Congress Cataloging-in-Publication Data

Sachs, Jonah.
    Winning the story wars : why those who tell—and live—the best stories will
rule the future / Jonah Sachs.
      p. cm.
  ISBN 978-1-4221-4356-8 (alk. paper)
  1. Marketing—Social aspects. 2. Storytelling—Psychological aspects.
3. Consumers—Psychology. 4. Social media. I. Title.
  HF5415.S223 2012
  658.8'02—dc23
                                          2011053284

To

Mira and Orion

the stars that now guide me

CONTENTS

CONTENTS

Prologue

A few minutes after I got home from the audition, my phone rang. I made a silent wish that it would be the director. It was.

"Jonah?"

"Yes?" I replied, trying to sound as if my nascent hopes for a career in front of the camera weren't trembling on his whim.

"Good news. I think you're right for the part. But there is one thing. "

"OK . . . "

"We're not going to use your voice—you'll be dubbed. I like the way you did the lines and you look perfect, but you sounded a little too, uh, squeaky."

"Squeaky?" I felt the excitement drain out of me.

"Look, Darth Vader is supposed to be the scariest guy in the galaxy. You're just not that scary."

I was in little position to argue. At nine years old, Louis Fox was a year older than me. He was the one with the camera, the mimeographed *Star Wars* script, and the mother willing to drive us on

1

endless location scouts. It was his idea to remake *Star Wars*, shot for shot. I was just a third-grader with a high-pitched voice.

"OK," I squeaked. "I'll do it."

The project, not surprisingly, took a while to get off the ground. Louis and I spent the first summer poring over catalogs filled with masks we could not afford, checking out dirt patches that failed to meet even our low standards for an extraterrestrial desert, and unsuccessfully trying to convince his bookish sister to play Princess Leia.

In fact, for twenty years, the project was on hold. But in 2005, we finally launched our own version of *Star Wars* on the Internet. Within a year, it would get more than 20 million views, be screened at film festivals around the world, and earn us a fan letter from Lucasfilm. And, just as he'd always planned it, Louis got to do the voice of Darth Vader. Only it wasn't me that he was dubbing over, it was a Russet potato playing the part of the Dark Lord.

Our movie had morphed considerably over the years from a two-hour retelling of the classic sci-fi fantasy into a five-minute advertisement for organic food. We called it *Grocery Store Wars* and it starred a complete cast of bad puns—Cuke Skywalker, Chew-broccoli, and of course, the infamous Darth Tater. Not exactly what we'd had in mind, but it was hard to argue with the results.

That disappointing phone call of two decades past was on my mind as I paced the hotel room, trying desperately to turn the presentation I had prepared into something coherent. I was about to give a lecture to five hundred eager marketing professionals looking for clues as to why *Store Wars*, and its equally popular predecessor *The Meatrix*, an exploration of the evils of industrial meat farming, had been so successful. These short spoof pieces were an experimental mix between entertainment and advertisement, and they had gotten the Internet to deliver on its promise of explosive results for very little money. Everyone knew that free distribution and easy sharing had torn down the barriers to the media marketplace. You didn't need to buy a spot on TV or rent a billboard to reach millions anymore. In those days, just before YouTube, everyone was trying to figure out how to use video to go from zero to world-famous in sixty seconds. And we had done it. We had created a piece of Internet history—twice. And I had absolutely no idea how.

I pictured myself on the ballroom stage, my movies projected behind me. At twenty-nine, I figured I looked about right for the part of young online marketing guru. And then I'd open my mouth and the words that would come out would make me sound just as I had at eight.

"Our ads work because they're funny." Squeak. "They work because they're spoofs of movies people really like." Squeak, squeak. "They're not too long?"

I had always done my work on feel, following my gut to whatever excited me creatively. I paid little attention to research or process—or to reflection, for that matter. This way of working had served me well. Louis and I had built a successful national creative firm focused on social change. We'd done a number of notably successful projects that pushed forward the causes of human rights, environmental protection, and socially responsible business. We just had no idea why some of our projects had become cultural phenomena while others just fizzled. And I hadn't bothered to try to figure it out before I agreed to this talk. I had just followed my gut to the edge of a cliff.

I was hit with a wave of regret that every creative person I know encounters regularly. It's the feeling of being a fraud—a vehicle for occasional, random, and unrepeatable success. To make matters worse, I felt I had stumbled onto the wrong stage. I had never identified myself as a marketer or intended to be one. Instead, I saw myself as a creative person with a passion for ideas—ideas I wanted to share to help make the world a better place. I had not yet realized that today's media landscape of unprecedented competition between messages has made us all marketers. Anyone who wants influence now—whether it's to push forward a social cause, to sell products, or simply to change the way people think—has no choice but to step into our global media marketplace and embrace this unlikely new job title. I embrace it now, but I hadn't then.

I needed to find my bearings—and fast.

It was in that sorry state that I googled both *The Matrix* and *Star Wars*—the two films on which my successes had been based—to see what, if anything, they had in common, hoping for some clue as to why they were so powerful that even spoofs created years after their theatrical releases could capture the imagination and compel the actions of millions.

That one search changed everything. It was the tornado that swept me up out of my black-and-white world of communications and deposited me into a Technicolor realm of endless possibilities for breakthrough, crushing my Wicked Witch of self-doubt in the process.

What I discovered was that both films had been written, intentionally, to reflect ancient mythological formulas. These stories were merely recent adaptations of stories that have persisted in the human consciousness for millennia.

Okay. I discovered something that an awful lot of people already knew. The fact that George Lucas read the work of Joseph Campbell, a giant in the field of comparative mythology, to combat writer's block while he worked on his script is a familiar bit of film lore. And *The Matrix*'s Wachowski brothers had followed Campbell's *hero's journey* formula to a tee. But while film critics, scholars, and storytelling enthusiasts had been well aware of the influence of myth-based narratives on cultural meaning making, I had been in the dark.

I followed my search through weird sci-fi fan sites, scholarly texts, and ancient sources themselves where I began to grasp what myth experts had postulated: *human beings share stories to remind each other of who they are and how they should act.* These tales are deeply ingrained in our DNA, and no matter where or when you were born, certain patterns of stories will influence you enormously. When we hear stories based on these patterns, we feel more like we're remembering something forgotten than learning something new.

The stories that work tend to be about reluctant or unlikely heroes (think Dorothy, Frodo, or Rosa Parks) lured into a dangerous quest of self-discovery. Hearing these stories excites and entertains us on a conscious level but also subtly influences our very conception of what is possible in our real lives, because each of us is a hero in our own personal myth. Just as a child looks to her parents to learn to negotiate her new world, adults look to myths for guidance in their much more complex lives.

I thought back to those days in the mid-1980s, when Louis and I felt such a deep need to help defeat the dark side of the force that we had devoted ourselves to re-creating the world of Jedis in our yards in upstate New York. I went back even earlier, to the first time I heard the story of Lucy entering the enchanted wardrobe that led to the troubled land of Narnia and how, as a six-year-old, I had come to understand that one day I'd have to leave the safety of my parents' home to try to do something to help make the world a better place. I then fast-forwarded to the creative sessions in which we thought of *The Meatrix*, and how perfect the metaphor was that we borrowed, along with its name, from *The Matrix*: it was undeniably true that some social ills—in the case of our project, factory farming—were so horrific that only a massive cultural trance could hide them.

Each of these stories is about something larger than a hero kicking ass and grabbing treasure. They are stories of social change, of the victory of humanity over tyranny, of the natural world over soulless machines, of people restoring ethics to a corrupt society. Human rights, environmentalism, corporate ethics—these were the very same battles that I, as a socially minded advertiser, was in the game to help fight.

So many of the stories that have really stuck, that have shaped culture, are about one thing: people reaching for their highest potential and struggling to create a better world. If the test of time is our judge, stories with this formula have a near-monopoly on greatness.

It turns out that a small group of storytellers have known or at least sensed this all along, building wildly successful brands, entertainment, and political messages that burst through the media din and become legendary by understanding the formula. They are practicing an art that has evolved into a quiet but powerful coun-terforce to the much-decried practice of influencing audiences through fear and insecurity that dominates our media market-place. These storytellers are creating a practice of marketing that can be a powerful force for good. Without knowing it, I had become one of them.

That day in the hotel, with only the barest hints of what I would discover later, I was able to begin explaining my storytelling suc-cesses. I stopped reading with the intense feeling that I was remem-bering something long forgotten but incredibly familiar. I pulled up my PowerPoint presentation and erased all my gropings and half-formed explanations. I created a blank slide and placed a red pill on it—you know, the kind offered to Neo in *The Matrix* to show him the real world. And then for that audience waiting down-stairs, I improvised a version of the gospel I've been spreading ever since. It goes something like this:

We live in a world that has lost its connection to its traditional myths, and we are now trying to find new ones—we're people, and that's what people without myths do.

These myths will shape our future, how we live, what we do, and what we buy. They will touch all of us. But not all of us get to write them. Those who do have tremendous power.

And where there is power, there is struggle for it. That's why, just below the surface, just beyond what the uninitiated can see, there are wars going on. The soldiers are Tea Party demonstrators and champions of "the 99 percent," climate change activists, makers of computers and sneaker brands. They seem to be fighting over ideas and dollars but they are really fighting for control of our stories. The best of them, those who know this and can convince us that their story is true, are blowing everyone else to smithereens.

These are the story wars and this is your invitation to be part of them. Understanding the story wars can make you a more effective communicator and a savvier media consumer.

*But that's not the only reason I want to enlist you. I want you to
be part of the story wars because our world is badly in need of
solutions in so many spheres—economic, social, and
environmental to name just a few. The ability to dream up and
spread these solutions lives or dies on the ability to tell great
stories that inspire people to think differently. Nothing is more
urgent than that right now.*

The book you are about to read is, in part, my journey to understand the patterns of my own successes and those of other iconic communications campaigns over the past several millennia. It has challenged me to learn lessons from both cutting-edge social media efforts and our marketing and cultural past. Throughout, I will offer you the formulas and patterns I've discovered to craft a story strategy for future breakthroughs. But formulas are helpful only when they stimulate rather than stifle creativity and instinct. If you expect to find in these pages cookie-cutter solutions to storytelling success or saving the world, you will be disappointed. Instead, *Winning the Story Wars* will offer insight and understanding, as well as tools to guide you, help you push past obstacles, and take courage as you set out on your own unique hero's journey to be heard. It is in this spirit that I invite you to join me on this adventure.

Part 1, "The Broken World of Storytelling," confronts the legacy of the *broadcast era*, which defined our media marketplace for over a century and stunted our storytelling landscape. Chapter 1 explores today's media landscape in which that broadcast era is giving way to something fundamentally new and yet surprisingly ancient in its character. Chapter 2 is a clear-eyed look at the common, unquestioned language of marketing that sabotages the stories we try to tell. Our path forward begins by recognizing what holds us back. Chapter 3 looks at a global society in need of new myths and a tradition of marketers filling that need as today's modern mythmakers. In chapter 4, we'll see how that role has been abused, uncovering the carefully crafted roots of the *inadequacy approach* that plays on fear, greed, and vanity to move minds and messages. This approach, once heralded by psychologists and political leaders as the most effective way to ensure a peaceful world, has led to a global society in the throes of ecological, economic, and even spiritual crisis. The old stories aren't working for marketers or for society.

Part 2, "Shaping the Future," lays out a clear path to solutions. This path will not lead us simply to create superficial story façades to slap onto our next marketing campaign. It goes much deeper than that, demanding that we question our core brand strategies and even the operations of our enterprises. With a well-designed story strategy in hand, we can then deploy timeless storytelling techniques to grab and hold audience attention and loyalty.

The solution we'll explore is a simple formula that anyone can use to craft a story strategy for a company or cause. It's derived from the wisdom storytellers have employed since the beginning of time but now appears long forgotten. For those who seek to rediscover it, this wisdom has been preserved in the "three commandments" laid out in 1895 by marketing's first great storyteller, John Powers: *Tell the Truth*, *Be Interesting*, and *Live the Truth*. Updated for our era, these commandments can guide us to tell stories that get noticed, create emotional affinity, and maintain credibility in a short-attention-span, meaning-starved, highly transparent world.

In chapters 5 and 6, we'll look at the common structure of successful myths as a first step to building a coherent story strategy. Myths have always told key truths in a particular language. They point to core values, create a clear moral of the story, generate a compelling pantheon of characters, and call on audiences to act in pursuit of their own highest potential. In chapter 7, we'll dive into the workings of the human brain to craft a model of storytelling that grabs attention and holds it in a world of rapidly diminishing attention spans. Finally, chapter 8 explores the perils and opportunities of telling great stories. Iconic stories create iconic expectations and, in our new era of profound transparency, brands must actually live out the stories they tell and apply the moral of their story not just to their audiences but to themselves. The pressure to live up to your story can also be seen as a transformational, positive force. It casts you, the marketer, in the role of innovation agent within your organization—the stories your brand tells can be a powerful force in leading your company to more responsible real-world behavior. It's a virtuous cycle that marketers can drive, shaping better companies and a better world.

Before I bring you any deeper into the fascinating landscape of the story wars, I should warn you that the story wars themselves are a myth. Like all myths that have come before, this one doesn't provide an unfiltered survey of the facts on the ground. Instead, the myth of the story wars organizes the realities of the chaotic and rapidly changing world we communicators face into something meaningful and understandable—a world that we can approach with confidence rather than fear or despair. This has always been the role of myth in uncertain times, and we need a good one now more than ever.

Now, one final note about you: though I refer to you, and to myself, as a marketer throughout the book, I hope this story will address you as a human being as well. Stories have always been powerful not just in shaping society, but in shaping individual lives. After all, we are each the heroes of our own life's journey, playing out what psychologists call our own personal myth. In reconsidering how we fight the story wars, I believe we marketers, those of us who professionally seek to influence others, have an important role to play in changing a media landscape that has done great damage to people and to our planet. *Winning the Story Wars* is an invitation for you to step into the role of hero and to play a part in the fight for a better future—finding deeper meaning and satisfaction in your own life story as a result.

PART ONE

The Broken World of Storytelling

CHAPTER ONE

The Story Wars Are All Around Us

The moment you open your mouth, your words risk being washed away in a flood of noise and clamor. Thirty-five hundred commercial messages are blasted at each info-addled American daily, and media markets all over the world are on pace to catch up. Inboxes are jammed with requests for orders, donations—any response at all. Recipients can't wait to delete you.

Empowered by social media tools and on-demand viewing, the public can choose to skewer, ridicule, or ignore our messages or, on a whim, send them directly to our most desired audiences—a privilege marketers once paid millions for. The familiar world of the *broadcast era*—in which the anointed few could purchase attention off of a rate card—is rapidly approaching its death. This is the battlefield of ideas marketers must now face—a free-for-all in which most messages struggle valiantly for their moment in the sun only to be dragged back down into the melee and crushed.

The battle over the meaning of America: Glenn Beck and Annie Leonard

Brad Jakeman, the former advertising chief at Macy's and Citigroup, sums up the common frustration of today's marketer: "The irony is that while there have never been more ways to reach consumers, it's never been harder to connect with consumers."

For those of us who want to be heard, the old paths that we have reflexively followed are disappearing fast. For many it's a terrifying experience—and fears are well founded. The average tenure for today's chief marketing officer is a minuscule twenty-two months. Crowdsource creative shops offer logos, branding, and campaigns overnight for peanuts, openly challenging the notion that professionals have any place at all in tomorrow's marketing landscape. Online ad firms tout algorithms and brain-scan technologies that promise to cut the need for creativity out of the equation altogether. Still, neither the old models nor the new ones vying to replace them consistently offer the channels to our audiences we so desire.

Under all this pressure, we must begin each effort staring into a deep chasm. On one side is the reality that audiences are more skeptical and resistant than at any time in history. On the other is the fact that these same audiences, when inspired, are willing and able to spread their favorite messages, creating a massive viral effect for those who win their love. We are expected to create communications that leap across this abyss, though any formula for doing so seems elusive at best. The nature of audience-powered success is that it can't be simply imitated and it can't be bought. Crossing the chasm demands the seemingly impossible of marketers—to be constantly fresh and original and to earn our place in the minds of those we wish to influence.

This is a book about crossing that chasm with the only strategic approach that has ever really worked—telling great stories.

The Rise of the Digitoral Era

After a hundred years of thinking in the broadcast model, in which marketing was assumed to be, at best, a tolerable intrusion into the content audiences really wanted, adaptation is painful.

These days, ad-industry magazines are full of articles about top marketers getting out of the business altogether. Yes, it's a time of great peril. But it's also one of amazing opportunity. Marketing now has the chance to be something far more than an intrusion into people's lives. We just have a lot of bad habits to break to get there.

As marketers, whether we're out to sell products or ideas, we have inherited the practices of an industry spoiled by TV, well-worn PR channels, and other paid media outlets that have lulled us into a creative stupor and dominated marketing for the last hundred years. That broadcast model is now dramatically withering into oblivion. And even though we're all aware that a shift to peer-to-peer, social media is under way—and unstoppable—few have even begun to grasp what it means.

Here's what I think it means: the *oral tradition* that dominated human experience for all but the last few hundred years is returning with a vengeance. It's a monumental, epoch-making, totally unforeseen turn of events.

How can this possibly be? The *oral* tradition? With multimedia texts and IMs and Facebook status updates, aren't we relying on oral communication far less than ever? Yes, of course. But our new digital culture of information sharing has so rejected the broadcast style and embraced key elements of oral traditions, that we might meaningfully call whatever's coming next the *digitoral era*. And while this new age will undoubtedly contain elements of both traditions—which we will explore momentarily—the digitoral era borrows much more from oral traditions than broadcast.

The Broadcast Tradition

When I say the *broadcast tradition,* I'm talking about everything from television back to radio back to the first bible printed on Gutenberg's press in the 1450s. In this model, information begins life in the mind of its creator but quickly makes the jump into a machine that relatively few people have access to. Because these machines—letterpresses, radio transmitters, TV cameras—are expensive, access to them is exclusive. This means that an elite gatekeeper gets to decide which ideas are allowed in and which die a quick, merciless death. Getting accepted by the gatekeeper—the priest, publisher, or studio exec—is usually the greatest hurdle broadcast information has to cross. If it's accepted, it's likely to find at least a modestly sizeable audience.

Once processed, broadcast media becomes clearly owned by the individuals who created and published it. More importantly, it becomes fixed. It's very difficult, and usually illegal, to change it. Audiences don't interpret it, mash it up, and retell it. They never take ownership of it themselves. They consume it—a marketer who talks about his audience as "consumers" is most likely thinking like a broadcaster.

In 1990, for a handsome and predictable fee, a marketer could buy a thirty-second spot on *Cheers* and reach more than 20 million viewers, guaranteed. No DVRs. No checking e-mail during the break. Either you were up at the fridge grabbing a Pepsi or you were watching an ad for it. And most reassuring of all, there was no chance that content of the show itself, which so relied on the marketer's support, would embarrass or contradict her message. The marketer who could afford such a slot had a palette of ways to spark the minimal attention she needed to keep viewers awake. She could choose to paint a picture of happy, satisfied users of her product (the soft sell) or make an enticing special offer or rely on product comparisons like the Pepsi Challenge (the hard sell). She could even pump up either strategy by embedding the whole package into a short story, as many of that era did. These strategies all found their days in the sun.

For all of its high-priced barriers to entry, the broadcast tradition makes life reassuringly simple for marketers. By artificially selecting what gets published, it goes a long way toward ordering the world's ecosystem of ideas into something resembling a modern industrial farm—monocultured, predictable, controlled.

The Oral Tradition

Ideas in the oral tradition, on the other hand, look like the wild "entangled bank" that Charles Darwin contemplated in *The Origin of Species*—chaotic, seething, freed from artificial selection. Here survival of the fittest rules.

In the *oral tradition,* ideas also begin in the mind of a creator, but their path to their audience is far less prescriptive. Instead of being processed through an elite device that replicates and delivers them directly, orally transmitted ideas must replicate themselves, passing from the mind of one listener to the next.

Evolutionary biologist Richard Dawkins has given us the famous idea of a *meme.* It's a useful concept in helping to understand how messages live or die in the oral tradition. Memes are units of cultural information—we can simplify the notion and say *ideas*—that act in our minds much as genes do in our bodies. As they replicate themselves from one host mind to another through communication between people, they change and adapt, often replicating imperfectly. They mutate. This mutation often keeps them relevant, but if they mutate too much, the original intent of the idea may be lost. Memes compete with other memes for survival because a mind can only host so many of them. If one is forgotten before it can be reproduced, it dies off. The most memorable, compelling, and adaptable memes survive. In the natural world, memes, or ideas, must ensure their survival by exciting listeners to keep passing them along, carrying the same core message in a chain of transmission.

So what's the most consistent way to make a meme interesting in the wilds of the oral tradition? That's easy. Just ask yourself what information has survived intact from cultures steeped in oral traditions. The answer, of course, is *stories.* The creation myths and hero tales of the pre-Colombian Americans, ancient Greeks, Semites of the Middle East, Egyptians, and Chinese dynasties remain surprisingly unchanged despite the thousands of years and mouths they've passed through. Even if you've never studied these ancient stories, you're probably intimately familiar with their plot lines; they form the foundation of many of today's most popular movies and books.

These stories are powerful memes. Most of them originated long before writing existed, and where writing did come on the scene, cultures used this new tool to record their stories even as they continued to transmit them orally.

It's not nearly as easy to keep an idea meaningfully intact in the oral tradition as it is in the broadcast tradition. Here, ideas are never fixed for long. Each holder owns the idea while it's in his possession. He may tweak it, comment on it, or link it up with other ideas. He may choose to forward it to his friends or let it die.

This may make the oral tradition seem too wild a world to master and thus, the world of marketing may feel hopelessly chaotic and broken. But it need not.

For millennia, as ideas have been passed from one mind to another, natural selection has clearly favored certain survival strategies. The fossil record of ideas reads like a how-to manual. Worthwhile ideas that have been deftly encoded in compelling stories have survived with their meaning intact.

Now, clearly, the types of stories that we find in modern marketing are not exactly the same thing as a Babylonian creation myth. So what do I mean when I say *a story*? Here's the definition we'll find useful for understanding the story wars:

> *Stories are a particular type of human communication designed to persuade an audience of a storyteller's worldview. The storyteller does this by placing characters, real or fictional, onto a stage and showing what happens to these characters over a period of time. Each character pursues some type of goal in accordance with his or her values, facing difficulty along the way and either succeeds or fails according to the storyteller's view of how the world works.*

We tend to listen to a well-told story because its characters serve as role models. Their fates strongly imply what will befall us if we follow a similar path.

Stories can be told as vast epics from the birth of a character to his death, as we find in the New Testament, or they can be invoked with a single image—a rugged cowboy with a cigarette dangling from his lips, no doubt scratching out an honest living on the American frontier. Their format is not what defines them. Wherever you find human-scale characters playing a larger role than facts or proclamations and a clear lesson you can apply to your own life, you know you're in the presence of the unique persuasion tool known as a story.

Stories rule the entangled bank of the oral tradition and great stories, well told, will rule the wilds of the media marketplace now emerging.

The Digitoral Era

So back to today's world of message fatigue, clogged inboxes, and social media rabble-rousers. The next time you bring an idea or campaign to market, you're probably going to tweet it and post it to Facebook or YouTube, where you'll rely on your audience members to pass it along. And even if you don't, someone else will. While your audience has your message in their hands, they're going to post it on their walls with their own twist, rate it or comment on it, and maybe create links to it from their blogs, which will range from slightly off-message to downright bizarre. If your message is catchy, audiences might provide their own soundtrack for it, spoof it, or just steal it for their own purposes. You might invite them to do all of this and measure your success by how readily they do.

See the connection between the oral tradition and our new digital landscape? Ideas today are never fixed: they're owned and modified by everyone. They move through networks at the will of their members and without that activity, they die. That's the *digitoral era* emerging.

To survive in this landscape—perceived as broken by many, but rich in opportunity for others—we can no longer treat our audiences as passive consumers of our marketing messages. They must be our partners. And we'll never create those partnerships by simply storming into our audience's lives with the annoying, manipulative sales pitches of yesterday. Of course, this isn't news. We've all by now gotten the message that we need to tell better stories, but after an initial burst of enthusiasm, most of us who try wind up bitterly disappointed. Dressing up old tactics in the superficial clothing of story—character, conflict, and plot—rarely delivers more than a yawn from jaded audiences.

The stories that will succeed in the digitoral era will be held to the same survival-of-the-fittest standards all oral tradition stories have faced. They will be bruised and battered in transmission, so their core message must be powerful, resonant, and resilient. Stories that will prevail in the story wars won't just entertain—they will matter.

Learn to tell stories that provide meaning and you will no longer find yourself gasping for air in the free-for-all of the digitoral era. Instead you will help your audiences understand themselves and their worlds. You will create armies of evangelists. And you will find yourself in the midst of conflict. Stepping into the world of meaning-making means stepping onto a high stakes battlefield where important stories compete. To thrive in the digitoral era, we must be prepared to understand—and then join—the story wars. After all, great stories and great conflict have always been inseparable.

A Dispatch from the Story Wars

Without a conflict, there is no story.

Your high school English teacher probably told you that. Without characters or forces acting in opposition to each other, there's no movement, nothing really changes—thus there's no story. But to understand the story wars, we must look at a more important and closely held secret: *without a story, there can be no conflict.*

Stories are how we humans arrange and recount our experiences of the world so that others will want to listen to and learn from them. They allow us to create order out of the chaotic, otherwise meaningless experience of our senses by editing out irrelevant details, defining a cause for each effect and providing meaning in the string of things we have seen, felt or even just imagined.

People who tell and believe the same stories hold the same values. They share a worldview. In fact, a worldview is just a collection of stories about how things have come to be the way they are and what we should do about them. A good story is therefore the fundamental ingredient in allowing humans to create a sense of *us*. Shared stories, shared values, shared worldview—*us*.

And this brings us back to conflict. Without a story, there can be no conflict, because without an *us* there can be no *them*. Without a *them*—well, who are we in conflict with?

Important stories have been at the root of conflicts throughout human history, and in our modern, digitoral world, the story wars are as alive as ever. Not long ago, I found myself in the middle of one raging on Fox News.

Glenn Beck smiles as he waves a small stack of papers at the camera.

"Is that sulfur I smell?" Then he sniffs the packet in his hand. "Yes. I think so."

The one-man media empire is just warming up, an impassioned commander rallying his troops. He's about to relate, in real time, the latest chapter of America's great story, a centuries-long battle for our nation's soul. More than 2 million Americans are tuned in, waiting to see how today's news will fit into Beck's epic narrative. He holds a curriculum from a project called *The Story of Stuff*. And on it, he detects the devil's fingerprints.

Satan did not work on *The Story of Stuff*. I know, because my studio produced the twenty-minute viral hit on the perils of overconsumption. But whether the movie was really born in the mind of a single-mother environmental activist (which it was) or in the diabolic mind of the Prince of Darkness is beside the point.

Beck owes his tremendous success to the fact that—like the great storytellers of the ancient oral tradition—he has constructed for his followers a powerful model of how the world works. Like the ancient myths that have built empires, the narratives Beck weaves work together to provide explanation, meaning, and a compelling story in a world that has come to feel increasingly alienating and chaotic to those who follow him. Once you speak the language of Beck's mythology, full of thrilling heroes and terrifying villains, any event—past, present or future—can be explained through it. And in that myth, the host of *The Story of Stuff,* Annie Leonard, who advocates for a more proactive role of government to protect human rights and the environment, is in league with the forces of darkness.

Beck doesn't have to explain what *The Story of Stuff* is. He knows his fans will recognize it instantly by now because he's featured it more than two dozen times on his show.

"It's going into your churches, and your synagogues. Some of it sounds great. Some of it—you know, it's truth mixed with evil stuff, to be real frank with you."

It would be easy for me to sneer at Beck's story or call him a conspiracy theorist nut job, as so many others have. But that's not my intention here. True, he's lumped my life's work in with the machinations of evil, but his claim makes perfect sense once you understand his underlying story—it's a story he has complete mastery over. His epic tale is the foundation for Beck's personal brand, one of the most valuable and influential in the world of political punditry. What's of interest to me, and to you if you want to achieve breakthrough communications success, is not the content of Beck's worldview but the storytelling strategy that has catapulted him to such unprecedented results.

Beck is a master marketer, successful out of all proportion to his category, if any category can be defined for him. By 2010, he was personally earning about $13 million a year from his books and magazines, $10 million from radio, $3 million from events, and (before his run on Fox ended) $2 million from TV. On an average day, more DVRs recorded Beck's show than any other cable news program. All this, and he was a central figure in the Tea Party movement that drove Republicans to victory in 2010. If you think of Beck as a newscaster or political figure, you're missing the point.

"I'm a brand," he told *Forbes* magazine. "I don't think you can make an impact in today's world without being ubiquitous." Few marketers have managed to be as ubiquitous as Glenn Beck. And precisely because he *is* a brand, the lessons of Beck's success have applications to all kinds of brands from retail goods to social causes.

———————

Annie Leonard is another category-defying marketer, a poster child for success in the digitoral era, with equally valuable lessons to impart. On the surface, Leonard's not a marketer at all, but an environmental activist with a passion for garbage. She stumbled into her marketing career with a message she was desperate to spread and with absolutely no funding or platform. Leonard had spent ten years investigating where the "stuff" that will become garbage is made, how that stuff is used, and what happens once that stuff-turned-garbage is dumped. She walked away from this investigation with a mountain of facts, data, and anecdotes and a clearer picture of our materials economy than perhaps anyone else on Earth. She also knew the system was out of control. But nobody seemed to care.

One day, a friend gently but firmly recommended that she stop shouting the facts and speak a language normal people could understand. The criticism turned into an instant revelation. She realized she had to start bringing what she knew down to the *human scale*: turn her rantings into a story anyone could grasp, not in the language of statistics, but in easy-to-picture little scenes. Populate her talk with characters and conflicts between them. Of course, this wasn't easy when dealing with something as abstract and invisible as a global economic system. Leonard had mountains of data and complex interrelations to shove into this format. But when she began to accept that challenge, people started taking notice. Without knowing it, she had started down the road of telling great stories and communicating a mythology of her own. A funder liked Leonard's story so much that she offered to pay for it to be adapted for the Internet so anyone could see it.

So the project came to my studio, where we turned Annie Leonard's sixty-minute lecture into a twenty-minute stick-figure cartoon. It proved irresistible. Millions of videos are uploaded to the Internet each day. Nearly all them are instantly forgotten. But *The Story of Stuff* sliced through the clutter and noise almost immediately. Sent out to a few bloggers, friends, and Leonard's small list of allies, the video went viral, reaching fifty thousand people in the first week. That number has now grown to well over 15 million. The movie launched Leonard's own media empire, which includes a *New York Times* best-selling book, screenings of her film in more than fifteen hundred classrooms, and a thriving nonprofit that has managed to organize over 200,000 fans acting on her behalf.

Where Glenn Beck achieved major icon status with the help of CNN and then Fox News, Annie Leonard achieved minor icon status with almost no support at all. The woman who created the sulfur-scented curriculum and the man who was just sniffing it both achieved success beyond all expectation. To understand that success is to understand the power of stories in the digitoral era. To understand why Fox News, perhaps the most powerful media organization in the world, would devote dozens of segments to battling the story of an Internet activist with no official platform is to understand the urgency of the story wars.

Decoding the War over Stuff

The concept of the story wars provides us with a powerful lens to understand what's happening here. Through that lens, we can begin to decode, and learn to emulate the components of any great story-based brand.

Creating these components begins by staking out a clear *moral of the story*. The winners of the story wars all have a single, compelling message that turns out to be the key lesson of every communication. Good morals are simple, repeatable, and memorable. For Amnesty International, the moral is, "Human rights abuses can't be carried out when people are watching." For Nike, the moral is, "Through hard work and determination, anyone can achieve amazing things." You get the idea. Morals like these underlie the literally thousands of stories these brands tell.

Next, these storytellers clearly define their *heroes, villains,* and the *conflict* between them to show how their epic plays out in the lives of characters we can relate to. And these epics invite their audiences to be a key character in that conflict, helping to bring a broken world to a better place.

If they do all of this, brands become vehicles for *explanation, meaning,* and *story.* In other words, they create myths that they can leverage to get attention and motivate action.

When powerful brands provide explanations, meaning, and stories that directly oppose each other, conflict breaks out. And this explains why Glenn Beck wants his followers to think Annie Leonard's message is evil. Let's use this story wars lens to decode the conflict between these master marketers.

In *The Story of Stuff,* Annie Leonard takes her audience on a humorous and ultrasimplified whirlwind tour of our materials economy at the scale of individual human experience. Along the way, we learn that all the stuff in our lives carries an enormous and invisible price tag. Leonard reveals that as consumption began to explode in the 1950s, US national happiness began to decline, and it's been dropping ever since. "We're destroying the planet," Leonard says. "And not even having fun doing it."

Such a head-on attack on our culture of consumption would certainly seem like sacrilege to many. To ask whether growth is good, as Leonard is doing, is to question some of the most basic assumptions about our economic system and its very purpose.

On the surface, we might just assume that this conflict got started because Glenn Beck is a defender of stuff and the unquestioned good of economic growth that goes with it. I assumed this to be the case and to see if I was right, I picked up a copy of Beck's number-one best-selling thriller, *The Overton Window.* My hypothesis couldn't have been further from the truth.

The book is about a plot to bring down America and install a worldwide socialist dictatorship. And it's masterminded by . . . a marketer, Arthur Gardner. Gardner revels in his ability to manipulate the public at will—instilling consumerism as a steppingstone toward total control.

Beck, it would seem, agrees with Leonard—but when it comes to the story wars, the story being told on the surface is rarely where the action is. What people respond to in the best marketing campaigns, what they build their lives around, are not the details on the surface but the moral of the story each brand epic creates or contests and the compelling characters who live that moral out. The battle between Annie Leonard and Glenn Beck is not about two people's view of stuff but about the very meaning of America.

After my "Glenn Beck loves stuff" hypothesis was crushed by *The Overton Window*, I realized I needed to get down to a deeper level to find the roots of this conflict, so I invited Leonard to lunch to talk with her about what *The Story of Stuff* was *really* about.

"The problem is that we are so individually oriented. We're so busy with our focus on the individual, we're totally forgetting to focus on the whole," she explained to me. "If we decide to all look out for each other, instead of just getting as much stuff as we can, we can have such a better quality of life." This is Leonard's moral of the story, and on that moral, she layers her heroes, villains, and conflict. In each tale Leonard tells, the problem begins with free enterprise—the ultimate expression of the individual's drive for success—run amok. The villains are always greedy, out-of-control corporations and corrupt government officials willing to go along for the ride. The heroes are always regular people who decide to cast off the label of *consumer* and embrace the role of *citizen*. These archetypal characters appear not as abstract concepts but as cute little stick figures that we want to reach out and hug—or flick, as the case may be.

Leonard lays out a clear journey for her citizen-heroes, who also happen to be her audience. Band together, she implores, and take the government back, making it an instrument of the collective will and a necessary balancing force in our out-of-control market system. Her audiences have responded by spreading her stories, voting them off the charts on video fan sites, and even making videos of their own that carry the same message—all hallmarks of digitoral success.

Leonard owes her now-iconic status to a marketing campaign based on a coherent mythology that provides explanation, meaning, and story in a neat package. *Explanation:* This is how our materials economy—totally invisible to you before—works. *Meaning:* This system is not delivering happiness, so it's time to look for meaning beyond consumption. *Story:* Her analysis has been boiled down from abstract economic theory into a world complete with villains, heroes, conflict, and high stakes. In fact, the stakes couldn't be any higher, because she's talking about the survival of human life on the planet.

I also asked Beck to lunch; he was not inclined to join me. But his mythology is easy to decode from his enormously consistent body of work. His brand epic, too, has a clear moral of the story and it is pretty much the mirror image of Leonard's: "The pursuit of the good of the individual is freedom and virtue. The pursuit of the good of the collective is tyranny."

Beck's stories always start with the same villain: progressivism or "the progressive cancer." Among the practitioners of progressivism: Barack Obama, George W. Bush, Stalin, Hitler, and his favorite target, Woodrow Wilson. The sin of progressives is favoring the will of the whole, or the state, over the will of the individual—uh-oh, Annie.

Beck encourages his fans to find progressivism anywhere the hero of his mythology—the average American, full of the individualist spirit—is hampered by the state, the ultimate instrument of the collective. It's an American story that dates back to the settlers on the frontier. These rugged men are embedded in our national conscience, and we see them as constantly threatened by big city elites back East, who are hopelessly out of touch with the pioneers' divine mission.

"Our Founding Fathers believed that it was the power of the State that was to be cuffed," Beck wrote. "While Progressives believed it was individuals who were cuffed to the greater good of the group. One of these two positions will eventually win out and that will dictate how future generations live their lives."

Here, too, we find all the elements of a clear mythology and a resonant story. Every day as he rolled out his blackboard with a new doorway to his worldview sketched on it, Beck gave his viewers not just the news but explanation, meaning, and story—in other words, a mythology to live by, an *us* to join. *Explanation:* America is defined by a battle between progressive elites and real, freedom-loving Americans. *Meaning:* Fighting this battle is the most patriotic and satisfying activity Americans can engage in (Beck says that he himself was saved from alcoholism and suicide by this greater purpose.) *Story:* The drama is embodied in compelling characters, conflict, and incredibly high stakes.

Beck's viewers can't get enough of this story, and that's why they enroll in his university, crash the blogs of his detractors, and even try to violently attack Leonard's funder, the Tides Foundation, as a man named Byron Wilson was inspired by Beck to do in 2010. Beck's brand hasn't just found an audience, it's created rabid evangelists.

I'm not sure if I agree with Beck that one of these two positions will ultimately win—they've been fighting it out forever. In the 1950s these worldviews collided in the stark contrasts of American ideals posed by storytellers like Frank Capra on one side and Ayn Rand on the other. And the conflict was ignited yet again between the Occupy movement and the Tea Party. What is clear is that these two myths are actively trying to snuff each other out and have long formed the great debate on today's American political scene. Thus the story wars rage on.

For all of their deep differences, these two marketers share another core belief that leads to their success. It's the belief that average Americans yearn to be part of something more than a quest for status or comfort or convenience. The stories they both tell open the door for all of us to be something more than a consumer. They *invite* us to be participants in a grand, unfolding drama much larger than ourselves. Beck's followers have begun to refer to themselves as "historians." Where most marketers would pigeonhole Beck's fans into a demographic labeled "anti-intellectual," Beck himself draws them into a wide-ranging (if bizarre) discussion of history, politics, sociology, and futurism. On the other side of the spectrum, Leonard asks disaffected viewers to believe again in the power of "We the People," to exercise their "citizen muscle," and see engagement with their community as the path to the kind of happiness consumption just can't deliver. Both of these storytellers reject the type of marketing we've grown so used to—the *inadequacy approach*—which appeals only to base emotions of fear, greed, vanity, and insecurity. Annie Leonard and Glenn Beck have tapped into the power of appealing to higher values and a need to get engaged with something larger than oneself.

The story of Glenn Beck and Annie Leonard shows that success in the wild digitoral era is indeed possible and, with the right strategies, can even be explosive.

All Wars Are Story Wars

Today's best marketers are creating cause and brand loyalty by telling stories that deliver a pattern of meaning for a society in need of just that. They build communities of purpose and give people an empowering sense of *us*. All societies have relied on core myths to guide them, and too many of ours have been stretched to the point of breaking. Our hunger for these stories explains many of the greatest marketing successes of our time and points to the enormous responsibility marketers carry as creators of modern myths. Why? Because the wars fought over stories have always been the most critical fights in shaping a society's future.

The drama playing out between Glenn Beck and Annie Leonard is part of the ancient pattern of powerful worldviews colliding. In fact, as far back as we can see, all wars have been story wars. Take your pick: the conquest of the Philistines by the Hebrews; the Crusades; the German invasion of Poland; 9/11. Countless wars have been fought over stories—stories of a people holding a unique covenant with God; a city standing on a holy rock; a master race with a destiny to rule the world for a thousand years; the heavenly delights in store for martyrs.

Powerful stories have spurred millions of men and women to acts—tragic and heroic acts—that have cost them their lives and fundamentally reshaped our world. The stories of the winners carry on and continue to define our reality.

Now, I'm going to make the (I hope) safe assumption that you're not trying to sell a war. More likely you're trying to sell an idea, a set of values, or a product. In other words, you're a marketer, not a military recruiter. So why all this talk of war?

First, knowing that people will leave their families, risk death, and kill to live out or defend a story tells you how powerful stories can be in moving us to action. We have evolved with tremendous resistance to the idea of throwing ourselves into struggles that can end our lives. It's called fear. And most societies reinforce that fear with strict taboos on killing. Yet a good story, well told, can wipe that all away. Stories have the power to radically alter people's behavior—and changing people's behavior so they'll think, buy, or vote differently, despite their fear of change, is what marketing is all about.

Second, war is the most visible and sadly explosive way that competing stories collide. Literal war shows us how high-stakes the story wars can be. Centuries ago, societies were small and—when it came to stories—pretty homogenous. Everyone in a tribe, village, or kingdom shared the same stories from birth. When new stories appeared on the scene, they usually showed up with a competing group of people with a competing set of needs. Differing stories would both amplify and justify conflicts between groups, and, at times, they still do today. But more often than not, in societies like ours, which contain a mix of dozens of different cultures, stories can compete furiously without neighbors constantly taking up arms against each other. Here the story wars become less violent, but no less important. We still need stories to define us and the more stories that coexist, the more furiously they must compete for our attention.

In our media-saturated environment, overflowing with brand messages, product pitches, election season attack ads, and movies designed for product tie-ins, our most powerful storytellers are no longer shamans, priests, presidents, or generals. Today's storytellers work at Pixar, creating animations about living cars that will become the year's hottest holiday gift item; at Starbucks, making an easy emotional connection for you with a coffee farmer in Nicaragua; and at American Crossroads, Karl Rove's media machine, crafting the tale of America's next citizen-powered revolution. Everywhere, marketing is challenging the power of traditional storytellers. This year, my local mall declared the supremacy of marketers over holy men by building its Christmas tree out of shopping carts. Nobody seemed to object.

The battlefield of the story wars has moved to the marketplace.

While it was once assumed that the fate of our world would be written in holy texts or constitutions, it now appears that it will be written, at least in part, in marketing campaigns. More than half of the hundred largest economies in the world are not countries but corporations. Marketing is the language through which they speak to the customers that sustain them. In the United States, marketers are becoming some of the defining players in our democracy. In 2009, the Supreme Court ruled that corporations have the unlimited right to spend money to influence elections. The following year, more money flowed into the kind of political advocacy groups corporations can support than the past five mid-term election cycles combined. Who was put in charge of those millions? Marketers. And, though terrorism and nuclear weapons continue to be existential concerns, the most serious threats we face as a species— climate change, resource depletion, species loss—are crises of overconsumption driven by—guess who?—marketers.

Even if stories are not driving you into literal battle, they are still driving each of us to make decisions that will shape the future of our democracy and our planet. With marketers in charge, today's story wars send causes, brands, and candidates into battle for the attention of their audiences. They recruit people into their own definition of *us* and get them to share that sense of belonging with others. They craft our inner worlds as well as the outer world we all share.

Winning the Story Wars is a book about hope in uncertain and difficult times. For marketers, the rise of the digitoral era has created a crisis. The traditional ways no longer work; suddenly, it's evolve or die. The good news is that our audiences may need us as much as we need them. People everywhere are looking for ways to make sense of a rapidly changing world in which traditional stories no longer hold resonance. By shifting gears away from the now-dysfunctional approaches of the past, marketers have the chance to reshape the media marketplace, orienting it to stories that have always worked in the oral tradition—those that call people to higher purpose. We can create patterns of stories that lift audiences up to become evangelists for our messages and call them to participation in creating a better world. After decades of antagonism between marketers and their audiences, the new media landscape offers the hope something far more satisfying for both sides. This book offers a whole new way to fight, and win, the story wars—with audiences as our allies rather than our targets.

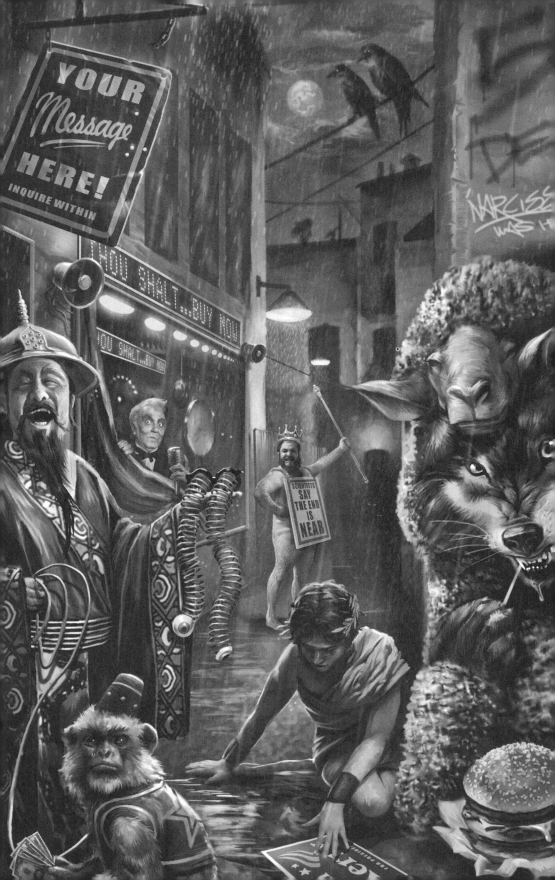

CHAPTER TWO

The Five Deadly Sins

Every hero has a backstory—a time before he struck fear in the hearts of his foes when he bumbled around making the same mistakes as everyone else. This chapter is about those mistakes. They are the five deadly sins that doom us to defeat in the story wars—vanity, authority, insincerity, puffery, and gimmickry.

In the movies, the backstory is transcended in ninety short minutes. In real life, most of us get stuck in it forever. Our messages get ignored, misunderstood, and muddled. Stabbing in the dark for solutions, we try to increase the emotional content of our communications, only to find that the emotion gets through but the message gets lost. So we shift gears and focus on the facts—our undeniable selling points—and find that our claims, though true, are disbelieved. We're in way over our heads, trying to fight the story wars woefully unprepared. Most of us are in desperate need of a mentor.

Of course, our mentors are all around us. Like us, the masters themselves have backstories. They groped, making the same mistakes we're making now, and then one day they emerged with a really great story, and everything changed for them. As a marketer trained under the assumptions of the broadcast era, as we all are,

---

Marketing's five deadly sins: vanity, authority, insincerity, puffery, and gimmickry

you must begin your journey to join the masters by confronting the most basic story-killing sins that hold us back.

Meet the Sins

By stunting the oral tradition's natural selection of ideas, the broadcast era stopped weeding sinful communicators out. So, like an invasive species, marketers who took shortcuts around telling great stories were allowed to thrive. But the sins have always been with us. They have, in fact, tempted storytellers for millennia. That's why cautionary tales have been crafted specifically to warn against them.

To help the lessons in this chapter stick, I'll tell some of those tales as I bring you into confrontation with each of the five deadly sins.

The First Sin:
Vanity and the Story of Narcissus

Narcissus was the best-looking hunter in the forest, and he knew it. So enamored was he of his own beauty that, upon seeing his reflection in a pool of water, he was irresistibly drawn to it. Some say he fell in and drowned. Others have him frozen by the pool, unable to look away from his own fabulousness, and eventually wasting away to nothing. Either way, there was no happy ending for the guy who could not get enough of himself.

Your brand or cause is a reflection of you. So, of course, you love it. That's good, because if you don't, you shouldn't be offering it to anyone else. But the sin of *vanity* sets in when you love what you're selling so much that you assume everyone else will too. You start to believe your idea will sell itself if you can just reach out and tell people about it. You're wrong.

When a marketer leads with "For thirty-five years we've been ..." or "We're the number-one blah blah blah" you're seeing vanity in action. His confidence in himself and his own relevance is blinding him to what needs to be done to connect with the people who are really important: his audience.

Utterly oblivious to the fact that what audiences really want is to see *their own* reality and values reflected in a message, the vain marketer gets on his soapbox and blathers away. Never quite feeling heard, he builds his soapbox higher and higher, reaching to the sky, farther and farther away from his audience.

Politicians are notoriously vain marketers. Case in point: John Kerry. He was so convinced of the clarity of his muddled message and so exasperated with his opponent's seeming ineptitude that he blabbered on about his own heroic service and the strength of his résumé. He was shocked, though he shouldn't have been, to find himself defeated by a weaker opponent with a better story.

It's impossible to provide one simple explanation for the outcome of an entire presidential election. But the news analysis in 2004 certainly tried, and if you read that analysis now, you'll see there was something close to consensus on the matter. Going into the campaign, George W. Bush was struggling on the issues. When he had entered office in 2000, about one in ten Americans thought the economy was in trouble. That number had risen to more than 50 percent by the time the 2004 election came around. And the war in Iraq had gone off the rails, stirring up a deep dissatisfaction among voters. The fact that Bush won was explained almost universally in this way: he found a way to connect with America. Kerry could or would not.

A few days after the election, a frustrated James Carville complained: "They produce a *narrative*. We produce a litany. They say, 'I'm going to protect you from the terrorists in Tehran and the homos in Hollywood.' We say, 'We're for clean air, better schools, more health care.' And so there's a Republican narrative, a story, and there's a Democratic litany."

Carville's words reflect the frustration of pretty much every Democrat at the time. Kerry pitched in a way that was all about Kerry. He listed *his* issues and *his* credentials. Then waited for thunderous applause.

Here, in the first three hundred words (that's about two minutes) of Kerry's acceptance speech at the Democratic National

Convention—the most important speech of his life—we find a treasure trove of me-focused marketing:

"I'm John Kerry and I'm reporting for duty."

"A great American novelist wrote that you can't go home again. He could not have imagined this evening. Tonight I am home."

About his mother: *"She was my den mother when I was a Cub Scout, and she was so proud of her fifty-year pin as a Girl Scout leader. She gave me her passion for the environment."*

And about his birth: *"Guess which wing of the hospital the maternity ward was in? I'm not kidding. I was born in the West Wing."*

The few *we-* or *you*-focused messages he uttered were sandwiched between, and setups for, all of these not-so-charming and not-so-relevant me-statements. That's vanity in action: Were we impressed? Maybe. Inspired? No.

Bush, on the other hand, kept his messages focused foremost on the values of the voters and a recognition of their need to see their world in tangible stories.

Here are some of the things Bush had to say in the first 350 words of his Republican National Convention speech:

"We have seen a shaken economy rise to its feet. And we have seen Americans in uniform storming mountain strongholds and charging through sandstorms and liberating millions with acts of valor that would make the men of Normandy proud."

"Since 2001, Americans have been given hills to climb and found the strength to climb them. Now, because we have made the hard journey, we can see the valley below. Now, because we have faced challenges with resolve, we have historic goals within our reach and greatness in our future."

"We will build a safer world and a more hopeful America, and nothing will hold us back."

And when he did utter the word I, *it was directed in gratitude to his audience: "I'm honored by your support, and I accept your nomination for president of the United States."*

See all those characters, conflicts, and values shining through? This is why Carville credited Bush with having a story. And by making his audience his starting point, Bush took the focus off of himself, stopped beating his chest, and made room for that story to come through. He painted a picture of a heroic nation in a struggle for a future of greatness. The substance of what he was actually saying wasn't all that different from what Kerry was saying. But Kerry had lost track of his story because it had been buried under this vanity. That's what the sins do—they bury our chances to tell stories.

Why is vanity such a story-killer? If you are the hero of your own story, as Kerry was, you wind up with only a single compelling character—yourself. Stories with one character standing alone on the narrative stage rarely work, if they can be called stories at all. And this is as true for brands and organizations as it is for politicians.

Start with your audiences and their needs, then introduce yourself as a catalyst for helping them meet those needs, and a story instantly begins to unfold: *Multiple characters* and, most importantly, your audiences in a starring role. *Conflict* between your audience's desires and their current state. And a *plot* or journey that you invite them to join you on to reach those desires.

Even brands with huge cultural cachet have come to flee the sin of vanity. Remember Coke's old tagline: "Coke is it!"? Or Pepsi's: "The Choice of a New Generation"?

These self-admiring statements are both meaningless and transparent attempts to sell you something. They start the conversation and immediately end it. What's the expected response here? Apparently Coke believes it's "it" and Pepsi thinks it's great for young people. How nice.

The soft drink giants have finally stopped talking about themselves and have started to talk to their audiences. "Open Happiness," and "Refresh Everything" put the action in the hands of the soda drinker, not the soda, and that is a step in the direction of telling stories. Instead of describing the superlatives of the product, these statements invite us to feel a certain way by using them. If Kerry made soda, he probably would have put "Kerry is it!" on his bottles, while the Bush Cola Company would have opted for something more like "Refresh America."

The Second Sin: Authority and the Emperor's New Clothes

The story sounded fishy from the beginning: A fabric so fine as to be invisible to a fool? The king who, to be honest, couldn't quite see the garment himself, felt off-balance as soon as the tailors presented it to him. But, they were the experts. When it came to clothes, these guys really seemed to know what they were talking about. Not wanting to seem a fool in front of such sophisticated men, the king reluctantly shelled out a few, well more than a few, gold coins. And here he was, wearing it in the parade. By the squeamish look on his subjects' faces as he went by, he could tell there must be more than a few fools like himself in the crowd. This whole thing had been a mistake. And then a child's voice pierced the air. "The emperor has no clothes!"

This is one of the most famous stories from one of the most famous storytellers of all time, Hans Christian Andersen. We find variations in the folktales of Sri Lanka, India, and Turkey. What's it telling us? Experts don't deserve our trust.

Just as our passionate belief in our own importance lures us into the sin of vanity, our presumed expertise in our own field tempts us to commit the sin of *authority*. We put the facts out there, assuming they'll speak for themselves. We list our features, parade our jargon, and flash our credentials. Then we scratch our heads as the crickets chirp in reply.

With far more data—and the technology to make meaning of that data—available than ever before, it is possible for experts to know things with much greater certainty. Still, there's an obvious reason why relying on people's trust in your expertise doesn't work. The public's been trained by swindle after swindle that experts are often the biggest liars or fools among us. Government experts have OK'd everything from lead in paint to thalidomide to DDT. Doctors recommended that we smoke Camel cigarettes. BP experts told us there was no way an accident could happen on the *Deepwater Horizon*. We're tired of it.

And there's an even more important pitfall for those who rely on authority. The more powerful we believe our facts to be, the less we remember to make an emotional connection, or any connection at all, with our audiences. It gives us the false impression that we can get by without a story. Nonprofit marketers, especially those working on climate change issues, are often guilty of this. Unlike a handbag designer, who knows that image is everything, many climate change campaigners roll out the science and the expert endorsements as if their marketing had been written by the debate club.

James Hansen, the man known as the grandfather of climate science, learned about the sin of authority after decades of trial and error. As a chief NASA scientist and early discoverer of the role of CO_2 in climate change, Hansen was the quintessential expert. In fact, as a scientist, *expert* was a role he cherished and intended to protect. So, no matter how dire the data he was collecting became, Hansen chose to dispassionately, and without comment, publish his findings. It's not that he wasn't worried about the fate of the planet. He was. He just thought the facts would speak for themselves.

After Hansen had practiced this strategy for forty years, his close friend Bill McKibben summed up its success like this: "I think [Hansen] thought, as did I, if we get this set of facts in front of everybody, they're so powerful—overwhelming—people will do what needs to be done," McKibben told the *New Yorker*. "Of course, that was naive on both of our parts."

Today, Hansen has come down from his ivory tower, and the septuagenarian is risking arrest by loudly protesting outside of coal-fired power plants. He's also joined up with the 350.org campaign, which organized over fourteen hundred simultaneous climate rallies around the world in 2009. Hansen's now devoting himself to emotionally symbolic action, putting himself on the line to call for change. And the story of a scientist driven to such extremes has given him a new buzz platform from which to drive his ideas home.

Will his new strategy work? It's certainly gotten him a lot of attention. But more importantly, it shows that for Hansen, and for the rest of us, relying on our own expertise and our deeply held beliefs in the facts just won't cut it.

The Third Sin:
Insincerity and the Wolf in Sheep's Clothing

Don't stop me if you've heard this one. You've likely forgotten how it ends:

> A wolf can hardly believe his luck. Out for a stroll one day, he stumbles on the prize of all prizes, a perfect sheepskin lying in his path. The cunning wolf knows a break when he sees one and slips into it. The fit is perfect. Mind-boggled at the possibility for endless eats, he wanders into the neighboring flock and licks his chops, searching for the tastiest morsel of the bunch. The disguise works! The sheep happily graze on, barely noticing the newcomer. But the real question is, thinks the wolf, will it fool the shepherd? He gets his answer a moment later when the shepherd, walking through the flock, picks the well-disguised wolf— and promptly slaughters him.

See the twist? The term "wolf in sheep's clothing" is most commonly used to warn us to beware of the dangerous person pretending to be who she is not. But Aesop had something else in mind when he wrote this a couple of millennia ago. The story is a warning to wolves: don't try too hard to fit in. You're better off being yourself.

The sin of *insincerity* is in many ways the flip side of the sin of vanity. The vain marketer can't stop talking about himself. The insincere marketer can't stop losing herself in hopes of pleasing her audience.

I've been in creative sessions that, right from the outset, doomed themselves to disastrous insincerity. With absolutely no time spent on the values or moral of the story of the campaign itself, the team gets laser-focused on the imagined, stereotypical, attributes of the audience they are trying to reach. The less the team really knows about the "target demographic," the more they adapt the messaging to hit squarely between its imagined eyes.

In the most egregious cases, this type of targeting backfires in a way delightful to everyone but the marketers themselves. In 2007, McDonald's was feeling good about its street cred after the successful launch of the tagline: "I'm Lovin' It." "Why stop there?" some marketing executive asked. And someone responded with a new edgy slogan: "I'd Hit It." While technically an expression that its target demographic was using, "I'd Hit It" is not something a young man would say about a burger unless he planned to use it in a way that might shock a few of the families seated nearby trying to enjoy their Happy Meals. The campaign was pulled as soon as the error was discovered, but it was too late. McDonald's suffered the deep ridicule of bloggers across the Web and the audience it was so desperately trying to reach.

Fiji Water's insincerity problems with its green campaign run even deeper. Fiji water may be a lot of things—pure, clean, refreshing—but it's not green. The water is pure precisely because its source is so far from its urban Western drinkers—in many cases, more than eight thousand miles. That means a lot of carbon to ship the heavy liquid to people who could simply get it from the tap. Fiji realized that it had a problem here because those inclined to spend extra money protecting their health with super-pure water were also inclined to protect the health of our planet by buying green products.

So Fiji decided to be the first "carbon negative" bottled water, and to shout loudly about its status with the highly publicized FijiGreen website. Through a complicated offset scheme, Fiji claimed that enough money from every purchase was being spent on carbon-reduction projects to more than offset the carbon cost of the product. This sounded unlikely. How could anyone offset the carbon footprint of a bottle shipped halfway around the world without charging a lot more for it? Fiji claimed to have done it. A class action lawsuit and campaigns by major environmental organizations are out to prove they have not. Amid a flood of negative publicity, fiji-green.com has been taken down. Trying to speak the language of a subculture it didn't belong to, Fiji set off the alarm bells of insincerity in the audience it most wanted to reach.

Here's what the problem of insincerity comes down to: great stories are universal because at their core, humans have more in common with each other than the pseudo-science of demographic slicing has led us to believe. Great brands and campaigns are sensitive to the preferences of different types of audiences, but the core stories and the values they represent can be appreciated by anyone. Universality is the opposite of insincerity.

Nobody seems to grasp the value of universality better than the story artists at Pixar. Where other animation studios target their films squarely at a child audience, Pixar aims for something higher—a human audience. I asked Nate Stanton, head of story at Pixar, how the company manages to achieve such universal appeal in its movies.

"We tell each other, 'Don't even bring up kids here,'" he explained to me. "If you're thinking like that, you're thinking the wrong way."

Nate knows that he's got to appeal to kids for his films to be a success, but it's the personal inspiration of the members of the story team that drives the writing process, not an insincere attempt to speak the language of their target demographic.

If we've got our storytelling fundamentals down, finding ways to speak the specific language of our audiences can be a powerful tool. But starting with this strategy as our foundation almost invariably leads to trouble.

Think of the campaigns that have moved you. Did they speak only to your age? Race? Gender? Party affiliation? I'm guessing no. In the digital era, our tribal affiliations are much more subtle than that. Don't lose sight of the fact that deep down, your story should speak a universal language, bust genres, and address your audiences as human beings.

The Fourth Sin:
Puffery and The Wizard of Oz

Pay no attention to the man behind the curtain.

The sin of *puffery* is brilliantly encapsulated in this unforgettable line from perhaps the most beloved movie of all time. It's the desperate plea of a man whose entire communication strategy relied on a single trick: speaking in the voice of God, or in this case, the voice of Oz.

The Wizard of Oz teaches a deeply resonant truth that anyone can relate to. The story is about four lost souls who each seek outside of themselves for something that has been within them all along: a heart, a brain, nerve, and home. They are briefly hoodwinked by the man who speaks in the voice of God, and do his bidding in the hopes that he can help them. But in the end, the wizard is nothing more than a humbug.

The story is a warning to puffed-up communicators that people *will* pay attention to the man behind the curtain. Even if the voice of God works for a while, it won't be long before those on the other side will wonder who's really behind it. Marketers need to heed this warning if they want to be storytellers and not just salespeople. To place ourselves above our audiences, issuing commands from on high without a trace of our own humanity shining through is to commit the sin of puffery.

In the early days of the broadcast era, the voices heard by the public were almost invariably godlike, whether they came from newscasters, politicians, or advertisers. We took it for granted that a booming male voice telling us what to do was appropriate. We hadn't quite realized that there was, of course, just a fallible human behind the curtain.

You can almost hear the slight hum of static on an old radio as you read these typical car ads from the mid-1950s and early '60s: "The move to Cadillac has never been more tempting, more rewarding, or more practical than it is at the present time." Or, "No matter where you're going, getting there is really a treat when you drive Chevrolet, the best looking, best driving car on the road. Try a handsome new, gleaming new Beauville!"

The puffed-up marketer, by virtue of having a platform to speak from, feels he can simply tell his audience what to think. Unlike the authoritative sinner who overwhelms his listeners with facts and statistics, a marketer practicing puffery simply sits back and issues proclamations. The voice is most often stiff, humorless, steady, and dispassionate. It is not the voice of the people who represent the message. It is disembodied—the voice of the message itself. Have you ever heard a good story told this way? Of course not.

TV news anchors were once dispassionate and venerable. They worked hard to appear unbiased. That generation is gone. The top-rated newscasters are now violently opinionated and shamelessly biased—Glenn Beck being an obvious example. Not only have they stepped out from behind the curtain, they've done so half-naked. I'm not happy about what Beck and Rush Limbaugh have done to journalism, but they are telling the stories around which America shapes its opinion.

The "voice of God" approach is clearly dying, but that doesn't mean that the sin of puffery is going away any time soon. While nobody seriously considers using the now-quaint 1950s voice, it's still a challenge for most marketers to replace it with a more human flair. But if we want to master the voice of the of storyteller, that's exactly what we must do—expose our humanity and talk to audiences as if we were offering them a pleasing tale in our own unique voice, not a commandment to do our bidding.

The Fifth Sin:
Gimmickry and King You of Zhou

Here's a story you're sure to know in some form:

> King You had made a classic error. The great Chinese ruler had
> traded in his old wife for a beautiful concubine who excited him
> in every way—until the blush of romance faded and day-to-day

life set in. The king loved to laugh, but the beautiful Baosi would not. And despite her obvious charms, their lives together had grown dull. King You had tried all the tricks he could think of to get a giggle, and desperate times called for desperate measures.

So one night, the king ordered distress beacons lit across his kingdom, warning of a nomad attack. Covering his wife's eyes, he brought her to the castle ramparts and then revealed the chaos ensuing below. Baosi gasped and then, realizing it was all a joke, she began to smile. When his noblemen arrived prepared for battle, the young queen could hardly contain herself. She burst out laughing, sending the warriors home in shame.

It all felt wrong, but King You was happy. And so week after week the couple indulged in their cruel prank. And then, of course, it all came crashing down. The father of King You's ex-wife decided to avenge his daughter's abandonment. When his armies reached the castle, King You desperately lit the flares, and of course, nobody came. The rest is ancient history.

Like all great stories, the tale of King You contains a lesson that anyone can understand: not all fun is harmless fun. King You's folly is one kind of funny—the dangerous kind. In the marketing world, it is the empty, overly-exploited, and fleeting chuckle at the *gimmickry* of a guy kicked in the crotch or chimpanzees in a boardroom. But there's a far more inspiring kind of funny that comes from hearing something we know to be true told in a way we've never thought of before. This is the humor we expect of our great storytellers.

Humor is a universal human emotion and one that brings people instantly together. Of all the ways that people can communicate, it may be the most instantly bonding. We laugh together at the same joke, and suddenly we are friends. So it turns out to be a great tool for forming what we know we are after as communicators: the creation of shared identity. But it only sticks if you do it right.

In our modern world of message clutter and the holy grail of "viral hits," most communicators look with envy on the hilarious campaigns that people watch gleefully and pass on to their friends. In fact, being funny appears to be the entire strategy of most TV and viral Web ads these days.

That's why each year, the exorbitant ads of the Superbowl look like a lineup of King You–inspired gags. There's a palpable desperation to get the audience to laugh, to feel some kind of quick emotional affinity for the brands paraded before them. Many of these ads bomb. And while a few are truly worth laughing at, the question we need to ask even of the passing successes is, "Are they funny because they're true?" The first few viral successes my studio created contained a heavy dose of laughter, and for a while I made the mistake of thinking that's what they were all about. In *Friends with Low Wages,* a cartoon commentary on Walmart's employment practices, people were amused to see Garth Brooks watching as an "associate" was ordered to lick a toilet. But that was just a gimmick that was part of a campaign that was explosively successful not because it made people chuckle, but because it made people laugh on the way to getting angry at something they believed was true and had not yet been said. I learned the hard way that humor was not enough when we later launched several, much funnier, movies that flopped.

Of course, there is nothing wrong with humor. In fact, it's a strategy that can help us avoid many other sins. Funny communications steer us away from authority and puffery. After all, stuffy experts who speak in the voice of God are never funny. But when we take humor as the beginning and end of our communication, we miss any chance to tell a real story. And we miss any chance to fight and win the story wars.

Vanity, authority, puffery, insincerity, and gimmickry—these five sins should feel sadly familiar to anyone on the creating or receiving end of marketing these days. In fact, they are the air we breathe. The obvious question, then, is, if so many of our peers are doing it, are these sins really so deadly? And can setting out on a new course really heal our broken marketing efforts?

The Mac Guy

August 5, 2007, 12:30 a.m. That evening, I sat next to a tired-looking businessman who stared without a trace of enthusiasm at a spreadsheet on his laptop. As the other passengers drifted off to sleep, I pulled my MacBook out of its case and began to work beside him.

This got his attention. He looked at my computer and then at me, then back at the machine. And finally, with something approaching a knowing leer: "Mac guy, huh?"

OK, here's my Mac guy backstory. When I was a freshman in college, I signed up to work at the campus newspaper. The first day, my editor-in-chief sat me down at a Mac Classic and taught me how to use it. I've been using a Mac ever since.

Not that long ago, in the days before Apple's devices became ubiquitous, I used to get the "Mac guy" question a lot. My answer to that question was—no. I'm no more of a Mac guy than I am a cornflakes guy, or a toothbrush guy, or a toilet paper guy. These are all things that help me get through my day. They're tools, and I appreciate them for how they help me but they don't define me—at least I don't want them to.

Still, I took the easy road: "Yeah."

He craned his head a bit to see the spreadsheet I happened to be working on.

"Your work must be a *ton* of fun."

If you're under seventy, look like you have a job, and use a Mac to do it, some people will inevitably see you this way. It's as if the computer called to them, "Hey look! This guy's living the life *you* always wanted to live. He's resisting mediocrity. He's breaking the rules!"

In other words, you pull out a Mac in front of some people, and they start telling themselves a riveting story. This is exactly what the marketers who have mastered the story wars teach people to do—tell a brand's story to themselves.

Of course, after all the back-and-forth product imitation, when it comes to enjoying life, there is almost no difference between a Mac and a PC. And using one is certainly no mark of open rebellion. Yet there was a time that, by using my computer in public, I was making a statement that was beyond the usual style or status people hope will rub off on them from their cool products. As a Mac user before the days of Apple dominance, I was deemed by others, and Apple hoped by myself as well, to be part of a creative, forward-thinking, joyful tribe that the company has claimed for itself by flat-out winning the story wars over the past twenty-five years.

Apple's march to story dominance began with its legendary "1984" Super Bowl ad. It ran only once, but to anyone who could see below the surface, it was a bold declaration, a battle plan for the story Apple intended to fight for over the next several decades. A sea of brainwashed drones stare at an enormous screen on which an Orwellian leader blabbers about the future. A sexy, athletic rebel runs into the auditorium and hurls a hammer at the screen, utterly destroying it and waking the masses from their stupor. It's humanity versus tyranny, spirit versus machine, a hero come to restore a broken world. It wasn't just the drones in the ad that were blown away. Everyone was. The moral of Apple's new story was clear: "Creative rebels are the most powerful force in the world."

In the 1990s, Apple extended its epic when the "Think Different" campaign slapped the company's logo over the likenesses of Gandhi, Einstein, Amelia Earhart, and Bob Dylan. These are our world's most famous rebels, resisting every constricting norm from colonialism to Newtonian physics, sexism to war. These rebels seem to resist conformity to anything—except perhaps the Apple brand. Define a powerful moral for your story and you're laying the foundation for a story-based brand. Make that moral irresistible with just two words, a logo, and an image—that's story wars mastery. Apple showed it doesn't take a four-minute video or even a thirty-second spot to bring forth a compelling narrative. Its audiences filled in the gaps that the single image and two words left.

Then Apple's storytellers made America laugh. Challenging us with the label of uptight nerdiness if we resisted Apple's grand rebellion, their ads got people to happily declare, "I'm a Mac"; these people had begun to actually live out the brand's story in their own lives. Apple has been so successful with its storytelling around joyful rebellion that the only thing that has undermined it is the near-ubiquity of its products—brought about, in large part, by this success itself.

So when that guy on the plane asked me if I was a Mac guy, he was asking me, driven by the work of powerful storytellers, whether I was part of some creative resistance that he too might take the leap and join. I, in turn, suspected he was secretly considering buying a Mac if he could only work up the courage to commit such a brazen act against conformity.

Once we got past the whole awkward Mac thing, the guy turned out to be a brilliant, if somewhat bored economist. We wound up talking for the rest of the flight, though I couldn't help but imagine that to him I'd always just be that "Mac guy."

Of course, it hasn't always been this way for Apple. Its marketers were once sinners too and, in their past, we find a tale of mistakes that nearly kept Apple out of the story wars altogether. Here's what came before 1984–1983 to be precise, and the advertising launch of Apple's ill-fated "Lisa." If you've forgotten this computer, you're not alone; if you remember the ads for it, you probably are. In contrast to the simplicity of the Think Different campaign, the first Lisa ad is nine pages long. It begins with this headline "Apple invents the personal computer. Again."

The ad proceeds through page after page of dazzling but confusing feature lists, insider history of how the machine was developed, and somewhat imperious commands for me to go out and buy the thing. Based on this ad, there was a zero percent chance that there would ever be a "Lisa guy."

Mac tells a story. Lisa is hopelessly lost in the sins of vanity, authority, and puffery. The difference in the success of their brands could hardly be starker, even though Lisa was widely considered a major technological breakthrough at the time.

———————

The five deadly sins that drown out our stories are a major reason the world is broken for marketers today. But we're not suffering alone. The world is broken for just about everyone else too, though for a very different story-based reason—the gap between our rapidly changing times and the shared cultural myths upon which a healthy society depends. It is to this myth gap that we will now turn.

The Simple Story Test

As you peel away the layers of story-killing sin on your communications, you are likely to find hidden stories emerging. Part 2 of this book is all about honing those stories to be both strategic for your brand and irresistible for your audiences. But if you're looking for a quick test to see if you're leveraging the power of stories, use these simple filters to check any communication you've created. The more you can answer "yes" to these questions, the closer you are to storytelling success.

TANGIBLE: Stories present information that makes concepts visible and human scale. They make people feel that they can "touch" and "see" an idea.

Does your communication provide a who, what, where, and when?

RELATABLE: Stories matter to us because their characters carry values that we want to see either rewarded or punished.

Do you find that you can identify with—or are in emotional opposition to—the characters in your communication because you understand what motivates them?

IMMERSIVE: Stories allow people to feel that they have experienced things that they have only seen or heard.

Can you learn something of clear value for your own life from the characters' experiences?

MEMORABLE: Stories use rich scenes and metaphors that help us to remember their messages without conscious effort.

Does your communication leave you with a lasting image—transmitted either in pictures or in text—that can be easily recalled and reminds you of the core message?

EMOTIONAL: Stories elevate emotional engagement to the level of, and often beyond, intellectual understanding.

Does your communication make you feel something rather than just think something?

CHAPTER THREE

The Myth Gap

June 16, 1945, 4:00 a.m. For weeks, he had been living off of hand-rolled cigarettes and ancient Sanskrit poetry. Starved, parched, six feet tall, and 116 pounds, there was almost nothing left—a wasted man in a wasteland.

He ran his fingers over the dusty earth; his back turned to the hastily constructed city of several thousand. Most of them were sleeping as if it was just another night at summer camp. He liked that camp feel. It discouraged the asking of too many questions. It softened the anxious curiosity of the wives and children, preserving the secrets that were everywhere.

A jeep rolled by, headed for the test site, and he waited for another flash of lightning. When it came, he could, for an instant, make out the vast New Mexico nothingness that had, even as a young man on summer vacation, made him feel at home.

"Like a nuclear bomb was dropped here," he thought, playing with the words for the first time.

It would soon come to be a horrifying cliché, used to describe anything from a flood-ravaged town to a child's unkempt room,

---

Marketing in the myth gap: the Crying Indian, Occupy Wall Street, and the Marlboro Man the expression of an ever-present, crushing fear shared by billions. But the words passed through Oppenheimer's mind first. On that particular day, only he and a handful of other exhausted men even knew the bomb existed.

That the "gadget," as they affectionately called it, would work was far from certain. The men had put together a pool to predict the power of the nuclear implosion they were hoping to create and guesses ranged from nothing at all to only-half joking predictions that the entire state of New Mexico would combust. Oppenheimer, the man responsible for the project's success, had played it safe in front of his men, gloomily predicting a blast equivalent to a mere three hundred tons of TNT. In the language of bombs, three hundred tons was hardly a game changer.

But in his private moments, Oppenheimer was feeling far less humble. He had been reading the *Bhagavad Gita,* one of the great foundational Hindu scriptures, in nearly every spare moment. Each time his thoughts wandered to the awesome power he was about to unleash, he brought them back to the story contained in the two-thousand-year-old sacred text. It was science that he used to design the bomb. It was a myth that he relied on to understand its significance and his place in the epoch-making moment about to unfold.

At times, he thought he must be living out the story of Arjuna, the reluctant hero-warrior, forced into battle against his conniving cousins. In the *Gita,* Arjuna appeals to Lord Krishna for help and is offered the benefit of either Krishna's vast armies or his bottomless wisdom. He chooses the power of the mind over the power of the physical world. Arjuna's story fit Oppenheimer's own nicely. That the wisdom of a few men could overcome the armaments of thousands, even millions, was what he had been hired by the army to prove.

Then again, he suspected that the bomb was more significant even than that. Perhaps his story was not that of Arjuna, the warrior, but of Lord Krishna, himself an incarnation of the Supreme Being. After all, until this moment, it had been only the gods who held the power to utterly destroy worlds. It had now become likely that that power would fall into the hands of man—and largely because of him.

The lightning had stopped, and he lit another cigarette with the glowing end of his last one.

"Krishna," he thought. "Why not?"

A jeep pulled up a few yards away, his brother Frank already in the passenger seat. Without a word, Oppenheimer stepped inside.

5:29 a.m. "Now!" the announcer shouted and the men in the bunker braced themselves—terrified that it wouldn't work, terrified that it would. Ten miles away, there was a flash and suddenly the predawn became day—the brightest and hottest any of them had ever known. A plume of flame raced skyward, seven miles high, and ballooned out at the top, glowing with an eerie light of purple and green. Forty-five seconds later, the blast reached the men, disturbing the otherwise perfectly still air. Thunder echoed and bounced across the desert, eerily repeating itself in a wholly unnatural way.

There was jubilation for several moments. But as the men slapped backs and called each other "sons of bitches," Oppenheimer's mind returned to the *Gita*. He would later vividly recall his thought of that moment—the thought of a man challenging the supremacy of the gods.

"I am become death, the destroyer of worlds." His words were the words of Krishna revealing his divine form.

But all he said aloud was: "It worked."

With a blast equivalent of 18,600 tons of TNT, indeed it had. Four hours later, another "gadget" known as *Little Boy* left Hunter's Point in San Francisco. In three weeks, two bustling Japanese cities would be as wasted as the New Mexico desert.

———————

Oppenheimer and his men had seized the power of the gods for humankind and they knew it, just as the rest of the world soon would. This bomb dealt a fracturing blow to a pillar of the cultural mythology the world had been living by for millennia. In the West, our shared traditional stories are largely drawn from the Old

Testament, itself drawn from far more ancient sources. These myths cast man as a humble and small being subject to the whims of the much larger power of God and nature. At least since the time of Galileo, science had begun to offer alternative explanations for the forces around us, but until that blast went off, science's enormous power had never been so undeniably manifested in the real world. No wonder Oppenheimer found himself in such a mythic state of mind leading up to the blast. No wonder he would later compare his team to Prometheus, stealing fire from the gods.

In the words of Isidor Rabi, who held the winning wager in Oppenheimer's pool: "A new thing had just been born; a new control; a new understanding of man, which man had acquired over nature." And Albert Einstein urgently warned: "The unleashed power of the atom has changed everything save our modes of thinking and we thus drift toward unparalleled catastrophe."

What Rabi and Einstein recognized is that changing times were deeply challenging our old ways of seeing and responding to our world. It's not technology that can save us, Einstein would repeatedly emphasize; it's a new mind-set. And the mind-set of a society is held in its shared myths. The myths of our ancestors were just not equipped to handle the bomb Einstein had helped Oppenheimer create.

How we choose to update those myths, our most important cultural stories, and how we choose to enact them, will in large part determine society's response to our rapidly changing times. Through the lens of the story wars, we're about to see that marketers now have a major part to play in this choice.

The detonation in the New Mexico desert—now a lifetime ago—marked a major lurch in the widening of our *myth gap*—the space between the realities of our moment in history and the shared stories to which we turn for explanation, meaning, and instruction for action.

It is this myth gap that we'll now explore—the rift marketers have stepped into where religion, science, and entertainment have faltered.

What Is a Myth?

It is both tragic and deeply ironic that our society commonly relegates the word *myth* to a reviled synonym for a lie. Today, when we speak of myths, we're more likely to think of busting them than looking to them for guidance. Yet to live without myths would put us in uncharted territory in the history of human civilization.

Myths are the glue that holds society together, providing an indispensible, meaning-making function. British anthropologist Bronislaw Malinowski said myth "expresses, enhances and codifies belief, it safeguards and enforces morality, it vouches for the efficacy of ritual and contains practical rules for the guidance of man." What we value and what we do not are codified and shared in our myths and this makes them enormously powerful—and necessary.

When myths are functioning properly, they bring us together and get us to act by using a specific formula that appears to be universal across all cultures.

Myth Ingredient 1:
Symbolic Thinking

Myths are neither true nor untrue, because they exist in a separate space and time. They need not conform to the literal constraints of reality. In fact, most societies have set the scene for their myths in a separate reality altogether—either long ago or far away. This sacred, imaginative realm informs the literal world but exists apart from it.

Using a symbolical language, myths allow us to break free from the often befuddling stream of facts that reality sends our way. They allow us to see the world through powerful symbols that stand in for and remind us of deep truths—truths that are often hard to grasp in literal language but easily evoked in symbols. You can think of the mythic realm like the realm of your dreams—not exactly *real* but deeply relevant to explaining reality and guiding life. In fact, Joseph Campbell called myths "public dreams."

Existing in the symbolic world makes myths *flexible*. New experiences of reality, even an earth-shattering invention like the atomic bomb, don't necessarily disprove them. The *Bhagavad Gita* has provided deep meaning on the proper way to live life for millions of people, including Robert Oppenheimer. It does not demand, however, that you believe the battle between Arjuna and his cousins really existed. Hindus can openly debate the symbolism of this story without fearing the charge of heresy. For most of human history, myths have survived through changing times because they did not demand to be seen as a *literal* retelling of events.

Myth Ingredient 2:
Story, Explanation, and Meaning

Myths provide *story*, *explanation*, and *meaning* in a single neat package. Take one of our most powerful myths, from which so much of our cultural history has derived—the first book of Genesis:

STORY: God created the world in seven days and gave man dominion over it.

EXPLANATION: This is how everything we see around us came into existence.

MEANING: So God deserves our gratitude and obedience.

The same elements can be found in modern foundational myths too, like the myth of the American dream.

STORY: America was clawed from the tyranny of British class and privilege and formed into an exceptional nation by men who believed in liberty, merit, and self-discipline.

EXPLANATION: That's why opportunity for success and prosperity is open to every American.

MEANING: So if you work hard, you too will be rewarded.

Any myth can be broken down this way. There is no right or wrong way to interpret a given myth. But if it is a myth and not simply a tale told for amusement, you should be able to find story, explanation, and meaning packaged within.

Myth Ingredient 3:
Ritual

Stories that provide compelling explanation and meaning can't help but hit us with a powerful moral of the story. And the first thing we do when hear a good moral is to wonder how we can apply it to our own lives. What believer of Genesis will not wonder: "What do I have to do to serve God?"

Because myths are set in a realm apart, humans have always sought to enact them in the real world through rituals. Rituals from a Passover Seder to a family ceremonially gathering to sign a first mortgage are how human beings make myths real.

————————————

When these elements are brought together—symbolic thinking, story, explanation, meaning, and ritual—the building blocks are in place. But not all stories of this kind actually become myths that shape society. For that to happen, these stories must be accepted by enough minds to approach a universal reference point. As we'll see, the *myth gap* has all but destroyed the universality of our myths.

The Opening of the Myth Gap

Myths tend to be extremely resilient, often persisting and evolving for millennia. But a myth gap arises when reality changes dramatically and our myths are not resilient enough to continue working in the face of that change.

Change has been accelerating at an ever-increasing pace over the last hundred years, and Oppenheimer's bomb caused only one tectonic shift in global consciousness. In the United States alone, we might also point to the civil rights movement, the Vietnam War, Watergate, the discovery of the ecological crisis, and the 2008 global financial collapse. It would have taken some extremely flexible mythology to continue to provide universal guidance in the face of all of these shifts.

As it turns out, our religious myths have not, for many, proven to be nearly flexible enough. And while we might have turned to science and entertainment to provide alternatives, these realms also have not been able to fill the gap with new myths. This has left the door wide open for marketers, who have gladly stepped in. But before we explore that history, I'll take a moment to explain what the modern myth gap looks like.

The Gap of Symbolic Thinking

Our mythic landscape has become brittle because many people have rejected the notion of thinking symbolically—and that's unique to our rationalist modern society. Today, we demand to know if something is true or not. This is why science and religion compete so furiously. Either the world is six thousand years old or several billion. Either we are descended from apelike ancestors or created by God. To the modern mind, only one can be right, and the other is wrong. To the mythological mind, both can easily be true. Held to the standard of literal truth, traditional myths start to crack.

The Gap of Story, Explanation, and Meaning

Today in our extremely diverse society, we perceive the functions of story, explanation, and meaning as dispersed among the realms of religion, science, and entertainment. When it comes to closing the myth gap, no one of these is stepping up to provide the complete myth packages we need.

Here's why: religions continue to play a powerful role in providing explanation and meaning, but please don't call the teachings contained in their holy texts *stories*. Today's mainstream religious leaders fear nothing more than the perception that their teachings sink to the level of myth. Mainstream religious communities ask that their religious stories be believed literally—and that price of entry proves too high for many. Religious myths are far from dead, but this rigidity causes them to drift further and further from universality.

Science, too, which now offers a powerful alternative to religion in terms of explanation, has shied away from the discussion of meaning. And, mainstream science, like religion, chooses not to present itself as a collection of stories at all.

Movies and television dominate our vibrant realm of imaginative storytelling, and most carry only a single burden—the expectation to entertain. Some entertainment is so popular as to achieve the status of universal cultural reference point. But few of our entertainers accept the responsibility of providing audiences with a genuine explanation of how the world works or offering deep meaning.

While pockets of forward-thinking religious leaders, scientists, and entertainers have attempted to reunify story, explanation, and meaning in their work, they all remain firmly out of the mainstream. And for a myth to function in society, it can't exist on the fringe. Where ancient and traditional society could turn to shamans and sages who took pride in combining story, explanation, and meaning, these sources have now disappeared or lost their widespread legitimacy.

The Gap of Ritual

Today's religious rituals are far too diverse and conflicting to provide our society any kind of universal glue, and they have had trouble evolving fast enough to meet changing realities. Entertainment isn't much help, since it emphasizes passive viewing, not active engagement, while science rejects the magic of symbolic action altogether.

—————————

With gaps like these opening up everywhere in the twentieth century, we need a new generation of effective storytellers—those to whom we can turn to update fraying myths and rituals and, when necessary, introduce new ones. As Robert Oppenheimer helped catapult us into the anxious age of the myth gap, we looked to our traditional mythmakers. They were unable to deliver the updated myths we so desperately needed.

The Marketer Becomes the Mythmaker

Of course, the opening of these gaps has been profoundly uncomfortable. Psychologist Carl Jung signaled an early warning about the myth gap just before the outbreak of World War I. Myth, he said, "is what is believed always, everywhere by everybody; hence the man who thinks he can live without myth or outside it, is an exception. He is like one uprooted, having no true link with either the past, or the ancestral life within him, or yet with contemporary society." In other words, societies without myth might easily fall apart. And a world full of such mythless men is a dangerous place.

Not long after Jung began to fret about men without myths, industrialists came face to face with an existential crisis of their own. World War I had mobilized the American economy to produce a tremendous quantity of material goods. Once the machine got rolling, it was no simple matter to turn it off, even once the war ended. The job and stock markets of an urbanizing America absolutely depended on continued production, or economic freefalls would ensue. But production of what? There was simply not enough demand to meet the supply. The myth gap was matched by an equally disturbing *demand gap*.

Thus the opportunity for a new kind of mythmaker—the *marketer*—presented itself. In fact, American political leaders of the time practically begged marketers to step in. As a result, the marketer went from a product pitchman to a major player in our cultural destiny.

Let's go back for a moment to the early part of the twentieth century: Puritan values and rituals, derived straight from the book of

Genesis, had built an America whose story, explanation, and meaning was based on thrift and modesty. (That history is illustrated, for example, by Benjamin Franklin's simple and wildly popular aphorisms, which had taught a nation to work hard and save heartily.)

To fill the demand gap, society itself would have to be revolutionized—transformed into something entirely new. Here's a perfect example of a myth challenged by vastly changed circumstances that had to be either updated or replaced. Just as Einstein called for a new mind-set to avert nuclear disaster, leaders twenty years earlier were calling for a new mind-set to avert an economic one.

During World War I, the marketing industry had flexed its muscles for America's leaders by turning the majority of its attention to the war effort, and it had delivered powerful results. As the new threat of soft demand emerged, our leaders again turned to marketers and in clear terms asked them to do what religion, science, and entertainment had failed to do: activate new myths to keep the economy going.

Listen to Calvin Coolidge addressing a gathering of top advertisers: "[Advertising] is the most potent influence in adapting and changing the habits and modes of life, affecting what we eat, what we wear and the work and play of the whole nation. Advertising ministers to the spiritual side of the trade." And Herbert Hoover: "You have taken over the job of creating desire and have transformed people into constantly moving happiness machines—machines which have become the key to economic progress." Coolidge and Hoover, the top political leaders of their day, were inviting marketers in no uncertain terms to create new explanations of how to live, new meaning and new rituals. In other words, marketers were being asked to step into role of modern mythmakers.

Marketers, of course, were uniquely suited to accept that role because they had the tools to close all the gaps that religion, science, and entertainment had left open. Since the late 1800s, the marketing industry had known about the power of telling stories in their advertisements. By the turn of the twentieth century, story-based campaigns like "Spotless Town" had rocketed Sapolio soap out of bland commodity status and into a highly coveted product. The poem-based stories of a fictional town built around the brand had become a regular dinner-table discussion topic in American homes. Stories like these were all about *thinking symbolically*. Nobody thought that Spotless Town, the Jolly Green Giant, the Morton Umbrella Girl, or the Marlboro Man were real, but they were still seen as powerfully instructive in the real world. Tens of millions of American smokers would switch brands in order to emulate the rugged role model they knew was fictional. This is the power of symbolic thinking that drives myths. Denied it elsewhere, people flock to these symbolic stories when they are put on offer in the marketplace.

The stories marketers tell have always done the work of myth in providing *explanation* and *meaning*. Every new product launch, from liquid dish soap to the iPad, has been a new practical *explanation* of how to live an ever-changing modern life. These explanations update as fast as the circumstances of our lives do, sometimes even faster. And from its most primitive days on, marketing has been about allowing a product or service to confer *meaning* on the purchaser. Even our take-out coffee container is a signifier of meaning and belonging. Looking at the cup, we know what tribe we are part of—Starbucks paper cup? Mainstream good lifers or aspiring to it. Dunkin's Styrofoam? Downscale and proud. Reusable steel travel cup? Eco-conscious and responsible.

And ritual? Well, of course. What's the good of a marketing story if it doesn't give audiences a way to live that story out? You might say that introducing a new ritual is the basis of every marketing campaign. Shopping has become the single ritual we universally share.

Symbolic thinking. Story, explanation, meaning, and ritual. Marketers would get the myth formula down cold. And thanks to a masterful class of marketers, the demand gap was decisively overcome as America shifted into hyperconsumption mode. The Puritan values of thrift and modesty were smashed, abandoned for easy consumer credit, conspicuous consumption, and deep personal relationships with brands. In terms of epoch-marking changes, this has been as profound a shift as the atom bomb.

The marketers who emerged as the new masters of the story wars had the complete package, ready for universal application. Cheered on by the highest powers, they began to update old myths and imagine new ones. History provides plenty of close-up looks at exactly how it's been done.

Cigarettes and the Myth of Adam's Rib: "Torches of Freedom"

Unto the woman he said, I will greatly multiply thy sorrow and thy conception; in sorrow thou shalt bring forth children; and thy desire shall be to thy husband, and he shall rule over thee.

—Genesis 3:16

By the beginning of the twentieth century, America's traditional agrarian life was being challenged by a new dominant force—the modern city.

Compared with life in the growing metropolises, life on the farm was only a stone's throw from the spot outside of Eden where Adam and Eve made their homestead after that little misstep in the garden. The scenario included a father who toiled on the land, ruling over his small dominion, and his wife as his helpmate. To a society based on this way of living, Genesis 3:16 provided reasonable story, explanation, and meaning. Everyone was familiar with it and almost everyone was living it.

But as women found independence from the old order and gained access to the educational and work opportunities that cities offered, "thy desire shall be to thy husband" was no longer a necessity for survival. In fact, to some of these women, it had stopped making sense at all. One culture-rocking outcome of this emerging rejection of Genesis 3:16 was the notion that women should have the right to vote. The idea that Eve might not agree with Adam on matters of public life was an 18-kiloton assault on a myth that had gone largely unchallenged for almost two millennia.

By the turn of the twentieth century, a new myth—that of the American woman on equal footing with the American man—was struggling to take root in the popular imagination. A small but influential group of urban suffragettes had begun marching in the streets, demanding the vote and sparking a major debate across the nation. These few women were prying open the myth gap, but it was a marketer, Edward Bernays, who would fill that gap by giving every American woman a ritual by which to live the suffragette's story—not by joining the marchers, but by smoking.

Bernays, Sigmund Freud's nephew, was the inventor of the field of *public relations,* a phrase he coined himself. Unlike other marketers of his day, Bernays saw marketing not as an exercise in providing products people desired. Instead, he claimed to be able to create new desires using his uncle's fresh insights into psychology.

In 1928, George Washington Hill, the president of the American Tobacco Company, approached Bernays with a problem—the old stories about American womanhood were encouraging women to be far too *modest.* These stories were the source of serious taboos against women smoking in public. Only a few years before, a woman in New York had been arrested for lighting up on the street. Just like voting, public smoking was a privilege of men, and that was bad for business. Bernays had a solution.

If the smoking ritual Hill was trying to sell wouldn't work with the old myth, why not attach it to a new story with tremendous momentum? Only eight years earlier, the 19th Amendment had been ratified, giving the suffragettes a monumental victory. Of course, they had no intention of stopping with the vote; the push for equality had only just begun. Perhaps providing the new story these women were writing with a ritual—smoking—could elevate their story to the level of myth. And more than a few cigarettes would be sold along the way.

The idea first occurred to Bernays after he brought a cigarette to a top Freudian analyst. "The cigarette," the analyst told him, "is a symbol of the penis."

"Well," Bernays reasoned. "If women are wanting everything men have, what could be more primal than wanting a penis?"

With penis envy on the brain, Bernays scribbled out a strategy to get women smoking by tying the cigarette to an emerging story that turned Genesis on its head. Women who wanted everything men had would be taught to want cigarettes, too.

Bernays hired a bunch of glamorous young women to march in the New York Easter Day parade posing as suffragettes. At a given signal they were to reach under their skirts, pull out cigarettes and light up, calling them "Torches of Freedom." The phrase stirred Bernays's soul as soon as he penned it.

He tipped the press off ahead of time about the planned rebellion. The stunt went off without a hitch, and it rocked the American imagination. Papers across the nation ran stories about these "suffragettes," and advertisements to drive the point home quickly followed. The taboo against women smoking in public came crashing down. Within a decade, there would be dozens of national brands designed and marketed specifically for women.

It was the suffragettes who helped to open the myth gap, putting a face on this renegotiation of Old Testament values. They became major characters in the powerful new mythology of American womanhood that continues to transform society to this day. And it was a marketer, Edward Bernays, who helped to activate this emerging mythology so it could be universally shared and lived by all American women. It would powerfully and conveniently connect millions of women to a new story, explanation, and meaning every time they went through the ritual of lighting up.

Litter and the Myth of the Wild Frontier: The Crying Indian

And God blessed them, and God said unto them, Be fruitful, and multiply, and replenish the earth, and subdue it: and have dominion over the fish of the sea, and over the fowl of the air, and over every living thing that moveth upon the earth.

—Genesis 1:28

Just as the Genesis story teaches a man to rule over his wife, it's also pretty clear about how mankind should deal with the Earth: Subdue it. As soon as our Pilgrim forefathers first beheld the marvelous expanse of seemingly uninhabited forests that would be their new home, Genesis 1:28 was instantly reactivated. To people coming from a crowded, deforested European continent, this was like a return to the Garden and a chance to carry out God's commandment anew. The idea of a virgin wilderness awaiting human hands has been at the heart of American mythology ever since.

So, from the beginning, American heroes have been pioneers, hunters, and cowboys—Davy Crockett, Johnny Appleseed, Annie Oakley, John Wayne, Rambo—men and women willing to step out of the safety of civilization and onto the frontier, clearing the next patch of ground for the use of civilized people. Our stories from Westerns to space epics take place on the frontier because that's where our core Genesis-based mythology can be lived out.

In the language of the frontier myth, leaving nature unexploited by human hands is not just a waste; it is an act of immorality, a rebellion against God's commandments. Thus the myth of the frontier became a powerful guide for action in two ways: It instructed Americans to continually push the frontier outward, exploiting land not just for economic gain but for spiritual redemption. And it justified the removal of "immoral" native people who were brazenly failing to subdue the land they inhabited.

Into the 1960s, this two-part frontier myth held enormous, near-universal cultural resonance. Intact, it made for powerful story wars marketing fodder. When Leo Burnett took over the Marlboro account, filtered cigarettes were seen as a lady's product (Bernays must have been proud). By introducing the rugged Marlboro Man, Burnett gave the frontier myth a new symbol and a universal ritual through which any male could assert his cowboy masculinity. The Marlboro Man singlehandedly made his cigarette the best-selling brand among male smokers for generations. Most Marlboro ads consisted of nothing but a single image and the brand name. The myth did all the heavy lifting. The Marlboro Man is *still* regarded as the most iconic brand spokesman in advertising history—and he never uttered a word.

Around the same time the Marlboro Man was born, the Kennedy administration was leveraging the "savage" part of the frontier myth to justify engagement in the emerging conflict in Vietnam. As American myth expert Richard Slotkin points out, John F. Kennedy's ambassador to South Vietnam, Maxwell Taylor, described and justified military actions as moving the "Indians" away from the "fort" so that the "settlers" could plant "corn." Soldiers responded deeply to the mythic lingo, for years, they would commonly describe Vietnam as "Indian country" and search and destroy missions as a game of "cowboys and Indians." Even once the literal American frontier had been closed, its mythological resonance was alive and well, endlessly providing story, explanation, and meaning. Everything from smoking to war could be seen as a ritual enactment of it. And then things began to go terribly wrong.

In 1962, Rachel Carson's *Silent Spring* hit the *New York Times* best-seller list and launched modern environmentalism. The book focused on DDT—the ultimate Earth-subduing pesticide that had made it safe to "plant corn" in the wilderness. The book sensationally revealed the chemical's unintended and devastating ecological side effects. We were suddenly confronted with an all out story wars attack on the biblical exhortation to subdue nature. Many awoke for the first time to the possibility that in beating back nature, we were beating back ourselves. Perhaps it wasn't man versus nature after all. Perhaps it was man *and* nature versus oblivion. We had once been at the mercy of God and the natural world, frightening and powerful forces. Just as Oppenheimer's bomb made us realize that we humans might be as powerful as God, *Silent Spring* was the first step in the realization that nature might be at *our* mercy.

The myth gap grew and eco-anxiety began to pervade the American public, growing more intense with each successive revelation: ozone depletion, species loss, and, of course, climate change. The man versus nature myth, once so universally shared, began to divide society. Environmentalists have been toiling ever since to update and rewrite the myth. Those who oppose the "treehuggers" seem to cling to the myth ever more fiercely, rejecting any scientific evidence that might question the march of economic growth.

As our relationship to nature on the frontier began to crack, so did our relationship to its "Indians." The situation was deteriorating in Vietnam. Opposition to the war was rising steadily, and for the first time, the myth of America as an archetypal cowboy battling for good on the frontier was being loudly and widely questioned. This new thinking combined with the dawning realization brought to us by the civil rights movement that, long after the abolition of slavery, America did not always fall on the side of justice and freedom. The myth of the virtuous settler versus the immoral savage began, to many, to seem a relic of a disappearing age. Even Western films began to question past treatment of Native Americans; eventually the genre would shift 180 degrees, to the point where films like *Dances with Wolves* and *Avatar,* in which the natives are the centers of virtue, would become the norm. Instead of subduing the Indians, the cowboys of these new stories would learn from them and adopt their ways, becoming completed heroes in the process.

By the 1970s, with both core pillars of the frontier myth—the subjugation of nature and the savagery of Indians—deeply embattled in the story wars, there was a clear need for access to an updated version of the myth. The marketing masters behind the Keep America Beautiful campaign saw a chance to provide just that.

Despite its public service-y name, the campaign was largely a food industry attack on laws that would limit packaging waste or add deposits to disposable bottles. The campaign set out to undermine these efforts by firmly implanting the idea that litter prevention was a personal, not an industry, responsibility. The "Litterbug" campaign placed the blame for our garbage-strewn cities and highways not on wasteful packaging but on immoral individuals. Its tagline: "People start pollution, people can stop it." The statement, of course, hides the fact that for every can of trash that people throw away, seventy cans of trash are made upstream.

In 1971, with a flood of troubling ecological revelations pouring in and the war in Vietnam worsening dramatically, Keep America

Beautiful provided the perfect therapeutic response to the anxiety caused by the crumbling of our cherished frontier myth. Its marketers would call their story-ad the *Crying Indian,* and it is considered the most iconic, and possibly effective, PSA of all time—and a powerful example of story wars mastery.

The ad stars actor Iron Eyes Cody (actually, an Italian immigrant who made a career of portraying Native Americans). As the ad opens, Cody rows his canoe majestically, tense music rising. The camera pans up to reveal that he is on a bleak, modern industrial river—he is on subdued land and it is anything but virtuous. Within ten seconds, the myth gap is invoked. But can the marketers close it?

Cody pulls the canoe onto a littered beach and the announcer's voice warns: "Some people have a deep abiding respect for the natural beauty that was once this country. And some people don't." A car drives by and some jerk tosses a plastic bag out the window. We zoom into the Indian's face and a single tear rolls down his cheek. America, from all sides of the political spectrum, burst into tears with him.

But wait—here comes the tagline and something we can do to be part of this new story—a story in which nature is respected, our former beauty restored. It's a story in which the Indian is the hero, the cowboy in the car the villain: "People start pollution. People can stop it."

The Ad Council marketers working for Keep America Beautiful, like Edward Bernays before them, offered a symbolic ritual that was available to all. Litter prevention and eventually recycling would become healing acts by which people could overcome the anxiety of a broken myth and feel virtuous again—reconciled with their planet and with their past.

Tea, Tents, and the American Dream: Responses to Economic Crisis

Each man and each woman shall be able to attain to the fullest stature of which they are innately capable, and be recognized

by others for what they are, regardless of the fortuitous circumstances of birth or position.

—James Truslow Adams, who coined the term
the American dream

Of course, the anxiety created by myth gaps and the power conferred to those communicators who heal them continue to fuel the
story wars to this day. As I write, the most salient emotion on both
sides of the American political spectrum is anger. And that anger
has been the direct result of the fraying of perhaps our greatest national myth.

The American dream equates liberty with economic opportunity
for anyone willing to work hard, and it stands at the heart of the concept of America as an exceptional nation. But the 2008 economic
meltdown and the government bailout of the "too big to fail" financial institutions seemed to many to be laser-targeted at dismantling
the promises of the American dream. Jobs, pensions, and home
ownership—the average citizen's just rewards for hard work—had
evaporated. This cherished story suddenly appeared to be a lie.

Two movements focused that anger with sensational effect, driving thousands of Americans to the streets and dominating the
media: the Tea Party and Occupy Wall Street. Where countless top-
down efforts failed to capture the imagination of a seething public,
these two movements caught on. Characteristic of the digitoral era,
they may not look like marketing campaigns, but they are. Both
were intentionally sparked by nontraditional media outlets whose
aim was to create a brand that would focus political rage.

The emotional impact of these movements in the United States
came from the fact that they offered a modernization of the myth
of the American dream that fills an unbearable gap.

Their policy platforms, if they can even be defined, were
hardly new or distinct. It was their symbolic imagery that is
breakthrough—modern-day American revolutionaries and "the
99 percent."

The Tea Party invoked the genesis of the dream—when our
founding fathers declared emphatically that this land does not

belong in the hands of ruling elites. Their declaration of liberty, expressed in economic terms—the Boston Tea Party was, after all, an act of resistance to taxes—is the foundation of the dream. As recession began to unravel the dream, the modern-day Tea Party sought to inspire Americans to believe that the downturn's attack on their prosperity was actually an attack on their liberty. By wearing eighteenth-century garb and squarely pointing their near-violent fervor at a government too big and too out of touch, they turned the complexities of the financial collapse into a simple and familiar morality tale, reconnecting it to a story everyone was familiar with. By naming the dismantler of the dream, the party responsible for the myth gap, they identified a clear villain (the government) and a clear conflict (resistance). Suddenly, the collapse was no longer a force of nature but a battle.

Hundreds of thousands signed up to fight this battle and reaffirm the myth. Still flush with victory in 2010, Americans for Prosperity, a DC advocacy group, which had been a key organizing force in the movement, held a national training event for Tea Party leaders. They called it "Defending the American Dream."

Occupy Wall Street may have had very different policy aims, but its breakthrough message of "the 99%" also worked to reaffirm the values of the dream and to provide clear character and conflict. It's worth noting that the message of Occupy differed from the Tea Party in that it did not seek to reaffirm American exceptionalism—it saw itself as an inclusive global movement. Otherwise it filled the myth gap in very much the same way. "The 99 percent" resonated as shorthand for the American dream concept that economic prosperity should be available to anyone willing to work for it. It must not be the exclusive provenance of the powerful elite. Like the Tea Party, the 99 percent message focused public anger by identifying a villain and inviting its followers into conflict. Instead of an overactive government, the elitist villains of the Occupy myth are corporations (embodied in the symbol of Wall Street) and a government weakly following their commands.

Even as the physical Occupations began to slow, it was clear that the battleground was not the parks but the story about what America is.

That's why Republican messaging guru Frank Luntz said: "I'm so scared of this anti–Wall Street effort. I'm frightened to death. They're having an impact on what the American people think of capitalism." While most media outlets focus on the fight in the streets, Luntz clearly sees the more important fight for the myth.

Both of these movements worked because they stepped into the gap left behind by the fraying myth of the American dream to supply new story (they provide clear character and conflict), explanation (they tell us that the root cause of the complex meltdown is simple), meaning (they exhort us as average people to stand up), and even ritual (they invite us to tea parties and tent cities). Their therapeutic and viral power was not contained in their manifestos but in the new myths they provided.

Success in the story wars began for all of these campaigns—from Torches of Freedom to today's explosive political movements—in understanding the state of the myth gap at the moment of their release. Every marketer is looking to tap into the zeitgeist, and there is no more direct way into it than through the void created by fraying myths. This is where anxiety is welling up. This is where people are looking for therapeutic relief. This is where new ritual is ripe for the making.

Marketers as mythmakers. Is this something to be excited about? Terrified of? Though some may instinctively wish to return to a media landscape ruled by shamans, bards, or priests, that's not likely to happen any time soon. That marketers are some of our most powerful mythmakers is, for now, a basic fact of life. And marketers would be foolish not to take advantage of the power this confers—it's the most direct path to success in the work we do. In fact, this book is a call to fully embrace that mythmaker's role and join the story wars. But if we do, we must also accept the responsibility the role carries. As thinkers from Jung to Einstein to Coolidge make clear, these stories are not idle play. They can set the direction of a society's future. And as we'll see in the next chapter, the direction marketing has chosen to set needs some serious rethinking.

CHAPTER FOUR

Marketing's Dark Art

February 3, 2011. They had spent the night in the square. A million of them; some said more. They chanted, shouted, leaned against each other's backs when they needed rest. History suffused the atmosphere all around them. And though several of them had been murdered over the last few days, the protesters felt safety in their enormous numbers.

To the young woman sitting among the crowd, the turnout was a miracle—many would call it a miracle of her own making. Just two weeks ago, Asmaa Mahfouz had been in this same spot, feeling deeply let down. She had posted an invitation on Facebook for others to join her in demonstrating on behalf of four Egyptians who had set themselves on fire to protest the Mubarak regime. She even took the dangerous step of giving out her phone number. But more policemen showed up than protestors—only three of them in all. It was a harrowing experience.

Still, Mahfouz believed in bravery—her own and that of her fellow Egyptians. So a few days later she had posted a video, brazenly showing her face on YouTube, openly calling for revolution. It was

---

Edward Bernays and the roots of marketing's dark arts

only slightly less risky than self-immolation: "Don't be afraid of the government. Fear none but God. God says He will not change the condition of a people until they change what is in themselves . . . Come down with us and demand your rights, my rights, your family's rights. I am going down on January 25, and I will say no to corruption, no to this regime."

The video went viral almost immediately. Hundreds of thousands of people saw it, and hundreds of thousands of them showed up. Some were shamed into action by the sight of a woman—a woman!—stepping forward. Others were simply stirred by seeing a real face of the revolution, unafraid of the light of day. From that moment forward, the momentum had been unstoppable, and Mahfouz had been there for every moment of it.

Just before dawn, the crowd was about as quiet as a million people can be. It would be a long day, for the protesters and the government soldiers charged with the hopeless task of containing them.

Then there was a single crack, followed by several more. Now, sustained bursts of machine gun fire. The sound seemed to be coming from everywhere as bullets flew into the sea of bodies. Suddenly the crowd was electrified, Mahfouz's revolution reawakened.

———————

A few thousand miles away, shoemaker Kenneth Cole had a big day ahead of him too. His spring line had just launched online—some exciting new stuff mixed in with the classics. But with the Egyptian revolution in full swing, it was going to be a tough day to get any real attention. Not the kind of thing you can plan for, no one to blame, but a shame nonetheless.

Cole realized, of course, that his problems were nothing compared with those of the kids in the square. He had long been a philanthropist, an AIDS activist, a champion of the poor. He knew there was more to life than selling shoes. Still, there was social media marketing to do. And because Cole had always insisted on doing his own tweeting, the problem of getting buzz was his alone.

Maybe I can have a little fun with this, he thought. Everyone's tweeting about Egypt. Why not me?

If the goal was simply to get earned media, it was a stroke of brilliance—Cole was about to get more of it than he could possibly have imagined.

"Millions are in uproar in #Cairo," he tapped out with a smile. "Rumor is they heard our new spring collection is now available online ... —KC."

"Good one," he must have thought.

Not really.

Before we look at the public's predictable response to this cringeworthy tweet, we should note that Cole was trying to do what story wars combatants have always done. First, he sensed the myth gap opening up. For a decade, a powerful story about Arab people had been nurtured in the Western media. The Arab "street" was painted as alien and fanatic. Many used this story as the justification for American support of men like Mubarak and Ghaddafi. According to the story, without these strongmen in place, the people—fundamentalist at their core—would take over. Look at Iraq. There, American soldiers roamed neighborhoods that teemed with insurgents unwilling to accept the gift of democracy.

But suddenly, thanks to the revolution in Tahrir Square, the world was finally meeting real Arabs face-to-face, and these presumed fanatics seemed instead to be an idealized vision of ourselves— peaceful, democracy-loving, tech-savvy, ingenious. A new story of the Arab citizen was being born—it still is—and the revolution in Cairo would become a perfect story wars battleground because it was challenging a deeply embedded myth. Cole just wanted to be there as it happened, riding the wave to digitoral success.

So the tweet went out and the responses rolled in almost instantly—thousands and thousands of them:

> "People from New Orleans are flooding into Kenneth Cole stores."

> "Black Pants Down—our new looks are more slimming than a Somali diet!"

And directly to the point: "WTF is wrong with you?"

With the Egyptian uprising capturing the attention of every news outlet on Earth, the story of Cole's crass attempt to cash in on it and the gleeful mockery now hounding him was buoyed to the top of the headlines too. Within hours, major media outlets were all over the story, and the shoe company began the painful process of backtracking: "I've dedicated my life to raising awareness about serious social issues," Cole pleaded on Facebook. "And in hindsight my attempt at humor regarding a nation liberating themselves against oppression was poorly timed and absolutely inappropriate."

If Cole's marketing mistake seems like an isolated impulsive act, it wasn't. He is famous for pushing a clear moral of the story in his marketing: nothing in life is more important than shopping. In Tahrir Square, the world was witnessing perhaps the most uplifting, positive human story of the new century, and the marketer's response was "That's nice, go shop." Soon after 9/11, Cole had put up a billboard with the simple message: "God Dress America." What's new here is not the tactless tweet—that was totally predictable, given the language many marketers reflexively use. What is new is that audiences can now respond instantly. Cole learned the danger of his strategy because an outraged observer had decided to organize a reply, creating a fake KC account that garnered tens of thousands of followers. Its fans reveled in ridiculing Cole. In the broadcast era, audiences would have just been dumbfounded at Cole's astounding lack of judgment and taste—a few might have even written letters of protest—and then they would have moved on. In the digitoral era, audiences are speaking up and fighting back.

It's not just Cole who's learning that this common marketing language—one that promotes mindless consumerism while sneering at higher purpose—may be losing its grip. Less than a month after the #Cairo tweet, social shopping sensation Groupon aired a set of multimillion-dollar Super Bowl ads that made the same mistake—pushing too far the concept that nothing in life could possibly be quite as important as good stuff at a good price.

The most condemned of Groupon's three spots floated up to the top of nearly every "Worst Super Bowl Ads" list and led to universal viewer and blogger condemnation.

"The people of Tibet are in trouble. Their very culture is in jeopardy," the ad begins. It appears to be a charity appeal from actor Timothy Hutton, but then it takes an unexpected turn: "But they still whip up an amazing fish curry . . . and since two hundred of us bought at Groupon.com, we're each getting $30 worth of Tibetan food for just $15 at a Himalayan restaurant in Chicago."

The people of Tibet *are* in trouble, and their plight has become the passionate cause of hundreds of thousands of activists. Almost as if it had anticipated that backlash was just around the corner, Groupon had already committed to donate to a Tibetan advocacy group. But in the face of the ad, the gesture appeared empty. One viewer incisively summed up the effect of the ad on Twitter: "Groupon seems to have achieved the unique feat of paying $3M to lose customers who previously loved them."

As the negative attention rolled in like a tsunami, Groupon CEO Andrew Mason took to his blog, stammering his way through a circuitous explanation: "Our ads highlight the often trivial nature of stuff on Groupon when juxtaposed against bigger world issues, making fun of Groupon." The explanation didn't hold water, of course, and the outrage and ridicule continued to flow. Groupon would very publicly fire its ad agency, Crispin Porter + Bogusky, try several times to reexplain its position and then, eventually, just remove the ads from sight.

Groupon and Kenneth Cole both tried to explain away their bad-taste marketing efforts as lapses of judgment, foolish mistakes in the fog of war—and they probably genuinely believed these explanations. But they're missing the point. What we're seeing here are not isolated errors. These are examples of the kind of marketing messages that, as a society, we have been living with for decades. It's only now that digitorally empowered audiences have been able to object.

Messages like these deny the concept of higher human purpose. They have become the foundation of our dominant marketing language and thus our mythic landscape. And they speak the language of what I call the *dark art of marketing,* which emphasizes the act of consumption as the highest human purpose.

As we'll see, this strategy is not the only, or even best, way to fight the story wars, but for too long marketers have used it as a go-to tool whether selling fashion, a candidate, or even a social cause. As marketers have become mythmakers, the use of this approach has had a profoundly negative impact on our society.

This practice has a fascinating history—its roots going back to the days of Freud, Bernays, and the demand gap. If we are to complete our picture of the broken landscape of today's story wars, we must trace these roots and how they led to the dark art's modern expression.

The Dark Art of Marketing

Each of us has received more than 1 million marketing messages in our lifetime—many of us hit that number before we turned eighteen. We may consciously choose to act on any of these messages or to ignore them. But unconsciously, we can't avoid the psychological buildup of the morals of the marketing stories we hear. These messages come to inform our sense of self, the world, and our place in it. If everywhere you look there are stories designed to direct you to action, and these stories tell you that you are powerful and full of potential, you are likely to come to believe them and act out that belief. If the stories you are told have the opposite message, you will likely come to believe and act very differently.

Marketers have consistently tried to deny this idea. Whenever regulators have expressed concern about the impact of advertising on children or society as a whole, marketers have pointed to studies that show that these stories have little or no impact on how we live our lives. Yet, inexplicably, global advertising spends have reached over $400 billion dollars annually. Nobody spends billions without expecting impact.

So why talk about today's dominant marketing language as a dark art? Jung believed that for each positive psychological factor, there was an opposite shadow side. It's the foundation of George Lucas's concept of the "dark side" of the Force; the Force is powerfully positive, but misunderstood or misused, it is just as powerfully negative. When we look at the traditional function of myth in society, we can see just how clearly the morals of our current marketing stories are providing messages that are the exact *opposite* of the messages generally conveyed by a society's most important myths. In effect, they are embodying the shadow side of myth—the dark side.

What, then, is the proper role of myth? Studying thousands of foundational stories across dozens of cultures and epochs, Joseph Campbell found a common purpose for mythology, a theme that makes myth so valuable. He called it the *hero's journey*.

At the end of his life, Campbell told Bill Moyers that all myths are about "the maturation of the individual from dependency to adulthood through maturity and then to the exit; and then how to relate to this society and how to relate this society to the world of nature and the cosmos." Simply put, myths help us grow up. They guide the selfish, frightened child to become a mature, wise contributor to the community. Is it any wonder young children listen so eagerly to stories, demanding them at every turn? They want to learn to grow up. Have you ever noticed how the heroes of most classic tales are adolescents learning to be adults? Consider Homer's Telemachus, the Grimms' Hansel and Gretel, Carroll's Alice, Baum's Dorothy, Lucas's Skywalker.

As Campbell so famously discovered in our mythic record, stories about how to mature are the myths we rely on to face the difficulties of life, especially in changing and challenging times. We can clearly see the yearning for maturation all around us. No matter our political or moral orientation, most of us wish for a mature society, full of citizens that can think long term, run a respectful democracy, make compromises, and leave a healthy planet for future generations.

Held to the standard of delivering stories that help people and society mature, a great many modern mythmakers are falling terribly short. As marketers, we've inherited a very specific storytelling approach from those who came before us. Even if we consider ourselves wildly innovative and unorthodox, we come to our work fluent in a marketing language developed over the last hundred years. And that dominant language is based on an *inadequacy approach*. Inadequacy stories encourage immature emotions like greed, vanity, and insecurity by telling us that we are somehow incomplete. These stories then offer to remove the discomfort of those emotions with a simple purchase or association with a brand.

Instead of teaching us to engage in the difficult journey of maturation from child to citizen, the myths of our day keep us thinking like adolescents, consumers who wait to be told what we want and then supplied with satisfaction. Even participation in democracy, the very expression of citizenship, has been reduced for most of us to the convenient act of voting and maybe slapping a sticker on a bumper. With participation at the polls consistently falling at or below 50 percent, even these simple acts prove too much to ask of today's Americans.

Campbell described the child uninitiated by myth this way: "You are in no way a self-responsible free agent but an obedient dependent expecting and receiving punishment and reward." In other words, you are not a citizen. You are a consumer. To the marketers, like Edward Bernays, who first took on the role of mythmakers and rescued the American economy from the demand gap, keeping people in this adolescent state wasn't just good for business—it was a moral imperative.

Inadequacy Marketing Is Born

In the beginning of the twentieth century, Edward Bernays's uncle, Sigmund Freud, introduced the world to the notion that the human mind could be studied and understood as a science. And the peek inside the mind that Freud gave us wasn't pretty. In fact, it provided reason for major anxiety. Freud painted a picture of aggressive and sexual forces deep in the unconscious that universally drive people. Most of us try to suppress these forces but to little avail—they are rooted in our deepest selves and eventually will find expression. "Culture has to call up every possible reinforcement to erect barriers against the aggressive instincts of men," Freud wrote.

"Hence, too, its ideal command to love one's neighbor as oneself, which is really justified by the fact that nothing is so completely at variance with human nature as this."

Living in Central Europe at the outbreak of World War I, a horrific conflict of unparalleled violence, Freud saw evidence all around him that humans were dangerous and dark. In a world of machine guns and biplanes with bombs, it wasn't hard to reach the conclusion that mankind needed to be controlled and pacified in order to avoid further barbarity. World War II provided more heartbreaking evidence that this was true.

Our marketing forefathers were inspired by contemporary psychology to believe such maturity was ultimately impossible for the masses. To these men, encouraging people to go on a journey of self-discovery would have seemed a futile and even dangerous exercise. They saw themselves as acting for the public good, believing they were rescuing a society on the brink of economic and social collapse. So they set out to found a marketing language that would avert these twin crises, and the dark art of marketing was born. It would be a language specifically designed to create feelings of inadequacy, stimulate immature drives, and then assuage these negative feelings with consumer goods.

The men who designed and nurtured inadequacy marketing were not side characters in the early days of marketing from the 1920s to the 1950s. They were its central figures. Ernest Dichter, an eminent psychologist and founder of the once-popular practice of *motivational research,* argued that a "stable citizen" worked off his frustrations by spending money to gratify his desires. And of course, a stable citizen, harmlessly working off his dangerous drives by shopping, was the foundation of a stable world. Dichter's daughter would say that her father and his colleagues thought that "by helping people use products to have a strong positive sense of self, they were forging the greatest society ever."

Stanley Resor was the dominant adman of the 1920s and head of the J. Walter Thompson agency, still one of the world's major ad firms. Resor was one of the first to bring the nascent field of psychology to the industry, and he evangelized that it was a mistake to think that human beings were individuals full of potential and purpose. Instead, he believed, people were undifferentiated parts of a writhing mass, driven by vanity, hunger, fear, and lust.

And then, of course, there was Edward Bernays, who was deeply convinced of the validity of his uncle's theories. In fact, it was through Bernays's enterprising spirit that Freud first became popular in the United States. From the 1920s to the 1950s, Bernays was seemingly everywhere—leading the efforts of war propaganda, remaking the images of presidents, engineering a Central American coup on behalf of the United Fruit Company, selling cigarettes and cars. His office became the center of the Madison Avenue universe.

Bernays is credited with inventing everything from PR to product placement. He considered himself to be not just a businessman but an architect of society, and he wrote extensively about this aspect of his work. He taught that by stimulating inner desires and then fulfilling those desires, marketers had invented a way to manage the dangerous, previously uncontrollable masses.

Bernays used his role as a mythmaker to encourage people to see personal choice as a decision between products, not between ways of ordering community or society. In the world he was designing, the primary duty of the citizen would be to consume, and the hero's journey would take place in the safe confines of the supermarket, where nobody would get hurt.

Resor, Bernays, and Dichter are giants of marketing's early days and the most successful combatants in the story wars of their time. On the foundations they laid, the common language of marketing has been built, layer upon layer. Once you've examined its formula, you will begin to recognize it everywhere. And though it constantly evolves, the dark art has never moved far from its roots.

Dissecting Inadequacy Marketing

All inadequacy marketing stories follow a simple two-step approach. Once you know the formula, you'll instantly recognize it in marketing messages all around you.

Step 1: Create Anxiety

As we've seen, all story-based marketing campaigns contain an underlying *moral of the story* and supply a ritual that is suggested to react to that moral. In inadequacy stories, the moral always begins with "You are not . . ." and plays off of at least one negative emotion.

GREED: "You are not in possession of what can make you happy."

FEAR: "You are not safe."

LUST: "You are not attractive enough to be loved."

You get the idea.

In their early experiments, inadequacy marketers learned that they could easily invoke several of these emotions at once by designing stories in which the problems associated with each lack spelled disaster in the lives of relatable characters. Alternatively, they would tell stories about people we are meant to envy because they, unlike us, have been able to overcome that lack and fill the gaping void.

Step 2: Introduce the Magic Solution

Faced with the welling up of these emotions, the maturing lead actor of the traditional myth would resist the temptation to indulge them. Our books and movies always tell us this is what we must do: nearly overwhelmed by the tempting power of the One Ring he possesses, Frodo must throw it into the abyss or be reduced to a monster of greed. Jesus's final test is to resist the temptations of Satan for power, wealth, and the trappings of a worldly life. Snow White's stepmother must renounce her vanity or be destroyed by it—which she is.

The hero will always remind herself that nothing can ever truly satisfy greed, vanity, and lust. The moral of traditional myths is, of course, that these impulses must be transcended.

Overcoming these emotions is easier said than done; that's why maturation is difficult. So inadequacy stories provide a more direct and convenient response. They offer to magically soothe the desire with exactly what it's looking for and allow us to do so through the consumption of a product—no hard work required. They tell Jesus to give in to the temptations—treat yourself, you've earned it. They offer a miracle skin cream to the vain Queen. Hey, sixty is the new thirty.

To believe stories that tell us that objects can satisfy these deep feelings of inadequacy takes a tremendous feat of symbolic, mythical thinking. But these stories really work. Generations of us have come to believe that joy can be purchased in a Coke bottle, status in the body of a Cadillac, sex appeal in the gears of a Rolex. Safety can be achieved with a single vote at the ballot box for a get-tough-on-crime candidate. Reconciliation with the past can be gained by recycling. Of course, all of this would seem preposterous to someone not fluent in inadequacy marketing's mythic language. But once you speak it, as we all do now, these statements make perfect sense. In fact, they may be the only statements of universal truth we share today. They are our most intact, actionable myths.

Tell a story that will *create anxiety* then *introduce the magic solution*. These are the two steps of all inadequacy-based campaigns, and we can clearly trace their presence throughout the decades as the practice has evolved. In its early days, the inadequacy strategy was unvarnished and bold-faced. We might call it the *primitive inadequacy* approach. Here the stress is on the first step of the strategy: create anxiety.

As the inadequacy strategy became the dominant force in advertising, audiences began to get wise to the underlying messages of the primitive approach, and inadequacy marketing was forced to evolve into what we might call the *modern inadequacy* approach. Closer to the modern end of the spectrum, the stress falls more on the second step: introduce the magical solution. In the modern approach, anxiety may be subtly invoked or just assumed.

In the supposedly tongue-in-cheek *postmodern* inadequacy stories typified by Kenneth Cole and Groupon, consumption becomes important not just as a therapeutic response to anxiety but as a therapeutic response to caring about anything at all—shop therapy in the face of the inconvenient experience of being alive.

As we look at the building blocks of inadequacy marketing, you will no doubt hear the echoes of thousands of marketing campaigns that have populated your personal media landscape. You may even hear echoes of your own messaging efforts.

The Primitive Inadequacy Approach: Sad Edna

CREATE ANXIETY

In 1922, Gerard Lambert was fretting over sales. His father had invented Listerine, a good surgical antiseptic that had also found modest success as a cure for throat infections. But even this broader market was too small to make Listerine a business worth getting excited about. So Lambert sat down with admen Milton Feasley and Gordon Seagrove to brainstorm some new idea for the hard-to-market product. Bad breath was suggested, and when a chemist confirmed that Listerine would in fact work on "halitosis," they were intrigued. None of them had heard the word before but it sounded scary in a good, medical kind of way. Before long, they would come up with a plan to build one of the most successful personal care products in history. Feasley would call the campaign strategy "whisper copy" and "advertising by fear."

"Often a bridesmaid, never a bride," introduces an unhappy young woman, alone at thirty, deprived of the status, safety, and sex appeal she so desires. And to make matters worse: "Since halitosis never announces itself to the victim, you simply cannot know when you have it." Suddenly, a condition nobody had ever heard of became the fear of a nation. Through the tragedy of Sad Edna, America internalized a difficult, but important, moral of the story: "You are not safe, sexy, or in possession of what you want because halitosis is silently standing in the way."

Ad Age lists "Always a Bridesmaid" as number 48 on the list of the twentieth century's top campaigns—two spots better than the

Crying Indian. Of course, Sad Edna wouldn't just sell millions of dollars of Listerine. She would become a founding goddess in the pantheon of the new American myth of the sanitized body. This myth, in turn, would lay the foundation for a multi-billion dollar beauty industry.

INTRODUCE THE MAGIC SOLUTION

Thankfully, there is a ritual to enact that can ease the anxiety of halitosis. That ritual is, of course, the daily use of Listerine. In this example of the primitive inadequacy approach the emphasis is on creating the anxiety. The solution is quite straightforward. The magic of the campaign is not making readers believe Listerine helps cure bad breath—it does. The real magic is making people believe that Listerine will conquer the fears that the product itself has instilled.

Sad Edna may seem quaint by today's advertising standards, and it is true that inadequacy marketing has evolved significantly since. But the long shadow of the primitive approach is still very much with us. A 2011 ad released by Breezes Resorts and Spas asks viewers: "You ever get the feeling everyone's having more fun than you? They are. It's time to play catch up."

Even marketers with far more noble intentions than the cynical Feasley continually fall back on whisper copy and advertising by fear.

A couple of years ago, Greenpeace brought us a perfect example. The thirty-second spot features a young man walking through his office while his coworkers abuse him behind his back. One gives him the finger, another drops a fat wad of saliva into his coffee. A nasty note is plastered onto his back. He is an outcast, totally rejected by his peers. He is not safe. He is not sexy. He has no status. And then he walks out to the parking lot and climbs into an SUV. He doesn't even realize he's being abused; after all, since eco-hatred never announces itself, there is simply no way to know if you have it. But we can protect ourselves because we can learn from his mistake.

Greenpeace's ad agency fell back on a time-tested inadequacy strategy. I was pleased to see that the digitoral world did not treat this ad kindly. Even environmental activists decried it, and it was quickly removed from circulation.

The Modern Inadequacy Approach: Daisy

CREATE ANXIETY

You'll find it on the same *Ad Age* list as Sad Edna, at number 100—Lyndon Johnson's 1964 "Daisy" campaign spot. Unlike the halitosis ads, Daisy would have no need to *create* anxiety from scratch—Robert Oppenheimer had laid all the groundwork the ad would need twenty years earlier.

A child picks the petals off of a flower, counting them one by one. Then the picture freezes on the little girl's face. An announcer begins to count down from ten, and then there it is—the mushroom cloud that visited nearly every person's nightmares. We can only imagine the child as a tiny speck within the destruction wrought by the bomb. The world's fear for its safety, always lurking just below the surface, is brought to the television screen in vivid detail. Anxiety floods the Cold War viewer.

First Johnson quotes W.H. Auden: "We must love one another or die." (Auden is also, interestingly, the author of the poem *The Age of Anxiety*.) Then: "Vote for President Johnson on November 3. The stakes are too high for you to stay home."

The moral of the story of course is, "You and your children are not safe." Using the modern inadequacy approach, the ad does not have to *create* as much as *invoke* a deep, preexisting anxiety.

As we move further along the spectrum from the primitive approach to the modern approach, feelings of inadequacy may not be explicitly stimulated at all, but these marketing campaigns very much rely on such anxious feelings. Jeans ads that show unattainably attractive teenagers in sexual ecstasy play off of young people's fears of rejection, while Cover Girl ads starring a well-preserved Drew Barrymore play on women's fears that as their youth fades, so does their beauty and desirability.

INTRODUCE THE MAGIC SOLUTION

People tend to hate badgering, fear-based political ads like Daisy or George H. W. Bush's infamous Willie Horton ad because our rational minds know that a vote at the ballot box will not be enough to solve the enormous problems they allude to—and our intellect is offended even if our emotions are intrigued. Sure, Listerine can credibly cure bad breath, but can a vote for Johnson actually put the nuclear destruction genie back in the bottle? Our minds say no, but when our fears are effectively stimulated and we have no powerful, positive myths to instruct us otherwise, we have little choice but to respond.

The Postmodern Inadequacy Approach: Whopper Freak-out and Pepsi Max

Finally, we come to the very latest expression of inadequacy marketing. Here, marketers are counting on the fact that we are entirely fluent in the language of anxieties magically solved. We can skip right over step one, create anxiety, and head straight to step two, introduce the magic solution.

After being told incessantly that brands are the solution to all of life's problems, we may come to believe that nothing in life is more important. Taking this proposition to its most ridiculous extremes becomes fertile ground for endless marketing humor—while still pushing forth the value of the solution proffered. Inadequacy marketing laughing at itself, while simultaneously reinforcing its message, is exactly the brain bender Groupon's Mason was working so hard to explain.

"Our ads highlight the often trivial nature of stuff on Groupon when juxtaposed against bigger world issues, making fun of Groupon." Yes, in a way he was making fun of himself, but the real message, the deeper message is, "Who cares about Tibet when you can get cheap and delicious fish curry?"

When called out on their poor taste, purveyors of the postmodern approach beg us to lighten up, it's just a joke. But the moral of these stories is dead serious—the magic of consumption trumps all other human values. Citizen engagement is painted as an unhip, naive approach to life. Of course, there was nothing at all naive about the Egyptian revolution—it changed the world. And that's what made Kenneth Cole seem so out of step.

Postmodern inadequacy campaigns are everywhere, and they feature people so obsessed with a brand that they will do the most outrageous things to get their hands on its products or totally panic if they can't. Take, for example, "Whopper Freak-out," in which a hidden camera shows Burger King customers in every imaginable state of childish meltdown when they are told that the Whopper is no longer available. Proving that the digitoral world prefers the postmodern approach to its now-reviled primitive ancestor, this campaign was an online viral sensation.

Then there's Pepsi's "First Date" 2011 Super Bowl spot. It's totally dismissive of anything but the basest of human values. A young woman stares at her date and wonders how much money he makes and if he wants kids. She's seeking—what else?—status and acceptance. The man's mind just whirs away with a single refrain: "I want to sleep with her, I want to sleep with her."

"Oh Pepsi," we're supposed to giggle, you've got the sexes down *cold*. Then a Pepsi Max is placed on the table and the guy's mind shifts instantly to: "I want a Pepsi Max. I want a Pepsi Max." That's right, guys are just big kids who don't want anything but sex—oh, and the products they love.

Whopper Freak-out and First Date are emblematic of the kind of marketing stories we've all come to expect, and they can be funny as long as you don't look too deep. But understanding the dark art and the deep impact it has had on the planet makes it a lot harder to laugh.

The Crisis of Consumption

The challenges humankind faces today are as urgent as those that confronted our marketing forefathers—but they are very different.

Where the crisis might once have seemed to stem from an unwillingness to consume enough, it now appears we are consuming far too much. The signs of the *crisis of consumption* are popping up everywhere and they are irrefutable. Even if you don't believe in manmade climate change, it's impossible to ignore that key resources are beginning to dwindle, species are going extinct at an alarming rate, and forests and reefs are rapidly disappearing. We are hitting real limits at current levels of consumption, and worldwide levels are expected to spike as industrializing countries gain access to Western lifestyles.

The Global Footprint Network estimates that humanity currently uses 1.4 times the resources that the planet can regenerate annually and if everyone consumed like an American, we'd need four planets. As Einstein suggested, it's time for a new mind-set.

History has shown us that inadequacy marketing really works, especially in the audience-stultifying broadcast era. But continuing to drive the "consume at all costs" mentality of men like Edward Bernays and Ernest Dichter is plainly not sustainable. Not only that, consumption doesn't even deliver the happiness or refuge from anxiety it would seem to promise. Just as Americans began to consume vastly more in the 1950s, measures of national happiness were peaking. As our rate of consumption—measured in house size, number of cars, trash produced, dollars spent and earned—more than doubled, indicators of individual happiness stayed flat and then began to decline. Maybe that's because we're working more hours, we're more deeply in debt, and our anxieties are constantly being stimulated by our mythmakers.

One of the most powerful and persistent elements of the happiness through consumption myth is the metric by which we measure the "health" of our economy. If you listen to NPR's *Marketplace,* you will hear a little cheerful tune when the market goes up and a bluesy dirge when it drops. The Dow Jones, itself tied in the long term to the rise and fall of the gross national product, gives us a beautiful simplification of all the millions of factors that went into making today a happy or a sad one. We don't have to think about these factors, because the music and the myth behind it tell us how to feel. Driven by consumer spending, the GNP was an unquestionable good to the marketers who came before us. But the poverty of this cultural story was already being laid bare more than forty years ago—long before our current crises had even been imagined. As Robert Kennedy said so eloquently:

> *Our gross national product . . . if we should judge America by that—counts air pollution and cigarette advertising, and ambulances to clear our highways of carnage. It counts special locks for our doors and the jails for those who break them. It counts the destruction of our redwoods and the loss of our natural wonder in chaotic sprawl. . . . It measures neither our wit nor our courage; neither our wisdom nor our learning; neither our compassion nor our devotion to our country; it measures everything, in short, except that which makes life worthwhile. And it tells us everything about America except why we are proud that we are Americans.*

If what we measure is what we value, it seems our values just aren't serving us any longer. The good news is that we have the technology and communications structures to rethink our way of life and adapt them at a rate never before thought possible. We just need a society of mature people to engage in the discussion of where we go from here. And we need millions, if not billions, of us to insist that this difficult discussion be brought out of the fringes and into the mainstream. A world of willfully immature consumers won't get us where we need to go.

Joseph Campbell, the man who knew more about myth than anyone hence or since, might say that it's time for a societal hero's journey. In fact he pretty much did: "The only myth that is going to be worth thinking about now and in the immediate future is one that is talking about the planet, and not the city, and not these people, but the planet, and everybody on it. That's my main thought for what the future myth is going to be . . . Until that gets going, you don't have anything."

As mythmakers, we marketers have enormous influence in crafting society's stories. Our forefathers did it once, turning a Puritan-values-based nation into one driven by the joys of consumption. With all that we've learned, surely we can create another shift, one appropriate to the moment we now find ourselves in. And we can thrive while doing it. Where brands were once totally dependent on ever-growing consumption and disposal to drive their bottom lines, companies in all sectors now have many more paths to profitability—ranging from selling more services to collaborative consumption solutions, like ZipCar or Craigslist, to increasing energy efficiency or innovating methods of using less raw materials to create the goods we want and need. There is literally no business or organization that must sit on the sidelines of the discussion of how we will craft a better future.

You need not be driven, as I am, by a belief that consumption has brought us to an ecological and social crisis. You might see our current challenges through the lens of fraying values, out-of-control wealth inequity, incivility in politics, or any number of pressing modern issues. Whatever lens you're peering through, you're probably seeing that times are changing fast, challenges are being amplified, and there is tremendous need for intelligent, respectful conversation. These challenges simply cannot be effectively addressed by people who care only for convenience, safety, and status—and there's science to prove it. Studies show that there is a causal relationship between exposure to television advertising and the holding of *extrinsic* values. Extrinsic values are heavily weighted toward concern with the perceptions of others—care for social status, material wealth, admiration, and power. And holding these values has been shown to influence people's willingness to embrace their role as citizens. People who emphasize extrinsic values show higher levels of prejudice, less concern for human rights, lower levels of behavior to protect the environment, and higher rates of depression.

The world requires that the dark art stories that encourage this mind-set be abandoned. There are many Tahrir Square moments waiting to happen.

And so, we have completed our journey through a broken world. The rest of our travels through the story wars highlights and demystifies iconic victories by marketers who have rejected the dark art and, even more importantly, lays out a step-by-step plan for following and going beyond them, creating a new storytelling strategy that can send you on your path to story wars victory.

PART TWO

Shaping the Future

A Creation Myth
for Marketers

Yes, our world is broken, for marketers and for our audiences. But it is still within our power to chart a new course armed with new myths to guide us into the future. Here's one to get the journey started.

Philadelphia, 1875. John Powers paused, his hand trembling on the brass handle. He tried to still the tremor, promising himself that he would go no further until the rage inside him had calmed. But after a moment had gone by without any sign of the emotion passing, he pushed open the giant glass door and stormed into the old Pennsylvania station.

New life had recently been breathed into the railroad depot, and it was now something breathtaking—elegant, bustling, and full of the promise held by the fast-approaching new century. Clutching an overflowing portfolio, sweat dripping into his eyes behind his glasses, his pace nearly maniacal, Powers did not look like he belonged among the happy shoppers.

"Welcome to Wanamaker's." A young man stood in Powers's path, eager to direct him to whatever he might be in search of or, better yet, see him back out the door.

"Where is he?" breathed Powers, scanning the hundreds of display tables in the massive department store. Trousers, dresses, lamps, ties. He knew how to sell all of it.

"Who?"

"Wanamaker. Tell him Powers is here."

The young man looked skeptical, but a glare from the lunatic taking yet another step in his direction convinced him he had little choice. He ran off to see if John Wanamaker was in his office and if he had ever heard of a man named Powers.

At a table of neckties, merchandise was brushed aside to clear space for papers. Powers arranged about twenty sheets, each a carefully laid-out ad mockup, until he heard footsteps coming from behind.

"John!" Wanamaker extended a hand to Powers who shook it and held it firmly a moment too long. "Did we have an appointment today?"

Of course, Wanamaker knew why his advertising agent had come and that there was no avoiding yet another angry confrontation. It was the cost of doing business with the only man in Philadelphia, perhaps in the country, whom he could trust with the Wanamaker's name. The ads Powers wrote for him drove shoppers to the store in a way he had never believed possible; from the beginning of their partnership, Wanamaker's had grown in just a few years from $4 million to $8 million in annual sales. But it was something more important than numbers that held Wanamaker hostage to Powers's uncompromising temper. He was the only ad agent who got results by telling the truth, and that was what Wanamaker, a man of deep religious faith, demanded. Wanamaker's scruples were legendary. This was a man who had invented the concept of a price tag because he felt that if all men were equal before God, they should be equal in what they pay for an item. To Wanamaker, telling the truth was the number-one, unbendable rule in business.

This time, though, Powers had taken the truth too far for Wanamaker's taste, and that was why there would be angry words today.

"Mr. Wanamaker, these are twenty ads that I've prepared for you. Each perfectly represents the goods you sell here," Powers began through clenched teeth. "Each tells a little story that will, like every other ad I have ever written for you, bring customers in to buy those goods. So why am I being told that you won't approve *any* of them!"

Wanamaker reached for one of the papers laid out before him.

"'The price is monstrous, but that's none of our business,'" Wanamaker read aloud. "Or this one, where you describe my neckties as 'not as good as they look, but they're good enough— 25 cents.'"

"That one will work," said Powers, as he ripped the ad from his client's hand.

"You're turning our agreement to be truthful into a kind of joke, aren't you? You are an advertising agent. I pay you to place ads that will bring customers to my store, not drive them away!"

Powers bristled. He did not appreciate the term "advertising agent," and Wanamaker knew it. Ad agents were unscrupulous men who focused their energy on swindling their customers on both ends: wildly inflating newspapers' rates to advertisers and then bullying those newspapers by threatening to withdraw accounts if the content of the publication didn't suit their needs. For advertising agents, writing the copy was just an afterthought. To men like Wanamaker, agents were the bottom of the barrel, universally reviled. Powers considered himself something far more dignified—a copywriter—but as the first of his breed, that term was lost on nearly everyone. Still, Wanamaker should have known better. Powers began to collect his papers.

"The ties *are not* as good as they look. Carry better ones, and I will rewrite the ads. Perhaps what you would prefer is something in the Pinkham style. That might bring Wanamaker's just the feel you're looking for."

The ads for Lydia Pinkham's Vegetable Compound were instantly recognizable, widely copied, and totally unscrupulous. The most ubiquitously advertised face of the century, the late Lydia Pinkham glared from the pages of every major publication in the nation, extolling readers to write to her for help with their female problems:

> *A SURE CURE for prolapses uteri, all female weaknesses including leucorrhea, painful menstruation, inflammation of the womb, flooding, and for all weaknesses of the generative organs of either sex.*

At nearly 40 proof alcohol, the concoction was little more than a sure cure for sobriety. All the other claims were fluff, exaggeration, and lies. Still, patent medicines dominated the advertising landscape, spreading both fear of disease and false hope for its cure. Every other industry had followed suit.

The Powers style was the only alternative that anyone took seriously, and he used the exact opposite approach, advertising the goods at Wanamaker's in a quiet, down-to-earth tone. His ads were short essays that set a scene for his readers and found an unexpected, simple twist, often injected with humor, on the product he was discussing. He called it "telling the off-story." It worked, and he knew he could pick it up and take it anywhere. Wanamaker be damned.

Wanamaker placed a gentle hand on Powers's forearm.

"All right John, run that ad. If we sell those neckties, you can run the rest of them too. One ad. That's all I'm going to approve today."

Powers shoved the papers back into his briefcase, smiled, and without further comment strode out of the store. By the next week, the neckties would be gone. Clerks marveled at the steady stream of cheery customers thanking them for the honest advertising. Powers was on his way to becoming the first great figure in advertising history—well, the second, if you count Lydia Pinkham.

But twenty years later, he was still angry. He had won the battle over the ties that day, but he had been losing the war over the truth ever since. Wanamaker would eventually fire him, fed up with his unyielding attitude. Powers would move on to new clients, each time using stories rather than exaggeration to build an iconic brand, each time failing to get people to stick to the truth. He had long ago decided that the advertising industry deserved its reputation for fecklessness. Everyone wanted to know the secret of how "Honest John" did it, but once they heard it, they seemed to willfully forget.

So, when a reporter from the new advertising industry journal *Printer's Ink* knocked on his door, Powers took a special delight in turning him away.

"I don't care to be interviewed," Powers told the reporter.

As the young man turned to leave the old oracle's office, Powers reconsidered. He wondered if this would be his best chance to tell the truth to those who needed to hear it, perhaps a last chance to save advertisers from themselves.

His words would become Powers's *three commandments*:

The first thing one must do to succeed in advertising is to have the attention of the reader. That means to be interesting. The next thing is to stick to the truth, and that means rectifying whatever is wrong in the merchant's business. If the truth isn't tellable, fix it so it is. That's about all there is to it.

That's all there is to it. Scribbled in a journal, later reprinted in a small industry magazine more than a hundred years ago, John Powers had given us all we've ever really needed to know.

Be interesting.

Tell the truth.

And if you can't tell the truth, change what you're doing so you can. In other words, *live the truth.*

More than a century later, these simple statements are still our best guides to success in the story wars. In fact, in the digitoral age, they have become more relevant than ever. They are the antidotes to the five deadly sins and the weapons that can ultimately drive dark art marketing to the fringes where it belongs.

The rest of this book is an exploration of these commandments and a set of practical exercises for applying them to all of your efforts to be heard. They form the basic training we must undergo to win the story wars.

Here's how we'll build our formula for success:

We'll begin with *tell the truth* in chapters 5 and 6, allowing us to define our story strategy. Here we'll learn the principles that help us craft stories that will rise to the level of myths. As we've seen, people build their lives and identities around such stories. With top marketers in control of our myths these days, we'll need to learn to join them if we hope to compete in the story wars.

In this section, you'll learn to orient your entire brand toward storytelling by defining and defending a powerful moral of your story in every communication. In learning to tell the truth, we will find that some morals are truer than others. Those that form the basis of inadequacy marketing and speak to the consumer mind-set are simply not those favored by natural selection. Those that tell the truth as core myths always have—that call us to maturity and our higher nature—have prevailed in ancient times and are winning the story wars today.

In chapter 7, we'll learn techniques to deploy our strategy as actual stories. Here, we'll uncover three storytelling devices guaranteed by 100,000 years of evolution to grab and hold attention—I've come to call them *freaks, cheats,* and *familiars.* Applicable to any attempt to tell a story, freaks, cheats, and familiars are behind many of the most successful viral marketing efforts of the digitoral era. We'll decode three of these breakthroughs.

Chapter 8 explores the third commandment—Live the Truth—the call for marketers to lead their companies and organizations to act on the morals they choose to base their stories upon. Here we'll find that iconic stories create iconic expectations. And in the era of digitoral transparency, we either step up to those expectations or find ourselves crushed by them. Live the Truth puts the marketer in the role of hero with the power to transform the way businesses and organizations operate.

CHAPTER FIVE

Tell the Truth, Part I

The Art of Empowerment Marketing

As a teenager, I spent half of my time at my mother's house and half of my time throwing baseballs with my father. Baseball had become our obsession by default. Soccer had ended after a confusing and hopeless season of scoring on my own goal; basketball was dismissed after a single futile shoot-around. I was so short and slow-footed that my father, full of unrealistic dreams for his only son, was driven to a state of near despair. Then it dawned on him that, with enough practice, anyone could learn to pitch. So every day we were together, we went out to the backyard and I threw to imaginary hitters, one after the next.

By the time I was thirteen, I had developed good control and a terrifying curveball that sped toward a batter's head only to change direction at the last moment and fall right into the strike zone. I reveled in dropping six-foot pubescent boys to their knees—the perfect vantage point from which to witness the umpire signaling strike three. The pitch required only one thing—a good baseball. The texture of the leather and the height of the seams made all the

---

Abraham Maslow and the foundations of empowerment marketing

difference. I was so dependent on the quality of the ball in my hand that my fingertips learned to ascertain instantly if this one was capable of breaking or not. I came to believe that I knew everything there was to know about baseballs.

Then one day, I caught my dog ripping a particularly good one apart. Grabbing it from her mouth, I was stunned to see that beneath the ball's familiar cover was a tangle of tightly wound string. I remember feeling shock—not because I expected something else to be there. The shock came, instead, from the realization that I had never even considered what was beneath the surface of this perfectly familiar object.

I sat down next to my disappointed dog and began to unwind the thread. And then finally, to my delight and amazement, I reached a bouncy cork sphere wrapped in red rubber. As I was unraveling, I had been wondering how this lump of string could pop off a bat with so much life when it was hit just right. The hidden red ball was my answer—a secret of the universe had just been revealed to me.

———————

Much later, I learned that good stories are structured just like baseballs. On the surface, we find the story's visible elements: the setting, the characters, and the actions those characters undertake. These are the elements of stories we've all been familiar with since childhood. We know the cover and we think we know everything there is to know. But there is so much more.

Just beneath the surface, the story finds its structure in the moral of the story. The storyteller does not introduce characters and actions by happenstance. Each visible element exists to illustrate an overarching point, an *explanation* of a professed truth about how the world works. Just as the ball of string beneath the cover invisibly determines a baseball's size, shape, and weight, the moral of a story provides its structure, shape, and relevance. In a fable, this moral will be overt and even stated outright. In a more complex story, it will be up to the listener or reader to glean it from the tale. But no matter how hidden or obvious it may be, without this underlying structure, audiences will intuitively feel that a story is just a collection of random events. Without some kind of moral, we instinctively reject a story as poorly told.

And then there is the story's core, hidden one layer deeper at the center of it all. This core may even be hidden from the storyteller herself. Here we find the *values* implied by the moral. When we hear a story with the moral "Better safe than sorry," we know something about the storyteller; we know she values safety and predictability. When we hear a story with the moral "He who hesitates is lost," we know our storyteller values something entirely different—adventure and risk. The values at the core of a myth provide its *meaning* and, unless we are looking for them, these values often remain hidden from our conscious minds.

I've found these insights enormously useful, and we'll employ them to explore the iconic success of stories built from the core outward on truths about human nature. These are truths that inadequacy stories ignore and often seek to deny. We'll unpack the mythic formula of what I call *empowerment marketing*—stories told to help encourage audiences on their path to maturation and citizenship. The practice of empowerment marketing is based on two of the most influential theories in the field of human growth and maturation—Abraham Maslow's hierarchy of needs and Joseph Campbell's hero's journey. The hierarchy of needs provides us with a vastly expanded menu of universal values you can appeal to in your audiences beyond greed, vanity, fear, and self-interest. Using Maslow's insights, you can define higher-level values appropriate to your message, brand, and audience. Then, using what we learn from Joseph Campbell, you can turn those values into a resonant moral of the story and create a story structure that will appeal to the heroic potential in your audiences. These models show us a clear alternative to the dark, limited view of human nature inspired by Freud and brought to the marketplace by men like Edward Bernays. And because these empowerment marketing stories function in the way traditional myths always have, calling their listeners to growth and maturity, campaigns built on these models are asserting their supremacy in our new oral tradition.

So we begin our journey to heal our broken world.

Empowerment Marketing:
A Resistance to the Dark Art

For nearly a century now, inadequacy marketing has provided the favored weapons for fighting the story wars. And though the cautionary tales of Groupon and Kenneth Cole (see chapter 4) show how the digitoral age is putting chinks in its armor, the approach is anything but dead. In fact, its practice remains the automatic starting point for most of us, whether we're selling fish curry or social action.

But that's only half the story. For nearly as long, a countercurrent has run through the story wars. Empowerment marketing eschews every assumption made by the inadequacy approach. Acting much in the way myths have for millennia, this approach builds stories that point out the possibility for human growth and even transcendence. Empowerment stories often delight audiences by mocking the familiar anxiety provoking assaults of the dark art. They inspire action by painting a picture of an imperfect world that can be repaired through heroic action. And most importantly, they create deep affinity by acknowledging that human beings can be something more than selfish machines seeking status, sex, comfort, and convenience.

Media mogul Arianna Huffington, who sold her homegrown, virally powered news site to AOL for $315 million, knows a few things about what works in the digitoral era. She recently described what she called the most important trend in marketing: "the recognition by businesses that there's much to be said for appealing to consumers' better instincts, and engaging them with something other than materialism, sex, money, and self-interest."

"It's not a coincidence," she added, "that this trend is escalating at the same time social media have risen to the forefront in the worlds of both marketing and activism."

Huffington is right—social media platforms are amplifying the power of stories that appeal to better instincts. But it's misleading to call it a trend. These stories have always been with us and have always been powerfully resonant.

Now, to judge the importance of empowerment marketing by the frequency of its use is to deem it irrelevant. Its stories represent but a tiny handful of the thousands of marketing myths that vie for our attention daily. But if you evaluate empowerment marketing by its ability to create unforgettable, iconic campaigns, it reveals itself as the ultimate secret weapon for winning the story wars. In fact, its relative rarity is one element of its enormous appeal. Beleaguered audiences often experience empowerment marketing stories as a celebrated breath of fresh air.

Telling the truth—most importantly, the truth that human nature goes beyond our basest desires and orients to a higher potential—provides the foundation of a storytelling strategy that can build your next breakthrough communication—and your entire brand. It also offers the opportunity to participate in a revolution aimed at repairing our dysfunctional and negative media landscape. Of course, putting a new, positive sheen on marketing is not an end in itself. But reorienting our myths away from the adolescent, depressed consumer mind-set and toward the empowered citizen worldview is a powerful first step in reshaping our society for the better.

Before we use the empowerment marketing lens to understand some of marketing's most famous successes, however, I offer an important warning: breakthrough empowerment stories are not the exclusive property of responsible products or organizations. To understand the connection between effective stories and responsible behavior, we'll have to wait for our exploration of John Powers's final commandment, Live the Truth. For now, I ask you to put aside your judgments about any product, organization, or political cause being examined. Yes, there is hypocrisy in some of these campaigns. But at this point, I simply want to illustrate the great power held by these iconic stories and the resonance they inspire.

Tactic #1: Expose Lies of Inadequacy Marketing

The first tactic of empowerment marketing is perhaps the most powerful: tell a more resonant truth in the face of commonly accepted lies.

Think Small

In the late 1950s, nothing expressed the dark art strategy more aggressively than automobile advertising. American automakers assailed the public with campaigns insisting that status, taste, and social acceptance were magically achieved and expressed entirely through the car you drove.

At the top of the heap sat the Cadillac, whose ads were aimed not only at those who could afford its exorbitant $5,000 price tag but also at those aspiring to such heights. These ads didn't just sell cars, they sold a whole set of values—values about happiness, identity, and the good life. The subtle effect of these campaigns was to coerce Americans to work longer hours and sacrifice more to step up the ladder from a Chevrolet to a Buick to an Oldsmobile and one day, God willing, to the ultimate automobile, the Cadillac.

Here's what a typical Cadillac ad from 1959 promised under the headline "A Single Glance Tells the Story":

The 1959 Cadillac speaks so eloquently—in so many ways—of the man who sits at its wheel. Simply because it is a Cadillac . . . it indicates his high level of personal achievement. Because it is so beautiful and majestic, it speaks of his fine taste . . . why not visit your dealer tomorrow and arrange to have a new Cadillac tell its wonderful story about you?

Climbing the automobile ladder was hard work, and staying on top was even harder. Each year, employing the practice of perceived obsolescence, Chevrolet would roll out an entirely redesigned, and usually larger, model. A car that had been the height of fashion yesterday would look small, embarrassing, and worn-out tomorrow, communicating the exact opposite story its driver so deeply desired to have told. As you would imagine, all of this provoked a good deal of anxiety from the bottom to the top of American society.

Then in 1959, seemingly out of nowhere, simple full-page newspaper ads began to appear with an unadorned image of the Volkswagen Beetle and the headline "Think Small." The ad didn't say much more, except that the car was modest and efficient—it even called the Beetle a "flivver," contemporary slang for a piece of junk. People found the ads shockingly honest and hilarious, allowing them to publicly express an unnamed anxiety that marketers had been instilling in them for years. Will I make it to the top of the ladder? Who cares?

Spurred on by the outrageous success of these ads, VW's agency, DDB, intensified its assault on the Detroit inadequacy approach, in effect *celebrating* the joys of what others might call inadequacy.

"Live Below Your Means" advised one particularly revolutionary advertisement. The campaign celebrated the fact that the clunky design of the Beetle had not changed for almost two decades (when Hitler had first commissioned its creation—a small detail that was, of course, omitted).

The effectiveness of these ads has been endlessly chronicled, and fifty years later it is still widely considered the stand-alone best marketing campaign of the twentieth century, number one on the *Ad Age* list. It turned the strange, sluggishly selling car into the totem of the counterculture revolution. It helped a whole generation fill the myth gap left by disaffection with the suburban dream as they discovered new explanation and meaning in freedom and the open road—and a new driving ritual to enact their new story. Think Small is even credited with starting the creative revolution that turned advertising on its head in the 1960s. But the campaign does not owe its success to offbeat creativity or its celebrated use of white space on the page. The power of the new story VW was telling began at its core, with its values. While Cadillac was celebrating an endless quest for status and wealth, VW celebrated joyful modesty of material desire and truth in the face of insincerity.

Real Beauty

Nearly a lifetime after Think Small's breakthrough success, Unilever's Dove brand rediscovered the power of a direct assault on inadequacy. Dove would base a new campaign launched in 2004 on the insights of a study showing that only 12 percent of women are satisfied with their appearance and a mere 2 percent consider themselves beautiful. According to the study, a shocking two-thirds of all women age fifteen to sixty-four said they withdraw from "life-engaging activities due to feeling badly about their looks"; *life-engaging activities* include things like voicing an opinion, attending school, and even going to the doctor. Who's to blame? A vast majority of respondents blamed the media, at least in part, for creating and promoting messages that celebrate unattainable beauty ideals. Of course, these ideals are no accident—they are the carefully nurtured engines of anxiety that drive inadequacy marketing. Hundreds of millions of dollars are spent every year reinforcing them.

Dove's Real Beauty campaign dragged this anxiety into the light of day and in the process created one of advertising's early online viral sensations. A seventy-five-second video, titled *Evolution,* shows in silent detail how a normal, even haggard-looking, model is Photoshopped into the perfect cover girl. The spot reveals that her beauty doesn't come from her cleanser, her moisturizer, or any one of a bagful of products women are constantly being encouraged to apply. We learn that this kind of beauty is just digital magic. A dark art secret had been revealed in little more than a minute, and millions of women around the world rejoiced, passing it from friend to friend. The video got picked up and shown as content, not advertisement, all over daytime TV. Oprah, who herself had become the most powerful woman in media through a relentless focus on empowering stories and higher ideals, featured the Real Beauty campaign every day for a week. The video would earn its creators tens of millions of dollars of free media.

Just like Think Small, the surface of the larger Real Beauty campaign is certainly worth attention: real-looking women starring in beauty ads, feeling beautiful in their less-than-perfect bodies. But it is the moral of its story—that the beauty ideal is a lie and that real beauty comes from truth—and its core value—sufficiency of all women as opposed to inadequacy—that created such enormous audience affinity and resonance. Although the campaign makes this moral implicitly clear, Dove wanted to make sure it couldn't be missed. Giving their models a mouthpiece through the campaign, the women spoke out, clearly stating the values and the point of the Dove story: "I love the thought of being a part of an ad that would potentially touch many young girls to tell them that it is all right to be unique and everyone is beautiful in their own skin," said model Shanel Lu.

And even more to the point is Sigrid Sutter, quoting Keats: "Truth is beauty."

Tactic #2: Speak to the Hero, Not the Child

The second tactic of empowerment marketing emphasizes the power of the audience, casting the viewer as the hero with the brand or organization as a helper, speeding her on her way.

Courage

At the center of Nike's 2008 "Courage" campaign is a website gallery of athletes who through sheer will and perseverance overcame tremendous odds. And at the center of this gallery sits a sixty-second video that denies every tenet of inadequacy marketing. It begins with a title card reading: "Everything you need is already inside." Then, to the beat of the Killers' song "All the Things That I Have Done" and the chant "I've got soul but I'm not a soldier," the viewer experiences a hyperspeed montage of the perfection of nature, the innocence of children, the diversity of world culture, and overlaying it all, the painfully won transcendence of athletic achievement. Finally, of course, we get the tagline: *Just Do It*. With these three simple, and now universally recognized, words, the viewer is asked not to simply admire all of this perfection but to pursue similar achievement in whatever way he or she defines it. The *it* in "Just Do It" is intentionally nonprescribed and thus, for many, has become deeply personal.

Courage is but one of the hundreds of Just Do It messages that has catapulted Nike to iconic status in its industry over the last twenty years, but I've chosen to highlight this execution because it so clearly declares the moral of the incredibly resonant Nike myth. Reminiscent of one of Aesop's fables, Courage's moral is spelled out for the audience in unmistakable terms: "Everything you need is already inside." Stirring up feelings of inadequacy? This is the exact opposite approach.

It's important to not just understand but to *feel* the distinction between empowerment marketing and inadequacy marketing—because that's how your audiences experience them. So try this: watch the *Courage* video and then watch the 2010 Skechers Super Bowl ad featuring Kim Kardashian—a classic lust-focused inadequacy spot. It's a muddled lascivious mess of a message in which the reality star gives up her trainer/lover for a shoe that does all the work for her. Audiences rated it a painful flop. Notice how the two approaches instinctively pull you on a gut level in opposite directions—one toward a sense of empowerment, the other away.

Still, the Courage message goes further than uplift. Traditional marketing has deeply ingrained in us the assumption that audiences prize ease and convenience and avoid making sacrifices at any cost—case in point, a shoe that replaces the need to work out. Even the latest strategy briefs from marketers working on climate change warn against acknowledging the need for tough choices and trade-offs. Rather, they exhort cause marketers to focus only on self-interest and ease of action.

This is a destructive and flawed assumption. People are programmed to believe in heroism, and, as Christopher Vogler notes in his classic text on mythic structure in movies: "Sacrifice is the Hero's willingness to give up something of value, perhaps even her own life, on behalf of an ideal or group." The post-modern inadequacy approach insists that people have lost any interest in difficult but ultimately heroic action. The success of Just Do It, with its relentless focus on pain and failure ultimately giving way to success, powerfully indicates otherwise.

It's interesting to imagine how counterintuitive Just Do It would have seemed to our marketing forefathers. If everything you need is already in you, what hole is there for the brand to fill? I can just imagine a 1950s creative director laughing at a junior copywriter, the *Courage* brief in his hand and soon to be in the trash bin.

Apple's 1984

Since we've already explored the details of this campaign, I'll pause here only to place it among its empowerment marketing kin. First, like Just Do It, "1984" mocks the idea that a corporation can take care of us and give us what we need. The droning voice of conformity on the giant screen is not just a stand-in for IBM. Most audiences didn't care enough to rebel against the monolithic computer maker because at the time, computers just weren't that personal. The story was so resonant because the villain represents advertising's typical consumerist approach, an approach that audiences indeed feel a deep need to resist. After all, the book *1984* was written as Orwell's response to the increasing levels of social engineering he saw all around him in the supposedly free world. Through the action of the ad, Apple doesn't try to step in as a heroic replacement for IBM, a better Big Brother. Rather it casts itself as a tool for the creativity of those who resist.

On its surface we find a remarkably produced and familiar tale of dystopia and rebellion. And it was well timed, coming at a moment of myth gap in which the techtopia future promised in the 1950s appeared to be nothing more than an illusion. More deeply, we find a moral deeply contradictory to the dark art: creative nonconformists will rule the world. And at its core, we find the values of self-realization and creativity.

As Steve Jobs would tell his biographer before his death, "The people who buy [Apple products] do think different. They are the creative spirits in this world, and they're out to change the world. We make tools for those kinds of people."

Tactic #3: Forget the Consumer, Call on the Citizen

The final tactic of empowerment marketing comes down to this: inspired citizens make better brand evangelists than helpless consumers.

Yes We Can

I thought I detected tearstains on the hundreds of messages that filled my inbox, e-mailed from my nearly forgotten friends, colleagues, and even my grandfather. For a moment I wondered if the same spammer had hijacked every e-mail account on Earth. But each message contained a personal, heartfelt confession—some variation on the single theme "I *had* to share this with you."

I click the link, and within a moment I'm riveted to YouTube:

It was a creed written into the founding documents that declared the destiny of a nation. Yes we can.

will.i.am, frontman for the Black Eyed Peas, sings the mythmaking words of a sensational candidate for president who had just been defeated in the New Hampshire primary.

Yes we can, to justice and equality. Yes we can, to opportunity and prosperity. Yes we can heal this nation. Yes we can repair this world. Yes we can. Sí, se puede.

Scarlett Johansson, Kareem Abdul-Jabar, and John Legend are all singing, chanting, signing along with Obama's concession speech—a speech that promised hope, not the kind that would be delivered to us as consumers, but that we could work together to earn for ourselves as citizens.

We know the battle ahead will be long, but always remember that no matter what obstacles stand in our way, nothing can stand in the way of the power of millions of voices calling for change.

Yes We Can is the perfect expression of the digitoral era: a mash-up, produced without the knowledge of the candidate who once owned its words. It's a reinterpretation and retelling of a story that had the power to move a nation but whose expression on a single night of defeat might have been forgotten in the twenty-four-hour news cycle—if not for tens of millions of views online. It's too long and unconventional to be a TV spot, too bold to be an official campaign video—and too compelling to resist forwarding it along. will.i.am had put his name on the first digitoral political masterpiece.

> *We have been told we cannot do this by a chorus of cynics who will only grow louder and more dissonant. We've been asked to pause for a reality check. We've been warned against offering the people of this nation false hope. But in the unlikely story that is America, there has never been anything false about hope . . . We will begin the next great chapter in America's story with three words that will ring from coast to coast; from sea to shining sea—Yes. We. Can.*

The ad earned will.i.am an Emmy and extended his legend as a man who chose to capitalize on—rather than run from—the massive changes the Internet had brought to the music industry. Of course, the digitoral-savvy of will.i.am is only half the story. The real magic came from the story *Yes We Can* had created, and that story began with Barack Obama, the candidate who was telling the truth. I'm not talking about the surface truth pertaining to policy details. Barack Obama was telling the truth about human nature. He was on his way to winning an election by winning the story wars.

The stage for the truth Obama would tell was set in an America exhausted by politics based on the dark art. The events of 9/11 had given rise to the most powerful narrative of the decade, and it was a narrative that meshed perfectly with the story told by the man who came before him. Even before the tragedy, George W. Bush had been warning: "Today we live in a world of terror, mad men and missiles." It was an unsettling tone we would come to expect as a matter of course and for a while it offered enough explanation and meaning to keep a nation moving forward. But it could not hold for long.

With an economic collapse looming and unstoppable and two wars raging, fear was everywhere. Obama responded with: *Yes we can.*

Contained within those three words was a campaign that turned inadequacy marketing on its head. Obama's words glorified optimism over fear, collective sacrifice over individual greed, and engaged citizenship over prepackaged, convenient solutions. My social network wouldn't have been weeping if Obama had been addressing us as a mass of passive children needing to be coddled and directed. He touched a nerve with an empowering message highlighting our boundless ability to mature and transcend.

Obama's story spread wildly through the digitoral landscape. People believed that yes, they could, and became joyful evangelists. The Obama campaign raised over $500 million online alone. And, against all odds, Barack Obama became the president of the United States.

What is most commonly admired and studied about the Obama campaign is not its brand but its success in leveraging emerging online tools. But the two cannot be separated. Sure, the campaign recruited Facebook wonder boy Chris Hughes to do its online organizing and seemed to grasp the magic of widgets and ringtones faster than anyone else. But tools alone don't deliver resonance. *Authenticity* does.

"It's even easier to reveal inauthenticity in the online world," observed Jeff Gulati, a professor tracking the use of social media in campaigns and a student of the Obama run for president. "If it doesn't resonate in the offline world, it won't resonate in the online world."

While the tools accelerated the massive spread of the message, it was the message itself that drove Obama's online success. And that message was simple: "Change will not come if we wait for some other person," he told his supporters on Super Tuesday, "or if we wait for some other time . . . We are the hope of the future."

It's a powerful message of hard work, personal maturity, and community engagement. And it's a direct assault on inadequacy marketing.

And what about audience response to Obama's message—everything from professional masterpieces like will.i.am's music video to thousands of in-person get-togethers and personal fan sites? Should these be explained by technological savvy or by the power of Obama's positive, citizen-powered message? This element of Obama's digitoral success is part of a larger pattern of empowerment marketing: brands that aim to empower tend to seek out and invest in new channels through which they demonstrate respect for their audience's power and opinions. And audiences quite often respond.

Because the Obama campaign believed in the possibility of maturity and even brilliance in its supporters, its marketers turned control of large pieces of the campaign over to them. Mybarackobama.com was a particularly sensational success, allowing enthusiasts to write their own blogs, submit policy recommendations for all to see, and fundraise the way they saw fit.

Inspired citizens, it turns out, don't just make good customers. They make great partners.

The Story of Stuff

Chapter 1 offered an in-depth look at Annie Leonard's legendary online campaign, but there's one further insight worth noting as we come to understand the characteristics of empowerment marketing, and it, too, involves the strategic power of speaking to the citizen, not the child.

When Leonard approached our studio with her project, we brought a few inadequacy assumptions of our own to the first creative session. We watched her hour-long live presentation with excitement but also with some skepticism. "Twenty minutes?" we responded when she told us of her goal to cut the talk down for the Web. "People don't want to think that much. They'll give you five at most."

And when it came to the audience for the piece, Louis felt that the world was ready to hear the message but the rest of us agreed it wasn't going to travel much beyond the choir. Yes, Leonard had learned that her talk had to be *simplified* to reach beyond non–technical experts. That's what made her presentation great. But she was steadfast that the presentation not be *dumbed down.* If the system was interconnected and multilayered, the animation would have to be as well, even if that meant a narrower audience. If there were no easy fixes out there, no "10 things you can do" to solve the *stuff crisis,* then no simple solutions would be proffered. We were going to treat our audiences as if they had adult attention spans and an adult interest in understanding complex issues. We would frame the problem as serious, something that could not be solved with a click. Sustained collective action would be the only out.

We started the project with deep misgivings that there were enough mature citizens out there on the Internet to get the project off the ground. That was 2007. Fifteen million views later, I've changed my opinion. This doesn't mean that I'd recommend anyone launching a campaign to ignore what's interesting in favor of an earnest recitation of dry facts. But you don't have to dumb down your message, either. As you'll see, empowerment marketing provides plenty of tools for getting it out there with depth and nuance still intact.

The campaigns we've just touched on each created new myths, as marketers have done since the earliest days of the story wars. They identified a place where old explanations—about everything from status, beauty, political engagement, possessions—aren't working anymore. They tell stories that provide the possibility of new explanation and meaning in the gap that's been created. And they offer new rituals to enact these new stories—a unique interaction with your computer, a chance to volunteer with a campaign, a deeper commitment to sport. But these efforts go a step further than their dark art peers. By appealing to higher values and believing in the desire of their audiences to seek truth, take on challenges, and understand complexity, these empowerment marketing stories achieved iconic status and built some of the most successful campaigns of all time.

Maslow's Answer to Freud: a Foundation for Empowerment Marketing

At this point in our journey we have reached a threshold. We have dissected inadequacy marketing and seen its Freudian foundation. In the story wars, we have come to know our enemy.

We've also observed a small but remarkably successful resistance—iconic campaigns that contradict dark art assumptions. The digitoral era and our own consciences will demand that we create more of these, but how exactly do we do that?

Do we organize our own resistance simply by copying the elements of what has worked for past empowerment marketing breakthroughs? Do we charge ahead on instinct, replacing inadequacy values with values that we inherently feel are of a higher service to society? And if we want to heed Campbell's call to create myths that help people "mature," how do we define *maturity* without randomly judging what is "grown up" and what is not? Without a coherent theory, we risk creating stuffy, moralistic, and naive marketing campaigns—typical socially conscious marketing fare.

In my own work, I found myself stuck for a time at this same threshold, eager to build my stories on higher values, those that I'd observed to be held by most of the people I've encountered in my life. It simply didn't fit my experience that, as Freud wrote, "hatred is at the bottom of all the relations of affection and love between human beings." But I needed a model to explain why people might resonate more strongly with something higher—to prove that Nike, Apple, Obama, and Leonard weren't simply lucky flukes.

And then I encountered the writings of Abraham Maslow, once a blaspheming rebel in the field of psychology who eventually rose to be one of its kings as the president of the American Psychological Association. As a young man in the 1940s, Maslow desired, as Freud had, to understand human nature so as to help avoid the horrors of another world war. But as his study and fieldwork progressed, he began to experience deep misgivings about the limitations of the strict Freudian worldview.

It was while living among the Blackfoot people of Alberta, Canada, that Maslow's faith in Freud first began to waver. In the society of eight hundred individuals that he studied, he reported that there had only been five known fistfights in the past fifteen years. During his stay, he never personally experienced a single instance of hostility, and noted that these people were appalled by the aggression they observed in white society. The dark, violent nature, supposedly inherent in humanity, just wasn't present in this small tribe. Returning from this experience, Maslow was inspired to look at his own society's problems not from the assumption of mankind's moral inadequacies, but from the exact opposite vantage point: "I wanted to prove," he wrote, "that human beings are capable of something grander than war and prejudice and hatred."

Maslow launched his assault on psychological orthodoxies by pointing out a simple, yet overlooked fact—Freud had developed his theories primarily by observing his patients, and all of his patients had been mentally ill. "If one is preoccupied with the insane, the neurotic, the psychopath, the criminal, the delinquent, the feeble-minded, one's hopes for the human species become perforce more and more modest," Maslow would write. "One expects less and less from people . . . it becomes more and more clear that the study of the crippled, stunted, immature, and unhealthy specimens can yield only a cripple psychology and a cripple philosophy."

While everyone else was studying sick people, Maslow set out, as nobody had before, to study the healthy, mature, and "self-actualizing"—those who seemed to find satisfaction in life and fulfillment of their potential. Maslow looked for patterns in the psychologies of the living and the dead—his mentors, his students, John Keats, Ralph Waldo Emerson, Ida Tarbell, Frederick Douglass, Harriet Tubman, George Washington, John Muir— thousands of individuals in all.

And just as his contemporaries were describing highly specific symptoms of various neuroses, Maslow identified the common symptoms of healthy maturity. Maslow and his colleagues set the bar extremely high for self-actualization, and his early work was somewhat confounded by the rarity of those who reach this final goal. But what would be far more useful than the identification of such special individuals was Maslow's discovery that movement toward self-realization is a nearly universal drive. Self-realization, he wrote, is "a far goal toward which all men strive."

In Maslow's worldview, human needs are not confined to the basics of survival—food, shelter, sex. As soon as these needs are fulfilled, and—as further research has shown—even when they are not, "higher" needs make themselves known. A person who is starving may perceive that his only need is for food. But once his belly is full, he will begin to feel the need for safety and shelter. Once the safety need is met, he will begin to act on the need for belonging and esteem of his peers, and so on. Neuroses, in Maslow's opinion, come not from suppressing the aggressive drives of the id, as Freud supposed. They can just as easily arise from the suppression of needs that lead to self-realization. We are all on a lifelong journey to maturity, he taught. We may never actually get there, but at least some part of us can't help but strive toward it.

Maslow arranged the universal needs he observed into a hierarchy. It has evolved much over time and been interpreted dozens of ways, but in essence it looks like the schematic shown in "Abraham Maslow's Hierarchy of Needs." It's important to note that while a "hierarchy" may seem to imply that some values are better or more important than others, this is not the case. Maslow felt that all of these needs were essential to human fulfillment.

At the bottom of this pyramid, we find the *basic needs*. They begin with the needs of our bodies. Deny these and you die. At the top end of this "lower" group are the needs of esteem. Maslow also referred to the needs in these four lower levels as *deficiency needs* because if they are not met, the individual will feel anxiety and inadequacy. This is where inadequacy marketers love to dwell.

When our deficiency needs are mostly met, we gain a platform off of which we can strive for psychological maturity. At this higher level, we find what Maslow labeled the *growth needs*. It is here that individuals question simplistic prejudices and turn to the larger concerns of society. Here the selfish consumer becomes the mature

Abraham Maslow's

Hierarchy of Needs

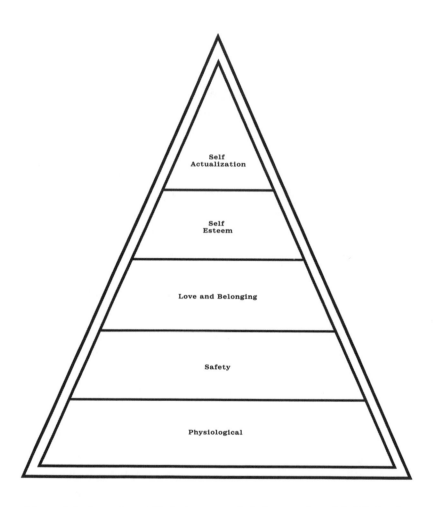

Self
Actualization

Self
Esteem

Love and Belonging

Safety

Physiological

citizen. Maslow also called these needs *being needs* to highlight that the object of these needs is not something to possess; rather, the individual moves toward the embodiment of these ideals. In this way, they are quite different from the deficiency needs, which might be delivered to and possessed by an individual.

It is on this pyramid that we may find a far more varied and exciting palette of universal values on which to base our marketing myths. And it is here, knowing that people strive to find a path to fulfilling higher level needs, that we find an explanation for the resonance of the empowerment marketing successes we've seen so far.

Maslow boiled the growth needs down to a collection of single words. With an eye toward making them useful for understanding and building empowerment marketing campaigns, let's elaborate on those we will find most useful. Beyond sex, status, and convenience, people are also driven by a need for:

WHOLENESS: The need to feel sufficient as an individual and connected to others as part of something larger, to move beyond self-interest

PERFECTION: The need to seek mastery of skill or vocation, often through hard work or struggle

JUSTICE: The need to live by high moral values and to see the world ordered by morality, to overthrow tyranny

RICHNESS: The need to examine life in all of its complexity and diversity, to seek new experience and overcome prejudice

SIMPLICITY: The need to understand the underlying essence of things

BEAUTY: The need to experience and create aesthetic pleasure

TRUTH: The need to experience and express reality without distortion, to tear down falsehood

UNIQUENESS: The need to express personal gifts, creativity, and nonconformity

PLAYFULNESS: They need for joyful experience

As soon as I came to understand Maslow's hierarchy, I knew I had discovered the foundation for a powerful alternative to inadequacy marketing. If we see these needs as *values*, as Maslow often referred to them, we find a whole new way to select a core for empowerment-based storytelling strategies.

The Values at the Core of Legendary Campaigns

With this palette of values in mind, let's rip the cover off some of the marketing myths we've seen on our exploration to this point, unwind their structures, and peer at the values hidden at their centers. Table 5-1 is my view of what we might find. Keep in mind that this analysis is the result of reverse engineering, surmising the deeply embedded values from the campaign outputs. You might assign different values from Maslow's hierarchy to each campaign but the pattern that will emerge, and that will be discussed in a moment, should remain abundantly clear.

TABLE 5-1

Campaign	Moral of the story	Core needs or values celebrated
Listerine	Halitosis makes you undesirable.	Safety, sex, self-esteem
Cadillac	Your car tells the world who you are. Get the best.	Esteem by others
Daisy (Johnson)	Vote for Johnson or you and your children will not be safe.	Safety
Whopper Freak-out, Groupon, Kenneth Cole	Nothing is more important than this product.	The denial of all values other than consumption
The Crying Indian	Using a trash can will allow you to rectify an uncomfortable past.	Wholeness, justice
Real Beauty (Dove)	Truth is beauty and the truth is, everyone is beautiful.	Truth, beauty
Courage (Nike)	Everything you need is within you. Work hard to achieve.	Wholeness, perfection
1984 (Apple)	Creative nonconformists rule.	Uniqueness
Obama's 2008 presidential campaign	Working hard together, we can solve our problems.	Wholeness, perfection
The Story of Stuff	You can understand a complex, broken system and once you do, you can help fix it.	Richness, simplicity, wholeness

Now that we've pulled them apart, we might order these campaigns according to their core values on Maslow's hierarchy. What do we find? First, of course, the empowerment marketing stories tend to aggregate at the top of the pyramid, while the inadequacy marketing stories cluster lower down in the deficiency needs. This makes sense when we remember how the two strategies work.

Inadequacy marketing, as we know, begins by creating anxiety. This is done by stimulating desires that, if unmet, will make audiences feel threatened and insecure—as if there is a hole to fill. As Maslow described, this anxiety occurs when the lower-level deficiency needs are threatened. It is also here that readymade, consumable solutions can be credibly offered. A marketer can truthfully offer to meet the physiological needs (Listerine *does* temporarily cure bad breath) and can even promise to magically deliver safety, love, and esteem. When the lens of myth is applied to inadequacy stories, the brand or organization behind the message tends to be the hero, delivering the needed elixir to the consumer— whether that be a product or a cause to support. The audience, on the other hand, is the damsel in anxious distress.

Maslow would have deplored this model and the ideal of citizen-as-consumer—the man who is considered well adjusted because he works out his aggression with his shopping choices. In fact, Maslow believed that many people get stuck focusing on basic needs at the expense of dedicating themselves to higher purpose because society continually stimulates insecurity at the lower levels: "Anything that increases fear or anxiety tips the dynamic balance between regression and growth back toward regression and away from growth," he wrote.

Freud wasn't all wrong. Fear and anxiety are strong emotions, and that explains why the dark art has been so successful. Still, even for those stuck in a state of deficiency, the desire to move toward self-actualization is there, waiting to be accessed.

Empowerment marketing campaigns, on the other hand, rely on growth—being—needs that can never be fulfilled *for* individuals but must be embodied *by* them. To work with this reality, marketers must help audiences to see themselves as the emerging heroes of the story. Everything you need is already inside, these stories say; we can help you on your journey to actualize your potential. I'm not implying, of course, that Nike doesn't benefit from and even encourage the notion that shoes can make you a hero. But the core strategy of empowerment marketing is not about magical fulfillment. It's about values and inspiration. Instead of offering to meet a deficiency need, empowerment marketers build stories around one of the growth values that are universal to human experience but rarely present at all in our consumer-frenzied media landscape. Recognizing that nearly everyone is striving for at least some of these higher ideals, empowerment marketers display these values in a way that stimulates audiences to renew or intensify their pursuit: See through the lies. Recognize your power. Push past failure. Dive into complexity.

The strategy works when audiences feel uplifted by the reminder that there's more to life than fulfilling base needs—take note, Kenneth Cole. Believing that the marketer is telling a deeper truth and sharing her deepest values, the receiver of the message feels uplifted. The message gains power and traction as she passes it along because she wants to share that uplift with her friends. Far from seeing the message as an intrusion, her friends will thank her for reminding them of their higher purpose. And everyone along the chain opens up to the ritual suggested in the message. Counterculture hippies became VW fanatics. Athletes bonded passionately to Nike. Voters fell madly in love with Obama. Educators defied the threat of dismissal to show *The Story of Stuff* in thousands of classrooms. And all of these groups evangelized these brands to widen their circles.

Before we go any further though, let's realize that we've stepped into dangerous territory, as we marketers are always apt to do. Empowerment marketing is not a wholly positive end in itself, and it is not easy to know what to make of campaigns that contain both dark art *and* empowerment elements.

Consider Edward Bernays's Torches of Freedom campaign. On the surface, we might deplore the ritual of smoking being inserted into the noble aims of women's suffrage. And you may remember the inadequacy foundation of that campaign—Bernays wanted to remind women they lacked something men had. But it would be dishonest to deny that the campaign also leveraged growth values like justice and wholeness. Clearly, some campaigns walk a fine line—noble words, manipulative intentions. In these cases, the presence of higher-level values can be more of a trap for audiences than a gift. Can empowerment marketing principles be abused in the story wars? Absolutely. Have they been abused by some of brands highlighted above? Again, yes. But as we'll see, an ever-more transparent digitoral landscape will not create a comfortable future for marketers who place a veneer of truth over a body of lies. We will look deeply at this subject in chapter 8.

In Maslow's pyramid we find a way to lay the foundations for an empowerment marketing story strategy—choosing from universal human values that stress truth over falsehood, the heroic nature of audiences and the citizen over the consumer. In chapter, 6 we'll discover how to build story structure around this core using the insights of Campbell's timeless hero's journey.

Before we move on to that next step, though, let's do some on-the-ground basic training to put these theories into practice for your cause or campaign. The Basic Training that follows offers concrete steps for choosing core growth values that will align with your audiences and your own deeper truth.

BASIC TRAINING

Identifying Your Values

You have arrived at the first of three Basic Trainings you can use to begin applying the lessons of the story wars to your brand or cause. Every great brand that has maintained its value over time has relied on a clearly expressed brand strategy that can be shared by all who communicate on its behalf. The document that lays out such a strategy is often a brand's most jealously guarded secret—and most valuable tool.

The first two trainings will help you define the underlying structure of your stories, while the third is a guide for actually writing stories that stick. If you take the time to go through these exercises, you will learn to reorient your brand strategy (or create one for the first time) with a focus on telling powerful and resonant stories. You will begin to flex your muscles as a storyteller and join the ranks of empowerment marketers who are reshaping our media landscape. I think you'll find the process deeply satisfying and worthwhile—it has been the most powerful tool I have discovered for guiding my own clients to story wars success.

Great stories teach truths about the way the world works and they stand for something. Our survey of the empowerment marketing landscape shows us how every brand has the opportunity to promote higher-level values and invite audiences to pursue them. You'll begin by identifying those values and making a commitment to them. This is not just a prerequisite for a self-identified "socially responsible business" or non-profit anymore. In the digitoral era, it is the surest path to success open to any brand willing to stand for values that matter.

Brands That Are Born with Values

For some brands, choosing higher-level values is easy because they are embedded directly into their own creation.

Patagonia, for instance, is a legendary brand among outdoor adventurers and a visionary leader in sustainability. Its values, one of which is Truth, are baked in because a passionate climber founded the company at a time when he was deeply concerned about the damage his sport was causing to pristine rock faces. As a young man in the early 1970s, Yvon Chouinard realized that there was a difference between loving to play in nature and authentically caring for it. Willing to face this hard reality, he invented an aluminum climbing wedge that could be inserted and removed without doing damage to the rock face. The success of this invention was an early step in the development of an ever-growing outdoor adventure line, driven by a single values-based dictum: "Build the best products while creating no unnecessary environmental harm."

Patagonia stresses the word *unnecessary* because the brand acknowledges the difficult truth that, just like climbing, the manufacture of outdoor gear will always cause some negative impacts. There's no way to avoid it, and the company wants its customers to face that truth. Thirty years later, one of its best-known initiatives has been the online tool, the Footprint Chronicles. Here Patagonia lays bare "the good and the bad" of its products up and down the supply chain. This is not feel-good environmentalism. About its Wayfarer board shorts, the copy says, "The fabric has no recycled content. We worked hard with our supplier to develop a recycled nylon fabric—and succeeded—but it's not commercially viable (a pair of shorts would cost $75)." Core customers, who value nature not as a concept but as a place they actually spend their lives, deeply appreciate the Truth value embodied in every highly transparent Patagonia marketing campaign.

Rick Ridgeway, Patagonia's VP of Environmental Initiatives and a member of the first U.S. team to summit K2, told me that he doesn't see brand communication as marketing at all but "sharing our core values with our customers." For brands like Patagonia, whose values were identified at the moment of creation, the work is to simply name those values and then relentlessly communicate them through great stories.

Brands That Embody Values

Other brands will find their values effortless to choose because they are a direct expression of their offering. Amnesty International, for instance, has built an iconic brand by offering activists a way to use their pens and keyboards to protect human rights. This is not a marketing ploy meant to drive donations. It actually works. By shining the light of public attention on human rights abuses—activities that thrive in secrecy—Amnesty has saved lives and stopped countless horrors. But the organization is not just providing something invaluable to those it protects; Amnesty also gives its members a chance to pursue the fulfillment of the higher-level Justice value—the need to play a role in bringing moral order to the world. Millions of activists have come to see writing letters in defense of prisoners as a gift to those in need and also as a gift to themselves, a doorway to higher purpose.

For brands whose offerings directly provide access to higher-level values, a powerful storytelling strategy begins by simply recognizing and naming these values then making a strategic commitment to put them, consistently, at the core of every communication.

Brands That Must Find Their Values

And then there are brands that want to tell resonant stories but were neither founded on obvious values nor have offerings that directly express them. Ben & Jerry's is an example of such a brand; the company built an ice cream empire out of nothing by being values-led.

Founder Ben Cohen didn't set out to find a more humane or sustainable or healthy way to make ice cream. He and his friend, Jerry Greenfield, just wanted to make a few bucks, and they liked dessert. Still, Cohen himself was passionate about peace and he wanted to see military spending redirected toward social programs. It started as merely a personal obsession but as his business got on its feet, he sensed that he was sitting on a tremendous platform for raising awareness—eventually there would be millions of pint tops and ice cream pop wrappers on which he could express his values.

At a time when American premium ice cream brands were falling all over themselves to sounds exotic and indulgent—touting made-up European-sounding names like Häagen Dazs, Glace de Paris, and Frusen Glädjé—Cohen and Greenfield broke through the clutter by putting their decidedly un-exotic faces on their packages and talking about what they cared most about.

Ben Cohen knew that a lot of ice-cream eaters wouldn't agree with reduced Pentagon spending, but he didn't care: "Companies do controversial marketing all the time to break through the clutter," he explained to me. "So if you can rise above it by taking a stand against nuclear weapons instead of using some sexy young girl, why not?"

Ben & Jerry's built a breakthrough brand, a brand Cohen insists wouldn't have been nearly as successful without its values, upon the passions of its founders—and these passions had nothing to do with ice cream. But audiences saw the values as authentic nonetheless because they were so personal. In fact, Cohen recalled the danger in trying to move beyond his personal passions into "values by committee." As the company grew into a giant player, Cohen surveyed his entire team to see what they valued, and the results were all over the map. In fact, the only issue they could agree on was the broad and uncontroversial "children and families." These results didn't feel actionable to Cohen and, before long, the company reverted to acting on the values of the founders.

"If you can form a relationship with your customers based on shared values, that is the strongest possible bond you can form," he explained. "But finding shared values means you have to *have* some values, they can't just be milquetoast, namby-pamby middle-of-the-road crap. You need to stand for something, so customers who believe the same thing can glom onto your brand."

Printed on the packages was a call to redirect 1 percent of the Pentagon budget toward peace initiatives. They sourced their Rainforest Crunch Brazil nuts from indigenous rainforest producers, protecting ecosystems by demonstrating these forests could be financially viable when left intact. And they never stopped talking about what they cared about. Perhaps more importantly, they gave their customers hope that, with every ice cream purchase, they themselves were expressing their higher-level values. Some of these expressions of values were unavailable elsewhere, like the pursuit of peace, which at the time seemed to have been buried with the 1960s. For millions of ice cream eaters, the brand stood for higher purpose while all other ice cream brands stood for vapid luxury.

Brands like Ben & Jerry's, which aren't founded in response to a higher calling and aren't providing something inherently values-based, face the empowerment marketing challenge as a need to choose values that their leadership can commit to and orient their entire team around.

It's likely that you'll consider these three types of brands—those born with values, those that embody them, and those that choose them—and immediately see your own story. Knowing where you fit is key, but wherever you are, you have the opportunity to identify core values on which to build your story strategy. Remember, these are the values you will share with your audience to inspire them. The goal will not be to simply show your audiences what *you* care about but to offer them encouragement to seek their own higher-level potential.

Here's how to begin.

STEP 1

Review the list of higher-level values shown in "The Values You Want to Live." You'll want to capture any that fit your aspirational brand. In other words, these values need not be an expression of where you are today but where you want to—and ultimately believe you can—go. Put each value in one of the following categories:

Values built into our founding story

Values expressed by our products or services

Values held by our leadership

Values we believe will most deeply resonate with our audiences

As the building blocks of your story strategy, and your future brand itself, the choices you make here will have far reaching impacts on your future—and as we'll see in chapter 8, you'll be called on to actually act on these values. But don't get locked up by the stakes. This is an iterative and evolving process. Like all brands, yours will be built on experimentation. Try out values you think fit. See how they impact your strategy as it gets built out over the next chapters. If the end result doesn't feel like where you want to go, you should start the process again, making needed adjustments.

The Values You Want to Live

Below you'll find a palette of nine brand-defining values derived from the being needs of Maslow's hierarchy. Note that they are not listed in order or importance.

WHOLENESS: The need to feel sufficient as an individual and connected to others as part of something larger, to move beyond self-interest

PERFECTION: The need to seek mastery of skill or vocation, often through hard work or struggle

JUSTICE: The need to live by high moral values and to see the world ordered by morality, to overthrow tyranny

RICHNESS: The need to examine life in all of its complexity and diversity, to seek new experience and overcome prejudice

SIMPLICITY: The need to understand the underlying essence of things

BEAUTY: The need to experience and create aesthetic pleasure

TRUTH: The need to experience and express reality without distortion, to tear down falsehood

UNIQUENESS: The need to express personal gifts, creativity, and nonconformity

PLAYFULNESS: The need for joyful experience

STEP 2

Narrow your field to three of these values—if possible, only one or two. Like all branding decisions, fewer inputs are usually better in the long run. But you don't want to narrow at the expense of your authenticity. Values that align across all four categories (founding story, offering, leadership, and audiences) are ideal choices, but not always possible to find. As Patagonia's Ridgeway put it: "If you're in the business of making landmines, you've got a big problem. But if you're making dessert, you've got a lot of choices of values that reflect your values. If you're making a product that reflects your own values, you've got it even easier, of course."

Ridgeway is pointing to an important truth: almost any brand can start becoming growth-values-oriented. Obviously it's easy for a nonprofit that helps volunteers deliver food to neighbors who cannot leave their homes. They have an offering that cultivates more Wholeness in the world as they ask people to step out of themselves and join into community with others. They are reaching out to those who seek more Wholeness in their lives. They are bringing people together into Wholeness. Easy.

But what about Listerine—a brand that owes its birth and success to inadequacy values? Does this brand have the same opportunity to create marketing around a Wholeness value? Consider this: Listerine was founded on a story of a woman, Sad Edna, who couldn't get close to anyone because she was inadequate. Today, the brand could flip that strategy 180 degrees pointing directly to the positive value that is the mirror image of Sad Edna. Listerine could now be all about *closeness* between people. It could be about people coming together to do great things. This seed of inspiration from the product might help the brand identify Wholeness as a core value. Their marketing might tell stories that focus on the uplift of Wholeness, and they might even partner with and support the elder-care nonprofit imagined above. Sad Edna becomes Citizen Edna and a new, digitorally relevant brand might be born. If Listerine has the opportunity to do it, so do you.

In the appendix, you'll find a blank Story Strategy Map. You are now ready to fill in the values section of this chart. Simply write in those you have chosen. With your values in hand, you can move outward from the center of our story strategy. In the next Basic Training, we'll explore the building of a story strategy's moral and identify its key characters.

CHAPTER SIX

Tell the Truth, Part II

The Hero's Journey

Sometime in the seventh century BCE. It was the tiny creases at the corners of her eyes that made him suddenly think of home. Had he really been away for forty years? Long enough to see his child-bride grow to be a mother — and someday soon a grandmother. Forty years following his flock over this gently rolling landscape through the endlessly cycling seasons. Eighty years since his birth in a land he knew he would never see again. Quietly, he slipped out of bed and walked outside to rinse his face.

"Moses the shepherd," he thought. What an unlikely end to the story of a man who had lived so many lives—as an orphan, a prince of Egypt, a fugitive wanted for murder. An unlikely ending, but it would have been a happy one—if only he was not reminded from time to time, suddenly and without warning, of the River Nile, of a kingdom lost, and of a people held in brutal servitude. He cursed these memories. They spoiled any hope for the peace a prosperous shepherd with two sons should expect—the just reward for a quiet life well lived.

A hero's path for marketers: the life of Moses

As he drove his flock toward the wilderness, Moses tried to convince himself that these thoughts of Egypt were useless, the impotent anger of an old man. Forty years ago, failure to just mind his own business had cost him his royal position and almost his life. Wandering through the slave quarters, still an untouchable prince, Moses had witnessed the vicious beating of an Israelite slave by his overseer. He was driven into a righteous rage that seemed to come from nowhere and he had killed the bully—a selfless, insane act. Had he been thanked in return? No, the man he rescued immediately ratted him out to Pharaoh, the king who had raised him as his own. It was a hard lesson for Moses. Like sheep, the Jewish slaves had been taught to love orderly bondage more than the unknown challenges of freedom. So he had become an outlaw—a prince who fled from home, never to return.

"Better to change what you can and let go what you cannot," thought the old man. It had become a mantra of sorts.

Mount Horeb was ahead of him. A rocky, steep climb to mostly untouched pastures. He contemplated the easier path winding around the mountain's base but, perhaps to test his old bones and the life still in them, he decided to hike upward instead.

Thus begins the hero's journey of Moses—as a founding story of three of the world's major religions, it has deeply informed the lives of heroes from Jesus to Martin Luther King Jr. to many of the Muslim students in Tahrir square. Joseph Campbell was the first to map out the universal story pattern of the hero's journey, but he discovered it only in the way that Columbus "discovered" the Americas. For millennia, it had been alive in the intuitions and traditions of shamans and storytellers around the world. "What the Shaman or seer brings forth is something that is waiting to be brought forth in everyone," Campbell said, to explain the power of such stories. "And so when one hears the seer's story one responds 'Aha! this is my story.' This is something I always wanted to say but wasn't able to say."

Stories that allow people to access and express their own inner truths—what could be a more powerful tool for creating evangelists in our postbroadcast world? Even though our circumstances may have no outward resemblance to Moses's, his story resonates for us. Who hasn't reached a moment in life that should have offered peace and rest only to be disturbed by the stirrings of some deeper, inconvenient knowledge? Who hasn't yearned for a return to a home that is now long out of reach?

The hero's journey has already proven its relevance many times over in explaining the successes of a couple of millennia worth of stories and legends, from *The Odyssey* and the *Bhagavad Gita* to *The Wizard of Oz,* and *Avatar,* the top-grossing film of all time. George Lucas used the formula as a step-by-step guide to crafting the universe of *Star Wars,* a brand that to date has earned more than $20 billion.

Of course, even if you don't have six movies, like Lucas, in which to unfold a complete epic, you can create resonance in all your communication and marketing efforts by using Campbell's insights. In my experience, the more of these insights you use, the more likely your audiences are to say, "Aha! This my story."

In this chapter, we'll explore the pattern of the hero's journey to help you identify characters for your story—the *brand heroes, mentors,* and *villains*—and the landscape they inhabit. This journey will also lead you to a discovery of your brand or organization's moral of the story. Here's what this part of our learning will look like:

Through a streamlined retelling of the hero's journey of Moses, we will get familiar with Campbell's story pattern. Campbell saw the journey as a complex multi-staged adventure, but for simplicity's sake, I have combined and renamed some stages, and left some out altogether (see "Joseph Campbell's Hero's Journey Map"). At each step of the way, we'll pause to translate the wisdom of the hero's journey into marketing terms. Here we're looking simply to gain fluency with the concepts. We'll leave it to the next Basic Training to get down to the work of applying these lessons to your empowerment marketing strategy.

Joseph Campbell's

Hero's Journey Map

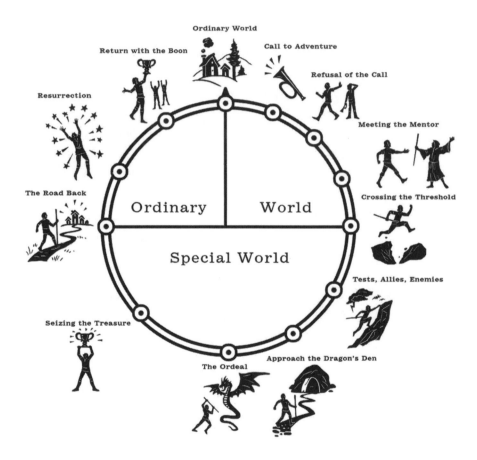

Ordinary World

Call to Adventure

Return with the Boon

Refusal of the Call

Resurrection

Meeting the Mentor

The Road Back

Ordinary | World

Crossing the Threshold

Special World

Tests, Allies, Enemies

Seizing the Treasure

Approach the Dragon's Den

The Ordeal

Stage 1: The Ordinary World and the Call to Adventure

In which our hero feels a stirring deep inside but has not yet conceived of the rich destiny that awaits.

An Unlikely Star: The Audience Is the Hero

The hero's journey begins with a hero-to-be living in a world out of balance. When we meet him or her, the protagonist may seem at that moment to be the unlikeliest of heroes—Dorothy is a little girl, Moses an old man, Frodo a cute little hobbit. The hero is often defined not by any outward heroic qualities, but by his or her very ordinariness.

In your marketing strategy, you will come to know this character as your *brand hero*—the person you imagine yourself speaking to as you design your storytelling strategy. As we'll see, a clear picture of your brand hero is absolutely critical because the stories we tell must allow this hero to see herself in the story—usually by starring a character with which she can easily identify.

By grasping the ordinariness of your brand hero, you are taking an essential first step in creating a successful story strategy. Your audiences will be unlikely to respond to simplistic "you can save the world" messages. In the early days of online activism, I observed no end to blatant hero messages going around: "*You* can rescue polar bears from extinction with one click!" was a typical e-mail subject line. And for a moment, people believed it. I admit, I did too. But several million clicks later, the polar bears are far worse off than they were a decade ago. Today "clicktivism," the idea of changing the world with a click of the mouse, strikes audiences as hopelessly naive. Like Moses, your brand hero has probably tried to change the world herself and been disappointed. You are going to have to show her how she can *become* a hero, not simply tell her she already is. Recognizing one's own hero potential is what the journey is all about.

I want to be clear that when I say *a hero*, I'm not talking about a caped crusader or fireman diving into a burning building. A hero is simply someone who is boldly pursuing higher-level values—creativity, self-expression, truth, or any of the other values on the upper levels of Maslow's chart—and is willing to make sacrifices in service of these ideals, or in the service of other people. Seen another way, heroes have cast off the identity of helpless consumers and are emerging as active citizens. The job of the empowerment marketer is to encourage this transformation.

The Choice to Muddle Through: The Brand Acknowledges the Hero's Agency

When we meet our brand hero, she is disturbed by the lack of balance in her world but likely knows she can manage to ignore it: "The threat is somewhere out there," she thinks, "and if I just look the other way, perhaps that's where it will stay." In the story of Moses, muddling through is the acceptance of a life in exile, living quietly as a shepherd.

This setup works in myth because it gives the hero *agency*, a chance to decide for herself whether or not to set out on the adventure. It works in marketing because it will square with the experience of your audiences. Few of us live in an action movie's constant state of life-or-death circumstances in which we are compelled to act. The shopper has the choice to buy the cheapest product, regardless of what it stands for. The voter can opt for immediate self-interest.

And, of course, the marketer can chose to stick with well-trodden approaches. Acknowledging the hero's free will is a strategy in stark contrast to inadequacy marketing. By instilling a sense of lack that cannot be ignored and must be fulfilled, the inadequacy marketer conveniently sets his *brand* up as the hero ready to save the day. We can create far more compelling stories by realizing that our brand is not the hero, our audience members are. And real heroes are more often pulled to adventure by an inner calling than pushed into it by absolute necessity.

The Call to Adventure: The Hero Is Ready for Something More

Yes, muddling through life is an option, but deep down the hero senses greater possibility. As Maslow discovered, we can ignore the pull to fulfill higher-level needs, but that pull is never extinguished.

Living as a quiet, married shepherd, Moses was likely fulfilling his needs for safety, comfort, and perhaps love. But thoughts about the injustices of his homeland kept intruding, disturbing his otherwise copacetic existence. These thoughts are an example of the "call to adventure" Campbell spoke about—the call to leave the confines of the comfortable and familiar to pursue values that lead to growth and maturity. In stories, the call may come in the form of a dream, the emergence of traumatic circumstances (as when the young hero is suddenly orphaned), a vision, a herald character (like the white rabbit), or the hero's conscience. In our modern lives, most of us experience the call as the pull of Maslow's growth needs—the desire to break free from soul-crushing work, to express ourselves more fully, or to stand up for what we believe in.

Stage 2: Meeting the Mentor and the Refusal of the Call

In which our hero encounters a compelling stranger who will change the course of his life but not before a bond of trust is formed between them.

Moses and his flock had almost reached the top of the mountain when something caught his eye. Just off to the side of the path, a fire was raging. Fire in the dry scrubby desert was hardly unusual. But this one was oddly confined to a single bush—nothing else nearby was burning. In fact, even the bush itself seemed unfazed by the flames.

Moses approached the curious fire cautiously, and as he came near, a voice called from within.

"Moses," said the bush.

As soon as he heard his name spoken, Moses felt his past come rushing back. He knew, in a flash, that he had not escaped the destiny of his earlier life after all—whatever that destiny might be.

"Here am I," the old shepherd responded.

"I am the god of your father," said the improbable bush. And then he told Moses about his plan. It went something like this: the old Pharaoh's dead and a new one has taken over—now's the time to act. You'll go back to Egypt, confront the new Pharaoh, and bring the people of Israel to freedom.

Moses thought this was a bad idea.

"Who am I?" he asked incredulously. "I stutter when I speak." This was true. "I'm a nobody in Egypt." True again. "Even the slaves will think I'm crazy." They would.

"And when I say God has sent me, they'll say 'Oh yeah? What's your god's name?' What will I say then?"

"I am that I am," was the poetic and infuriating reply from the bush.

This was only the beginning of a very long conversation. According to rabbinical lore, Moses and God spent seven days discussing the plan—Moses asking tough questions, God reassuring him and offering him strength. The whole thing was crazy, and Moses pointed out that it defied logic. The bush agreed. But, God said, he had more tricks up his sleeve for when they got there. Not that convincing, really.

Still, deep down, Moses wanted to be convinced. The call that God was offering him was, after all, the same call he had always felt deep inside of himself—a chance to reconcile his actions with his highest values.

Before the end of the talk, God noticed the shepherd's rod Moses had been holding.

"What is that in thy hand?" asked God rhetorically (he had, after all, created the universe and everything in it).

"A staff," answered Moses, a little taken aback.

God told Moses to place it on the ground. When he did, the stick transformed into a writhing serpent. The trick scared the daylights out of Moses, and only through God's strongest encouragement did the shepherd reach out to touch it, at which point it became a staff again.

"You're going to want to take that with you," God said as Moses gingerly picked it up off the ground.

So Moses went home. He packed up his wife and kids and ventured out of his world of safety and into a world of unfathomable challenge and the hope of unparalleled reward.

The Mentor Makes the Difference:
The Brand Becomes the Mentor

In this stage of the journey, we meet the next key character of our storytelling strategy—the *mentor*. This is the character your brand will come to inhabit. The mentor's role is to get the hero moving from her uncomfortable position living in limbo onto the path she must follow in order to meet her destiny. Without the mentor, the call to adventure may be nothing but a stirring, an unfulfilled potential. It's no accident that the word mentor comes from the Greek word *menos*—meaning *intention, purpose,* and *force.*

"Mentors in stories act mainly on the mind of the hero, changing her consciousness or redirecting her will. Mentors also strengthen the hero's mind to face an ordeal with confidence. *Menos* also means courage," writes Christopher Vogler, the screenplay sage and author of *The Writer's Journey: Mythic Structure for Writers.*

In the Moses story, the mentor character is God; in your own storytelling strategy, your brand will play the role of the mentor. It may seem strange to think of your brand in a role once occupied by the Creator, but there is an important lesson for marketers in looking at God's role as a mentor to Moses in this ancient story.

Notice how even God himself can't order Moses to take the journey? It took seven days for the Almighty to offer enough strength and inspiration so that Moses would take on the task. Issuing commands just wouldn't do it. Building up courage ultimately would. Here we see Campbell's notion of *the refusal of the call* at work, and it reminds us that creating change in people's thought patterns and behaviors is never easy. The mentor's role is to make change irresistible but not mandatory. God does this by accessing Moses's innate desire to right what he, deep down, knows is wrong with the world. This is the indispensible role of the mentor in the hero's journey.

Mentors come in all shapes and sizes; Cinderella's fairy god-mother, Dorothy's Good Witch, Morpheus, and Merlin are classic mentors. The palette of character types you have to choose from for your brand is enormous. Learning to whittle your brand mentor down to a single defined character is the next critical step on the journey.

By developing your brand mentor fully, you begin to understand the voice of the *storyteller* behind each of your stories. When he (or she) speaks to our brand hero, does the mentor inspire her to adventure with hearty pep talks? Optimistic visions of the future? Mystery? Quirky, offbeat humor? Understanding your brand mentor as a living, breathing character will answer all of these questions, help you place your brand where it belongs in your storytelling strategy, and bring consistency to your communications.

The Mentor Must Reveal His Name: Embracing the Wisdom of WWJD

Of all of the concerns and objections that Moses comes up with to respond to God's unlikely plan, one of the most powerful and famous is, essentially, "I need to know your name." To which God replies "I am that I am."

This exchange highlights a critical dynamic between the hero and the mentor, and thus between you and your brand hero. The hero yearns for a relationship with the mentor as an *individual*, not a nameless source of wisdom and authority. A key to effective storytelling is the notion that the mentor's concepts must come from the mouth of a relatable personality. This rule explains the runaway resonance of one incredibly powerful story wars meme—WWJD.

Beginning in 1996, long before everyone and his mother was sporting Lance Armstrong's yellow LiveStrong bands, Michigan pastor Dan Seaborn ordered up some bracelets with the acronym WWJD woven into them. The concept: before taking an action or making a life choice, ask yourself "What Would Jesus Do?" Not "What does the Bible tell you to do?" But "What would the *man* whose words inspired it do?" The four letters were short enough to be easily remembered and cryptic enough to attract curiosity from those outside of the campaign's inner circle. Seaborn instructed anyone who wore the bracelet to pass it along to anyone else who asked what the acronym meant—and then pick up another one.

What made this concept so powerful—and ultimately moved more than 15 million bracelets (some estimates put the number closer to 50 million)—is that it revitalized the *story* aspect of Jesus's life, emphasizing not his rules and decrees but his character as a human being. Young people found this direct relationship with Jesus as mentor far more appealing than the traditional practice of quoting scripture by chapter and verse. The breakthrough of WWJD vastly increased the power of the evangelical youth movement and funneled a new generation of adherents into the church, using an element of storytelling to make Christianity cool.

The success of WWJD offers an important lesson for building your storytelling strategy. If we are to create human relationships with our audiences, we must come to know our brand as a character, not as an organization, legal entity, or group of employees. We must become so familiar with our true character—our brand mentor—that we can ask ourselves "WW[Your Brand Here]D?" and be able to confidently and consistently answer that question. In fact, if you remember nothing else about achieving consistency in your brand, remember WWJD.

Until you've grasped your own character, there's no hope of bringing it to life for your audiences. So the next step in building your strategy is to thoroughly understand your own brand mentor. Carl Jung provides some help in achieving this self-knowledge with the idea of *archetypes*.

Jung believed that we are not born into this world as a blank slate, but with preset concepts—*archetypes*—that inform all experience and behavior. Because these archetypes are unconscious and can never be fully described, they are what Jung described as *primordial images*. Through experience of the world, a person will begin to attach conscious archetypal images to these inexpressible concepts. For instance, we are not born knowing anything about knights in armor or democracy protestors in Egypt but when we encounter such figures in image or experience, we readily attach them to a built-in archetypal concept of heroism. The more a character or image fits an unconscious archetype, the more powerfully it will connect to our emotions.

Myths tend to be full of characters based on archetypes. My own childhood *Star Wars* obsession began at age five, when I started collecting the movie's irresistible action figures. *Star Wars* is full of powerful archetypes: Darth Vader (the *Villain*), Obi-Wan Kenobi (the *Mentor*), Yoda (the *Oracle*) and Han Solo (the *Rebel*). Even my three-year old daughter, who has never seen *Star Wars* or heard about it from me, calls herself Princess Leia and her best friend next door Luke, absorbing these characters almost as if by cultural osmosis.

Archetypes are so irresistible to the human mind because although they appear to describe external, independent characters, they in fact describe the various pieces of our own psychic structures. One of the places we most often encounter archetypes is in our dreams. Here we find terrifying villains, beautiful seducers, and strange shapeshifters. If you've ever tried dream interpretation, you know that each of these characters is considered somehow a part of the dreamer herself. Each of us embodies every archetype, so any archetype clearly defined creates the chance for identification and self-knowledge.

If archetypes get people to sit up, take notice, and connect emotionally, it should be no surprise that they are indispensible to marketers. In their book, *The Hero and the Outlaw,* Margaret Mark and Carol Pearson do an exhaustive survey of brands that stick to a well-defined archetype in the minds of their audiences. They provide startling evidence that this approach leads directly to markedly better financial performance.

In the world of empowerment marketing, archetypes are particularly important because they are the perfect way to embody your otherwise intangible values. For instance, if your highest brand value is Playfulness, you may be drawn to an archetype like the

Magician, who joyfully breaks natural limits and makes the impossible suddenly possible. If your highest value, on the other hand, is Uniqueness, you may find better alignment with the *Rebel.*

In the Basic Training at the end of this chapter, I offer seven archetypes that I've found particularly helpful in building empowerment marketing brands. These archetypes can help you get more deeply acquainted with your own brand mentor and begin confidently answering "WW(My brand)D?" as you begin to design breakthrough stories.

Stage 3: Approaching the Dragon's Den and Seizing the Treasure

In which our hero journeys to the center of the magic world, encounters a frightful nemesis, and is aided by the mentor's magic gift.

How could he have been prepared for the sights and sounds of the metropolis? For forty years he had known nothing but sheep, quiet breezes, and a few gentle souls. Like a prisoner confined to darkness who is blinded by the light when he emerges, Moses found his old home to be a frightening clamor of activity and chaos. After four decades of chasing stray lambs, it was also exhilarating. Merchants shouted from flimsily constructed stalls. A street magician beckoned to him in a language he had never before heard. Harlots whispered from windows above. Slaves trudged by, peering up at him from heads bent low. None recognized their former prince.

His brother Aaron, who had been inspired by God to meet Moses just outside the city, seemed to take it all for granted as he guided the old man through the labyrinthine streets out into an open square. It was from here that Moses saw the palace, his old home, for the first time since that terrifying day when he had killed a man.

"Go talk to Pharaoh." It had sounded, well, not simple, but at least *possible* when discussed on that lonely mountaintop. But standing before the home of the king, Moses beheld what he guessed were thousands, if not tens of thousands, of soldiers guarding its four hundred doors.

The brothers approached the outer gates, resigned to the most likely outcome of this fool's errand—death. But what else could they do? And then something curious happened. The closer they got to the soldiers, the more obvious it became that these men could not see them. Even the two enormous lions that stood near the doorway they now approached did no more than sniff the ground a few feet away as they circled the awestruck brothers.

"Well, this is going better than planned," whispered Moses as they stepped into the palace. It was the last time in a long life that he would utter those words.

Everything about Pharaoh's throne room was designed to make petitioners feel like they were in the presence of a god—the kind of god who has more gold and power and weapons than everyone you've ever known combined. The kind of god who could snap his fingers and have your heart ripped out.

If the guards couldn't see the two elderly men approaching, the Pharaoh and his courtiers surely could. And they weren't much impressed as they sneered down at the uninvited guests.

With his head humbly tipped back to address the king who sat several feet above him, Moses skipped the preamble and got right to business: "Thus saith Yahweh, the God of Israel, let My people go, so that they may hold a feast unto Me in the wilderness." Silence. This was the not-so-clever ruse God had concocted for Moses. Pretend you're asking for a three-day break in the desert, then, when nobody's looking, make a break for it.

Pharaoh reacted as you'd probably expect—with an unequivocal no. He'd never even heard of this God whom Moses supposedly spoke for. Then, adding insult to injury, he ordered that from that day forth, Israelite slaves would be required to gather their own straw for the bricks they were forced to make, effectively doubling their work. Thank you very much for coming.

Thus begun a battle to the death of wits and magic between Moses, the underdog, and Pharaoh, the all-powerful. As God had promised, the magic staff would come in particularly handy. Moses gave the staff to Aaron, who turned the Nile to blood. Pharaoh's magicians could do that too. So Moses waved the staff and began summoning the plagues—frogs, gnats, flies, pestilence (which killed all of Egypt's livestock), boils, hail, locusts, and darkness. Each plague was worse than the one before, but none terrible enough to soften Pharaoh's hardened heart.

And then Moses threatened Pharaoh with what would seem the deathblow—the slaughter of every firstborn child and animal if Pharaoh failed to free the Israelites. And fail he did. So God brought the final plague upon him.

"Go! Go!" cried the king when he saw the carnage wrought by the God of Moses. The cowardly and selfish Pharaoh, himself a firstborn son, was fully expecting his own life to be extinguished at any moment.

With the hard-won treasure of freedom in his heart and the trusty magic staff gripped tightly in his hand, Moses fled Egypt with his people following close behind.

A Journey Through the Magic World: The Brand Creates New Possibilities

Once the hero has crossed the threshold out of his ordinary world, he enters a land both terrifying and thrilling: terrifying because it is entirely unfamiliar, with many unknown dangers; and thrilling because old roadblocks and habits no longer exist here. As Moses found, suddenly, anything is possible. Campbell likened this magic world of the hero's journey to the world of dreams, where even the most basic rules don't apply and where we encounter powerful symbols, rich in meaning that inform or guide us. At the threshold of the magic world, the thrill usually outweighs the fear. Think of the cantina scene in *Star Wars,* where Luke meets fantastic and wild creatures engaged in raucous debauchery.

Great storytelling strategies also create fantastic magic worlds where stifling old rules no longer apply. Candidate Obama's story was set in an optimistic world where racial tension melted away. In VW's magic world, advertisers stopped lying. In Annie Leonard's magic world, dry, complex issues became instantly graspable and fun. Just as Oz is presented in Technicolor, in contrast to Dorothy's black-and-white Kansas existence, the magic world of your brand should be far more alive and interesting than the familiar world your hero knows. Chapter 7 offers several concrete tips for creating stories that make this possible.

Meeting Your Nemesis: The Villain Is Just the Hero, Unrealized

A bad guy with evil intent can be interesting, sure. But the villain becomes personally terrifying to the hero when he represents the hero's own dark side. That's one of the reasons Pharaoh is such a perfect villain.

Pharaoh has three primary characteristics in this story, and they all represent Moses's worst fears about himself—fears that would have been realized if he failed to act. First, he is completely insensitive to the suffering of others. Doubling the burden of the slaves, he thinks nothing of working them, perhaps literally, to their deaths— and all just to mock Moses's demand. Had Moses stayed in Midian, he would have been turning his back on a suffering of others that he knew he should not ignore. Second, Pharaoh has no faith in God. He laughs at Moses's demands because he doesn't believe the God of Moses exists. Had Moses refused the adventure, it would have been a declaration of faithlessness in God's power. And finally, Pharaoh is a coward. He allows the lives of his people to be ravaged but does not relent until he fears for his own life—a coward just as Moses would have been had he ignored God's call. The fact that Pharaoh is Moses's dark mirror image is what makes him so horrifying.

The lesson here is simple: when pursuing our higher values, our greatest enemies may seem to be others who oppose us, but the real opposition comes from the fears and weaknesses within. And learning to confront our own weaknesses is the only way to ready ourselves to confront true opposition from the outside. In your empowerment marketing efforts, this insight applies not just to the brand hero but to the brand mentor as well. Each mentor arche-type discussed in the next Basic Training contains a description of that character's dark side. Being sensitive to the pitfalls of taking on a relatable character is a key to successful storytelling.

The Mentor's Gift: Naming What Makes the Brand Unique

Like the *Star Wars* cantina, the magic world starts out fun. But every step the hero takes through this land is a step closer to the dragon's den—the frightful belly of the beast she will have to pass through if she is to complete her quest.

Still, the hero is not unprepared. There is balance in the hero's journey. For every step she takes toward danger, she also takes a step toward her power. By the time she encounters the dragon—or Pharaoh, or the Wicked Witch—she is no longer such an unlikely hero. She also has an advantage that gives her a leg up—the mentor's gift. One of the primary functions of the mentor, it turns out, is to give the hero something—a magic object or tool—she can use to defy the odds in her hour of greatest need. The mentor, not being the hero of the story, doesn't go into the dragon's den with her, but he can be called forth in spirit through the magic of this gift. While the mentor's words make the call to adventure seem exciting, the gift makes the adventure's unlikely success seem possible.

In great stories, the gift is a staff, ruby red slippers, a light saber, or the sword Excalibur. In the world of marketing, the gift is the unforgettable concept or visual that indelibly marks the brand, making us feel "with this one, we can beat the odds because this one is different." The empowerment marketing examples in previous chapters all approached the gift from a different angle, but each brand does have a gift to offer, making the promise of defying the odds and breaking old patterns seem possible. Annie Leonard's gift is the magic whiteboard upon which clarity is instantly produced. Obama's gift is a set of amazing online tools, marking the campaign from the beginning as the dark horse with a real chance because it was so in step with the technology of the times. Apple's gift is beauty that can overthrow the beige tyranny of the business machine. WWJD was all about a magic gift, a bracelet.

Well-chosen brand gifts will not simply be a literal reflection of the message of the brand itself. Apple didn't choose a fist in the air to represent rebellion. Annie Leonard didn't choose to build her brand around a basic-looking flowchart to bring to mind simplicity. Even Moses's humble wooden staff might seem a strange talisman of God. The brand gift is a wild card addition that makes the rest of the storytelling strategy leap creatively to life.

Empowerment marketing's brand gift may sound reminiscent of the dark art practice of magically solving problems through use of a product. There are similarities here to be sure, but there is a key difference. Where inadequacy marketing stirs up anxiety and then offers an object to quell it, empowerment marketing tells the hero that the work is up to her. The gift simply makes a once-impossible adventure achievable, but it is still an adventure she must undertake as the lead actor. Obama's Internet savvy didn't excuse you from working hard on the campaign; it allowed you to work *harder*. Leonard's whiteboard doesn't solve the world's problems; it invites you to understand and engage with them. Apple is not thinking different for you; it's creating a beautiful tool that empowers *you* to think different.

Stage 4: The Road Back, Resurrection, and Return

In which our hero brings something of great value to the world and a lesson is finally learned.

An infant slave, a prince, a fugitive, a shepherd, then a prophet— and now a shepherd once more. But this time his flock numbered in the hundreds of thousands and they were far more unruly than even the testiest sheep.

The flight from Egypt had started off smoothly. Moses and his people had left not as slaves and fugitives but with their heads held high, the treasure and armaments of their oppressors in hand. Still, they ran rather than walked into the wilderness. After so many betrayals of his word, Moses wasn't about to give Pharaoh a chance to change his mind.

Of course that's exactly what Pharaoh did. Realizing he had lost his labor force, the stubborn king flew into a rage. His fear having suddenly evaporated, he set out with six hundred of his war chariots to bring the slaves back.

Back at camp, one of the Hebrews noticed a cloud of dust approaching from the west. Someone else screamed in panic, while others cursed Moses for his choice to settle in for the night with their backs to the sea.

"Turn and fight!" Moses shouted to his people, who far outnumbered the Egyptian army. But they rebelled. They wailed. They tried to bolt.

Moses was furious. Had they come this far just to hand back their hard-won freedom? He was angry, yes. Despairing, no. Everyone else expected death, but the shepherd was no longer a reluctant, excuse-making retiree—a man trying to dampen the spark of his call. He was now filled with a purpose that would not be denied. And so he turned to God once again. And God responded to him as a man who understood his own awesome power:

"And lift thou up thy rod, and stretch out thy hand over the sea, and divide it."

He didn't tremble. He didn't question. He simply acted and the sea parted.

Now he had the flock's attention. With death behind and their shepherd ahead, the people followed in awed procession as Moses led them to freedom. And as the last Israelite crossed the sea, the waters closed up again, drowning Pharaoh and his chariots. Moses had fulfilled his call.

Returning with the Treasure: Identifying the Boon

Having seized the treasure from the belly of the beast, the hero must leave the magic world and use that treasure to heal her own broken world. Campbell calls the treasure "the boon to society," and the term reveals a key feature of the hero's journey. The treasure that the hero wins in the magic world is not something she keeps for herself, but rather something that she shares with her community. Ultimately, the quest is the selfless act of a hero who has made sacrifices so her world will be a better place. Understanding your own *brand boon,* the gift to society you encourage your hero to bring back, will help raise the stakes in your storytelling strategy so that your stories feel relevant and gripping. It also amplifies the viral potential of your stories. The brand boon of Dove's Real Beauty campaign, for instance, is what made women open their social networks and share the message enthusiastically. Removing the images of anorexic or surgically enhanced and Photoshopped models from urban billboards and replacing them with images of real women with normal bodies—and in their underwear, no less—was not just a gift to the viewer, who immediately felt better about her own normal body. It was a political statement with overt messaging designed to heal society's damaging beauty ideals. Thus, sharing the message became a heroic act of sharing the brand boon, the gift to society. Nike, too, has discovered that individual achievement isn't a satisfying-enough end to the story. It's recently created a major destination hub for its brand, called Nike Better World, to provide a richer brand boon to society. The site is all about how sport is one of the world's most powerful tools to end violence, fight homelessness, and crush prejudice. The moral of Nike's story has been extended into hero's journey territory by tying athletic achievement, a pursuit in which anyone can participate, to the greater good.

The Truth Is Revealed: Articulating the Moral of the Story

The hero has the treasure in her hands, or at least in her heart. She's nearly crossed back into her ordinary world. But the story's not over yet. Suddenly, disaster looms yet again. The enemy, once thought defeated, comes back for a last showdown. This time, the odds don't look good. In fact, it is common for the hero to face an almost certain death at this final stage.

But marshalling everything she has learned from each trial, friend, and enemy encountered along the way, the hero takes decisive action and finally defeats her nemesis once and for all. The hero has fully matured to embody her highest-level values, and a miracle of near-resurrection occurs.

This last stage of the journey is critical because, until we experience it, we don't really know what the storyteller is trying to tell us. We haven't gotten the moral of the story yet. The moral of Exodus is that freedom is won through absolute faith in God. Moses dutifully follows God's advice to camp with his back to the sea, an obvious tactical mistake but a deep show of his faith. Then when they are attacked, he is the only Israelite with enough faith to not panic but to heed God's word and use his magic staff to part the waters. His faith saves the day.

Suddenly the whole story makes sense. His earlier doubts as a hero-to-be have given way to deeper and deeper faith, until finally the good shepherd is leading his sprawling flock to safety on faith alone. Think of how different this story's meaning would be if, at the last moment, Moses had decided not to listen to God's commandment. What if, instead, he had realized that what he really needed to do was to trust himself? He comes up with an impromptu, stirring speech to the Egyptians, and Pharaoh's heart is softened. Now the story has an entirely different meaning: "Everything you need is already inside, so trust yourself." Or Moses listens to God but nothing happens. So he humbles himself and appeals to his flock for help. Seeing that Moses is willing to abdicate his power, the community acts and slays the Egyptians. The moral would be, "No man, even a man of God, is an island." How the hero triumphs in this final trial tells us what the story is all about.

We might find any of these endings satisfying because they each bring forth a moral that embodies some piece of commonly held and resonant wisdom about life. If the moral is unclear, on the other hand, the story falls apart. Moses strikes his staff. The sea parts. The Israelites flee, with the Egyptians following close behind. Then suddenly, the waters close and everyone drowns except Moses, who miraculously makes it out alive. We would be left trying desperately to understand what the storyteller wants us to learn.

Unfortunately, this kind of muddled moral of the story mars so many brand strategies. Not only do brands fail to stick to any sense of their archetype—*who* they are—they fail to define a clear moral of the story—*what* they are trying to say. Each communication is just a confused attempt to make us smile at, lust after, or simply notice their offering. The story wars can only be won by brands that choose and defend a clear moral, and the culmination of each of their stories should be a proud declaration or clear implication of it. Smart inadequacy brands have been doing just that for decades with morals that tell us we are nothing more than our basest desires. This moral is clear, but does it truly draw us in now that we have millions of stories to choose from? Do these inadequacy stories contain commonly held wisdom about life? Or is it likely that empowerment marketing opens the door for far more resonant morals—those that square with our inner beliefs and hopes about the possibility for human transcendence? You know where I stand, but it is your decision to make for yourself.

And so, we have come to the end of our journey with Moses—a journey that has illustrated the larger hero's journey pattern. This formula, as Campbell discovered, has been the way mythmakers have communicated deep truths for millennia. Taken together with Maslow's insights about the drive for transcendence, we can build out a story strategy that heeds Power's commandment to Tell the Truth about human nature and potential in ways that audiences will respond to and share.

The following Basic Training puts these insights into action.

BASIC TRAINING

Designing Your Core Story Elements

In this training, the stories you tell for your product, cause, candidate, or idea will find a strategy for discipline and consistency. Before we dive in, let's review the component parts of what will become the rest of your story strategy:

BRAND HERO: The embodiment of the primary audience you seek to reach. Seeing members of your target audience as heroes-in-the-making and the implicit stars of your stories will orient your efforts toward inspiring and empowering audiences and away from messages of inadequacy.

BRAND MENTOR: The embodiment of your brand. Defining and then getting deeply acquainted with this character will help you craft a consistent voice and unique brand feel. Recognize that you are not the hero but the force that puts the hero in motion and you will empower your audiences to act.

BRAND GIFT: The creative wildcard that makes your brand special and makes your brand hero believe she can pursue her higher-level values through a relationship with your brand.

MORAL OF THE STORY: The moral is the core message that underlies, sometimes subtly and sometimes overtly, every story you tell. The moral can be dressed up in any number of plots, characters, and forms, but it should always be there providing meaning and consistency to your communications.

BRAND BOON: The contribution to the world that your brand hero will ultimately make. Empowerment marketing calls its heroes not just to fulfill themselves, but to heal, renew, and improve the world at large.

The Brand Hero

Step 1: Bring Your Brand Hero to Life

Create a character sketch of your brand hero, a person who stands in as a quintessential member of your target audience. Take time to really picture this person, whether real or imagined, as concretely as possible. What is her (or his) name? How would she describe her external persona and her inner sense of self? Write this description in the first person.

If you already have demographic information or have developed audience personas, that's valuable fodder for your story strategy. Traditional research can and should inform this process, but as you're about to see, we're going to go much farther into the realm of imaginative storytelling than traditional research can take us.

You may feel the need for more than one brand hero. And depending on the diversity of messages you need to create for various audiences, you may need to bring more than one hero into your strategic thinking. But keep in mind that you only get to have one brand and that brand needs focus for its stories. With the introduction of each additional brand hero, the creative pressures on your story exponentially increase and eventually your vision of your hero may become nothing more than a muddy mess. As frightening as it may seem to choose one brand hero, it is the most direct path to a coherent strategy. Remember, we're dealing in human universals here, so a single well-defined hero does not necessarily exclude everyone else. If at the end of the exercise, you decide to go back and add another brand hero, make sure you're doing so to solve problems that cannot be otherwise addressed.

BRAND HEROES IN THE REAL WORLD

> DOVE REAL BEAUTY: A woman who feels a profound sense of discomfort with her body image. She senses this feeling is being stimulated from the outside but rarely pauses to think about how and by whom.

> APPLE: A young man who sees himself as creatively inspired and pulls against what he believes is a culture of conformity.

> THE TEA PARTY: A middle-aged couple who are furious about what is happening to America. They see their country going in the wrong direction but are having trouble naming the source of this problem or solutions to it.

Step 2: Write a Letter from Your Hero About Her Broken World

Write a letter from your brand hero to one of her close friends or family members. In it, reveal the broken world your hero is muddling through. In writing this letter, you might ask yourself: What old stories or explanations are no longer making sense to her? How would she describe her inner call to adventure—that inkling that something more is possible? Why has she not yet followed it?

Write this letter in a story language that frees you from mundane business-speak. Make it feel like the beginning of a very personal adventure. A great way to warm up for this exercise is to read a classic text that sets up its own broken world in story language. Here are some quick and easy ones: *The Lorax*; the opening chapters of *Harry Potter and the Sorcerer's Stone*; the first chapters of *The Odyssey*; the title crawl of *Star Wars*.

Step 3: Capture What You've Learned

Turn to the chart in the appendix and write the name of your brand hero and a short description to remind you of who this character is. You'll want to keep your broken world letter handy for a more in-depth view of your brand hero when needed.

The Brand Mentor

If your audience members are your heroes, your brand itself is the *brand mentor*, the character who guides the hero to adventure. So the purpose here is to get to know what kind of mentor your brand really embodies.

Step 1: Uncover Your Brand Mentor's Archetype

Just as you created a brand hero sketch, you will now create a sketch of your brand mentor. The character sketches below will help you uncover your archetype. I use the word "uncover" rather than "choose" because this is a process of deeply observing both who you are as a brand and who you aspire to be. It is about putting a name and a face to your authentic core. In considering the archetypes below, think not only of how you see yourself but how, when you're at your best, your audiences hold you in their hearts and their heads.

Note how each archetype embodies certain values. If you see an archetype here that embodies some of the values you've already chosen, this may be a clue to the character at your authentic core. Conversely, you may immediately gravitate toward an archetype based on its personality and reconsider your brand values—if they are not already baked deeply into your organization—to match it.

Play with both directions and see which generates the most creative excitement. You may be tempted to combine archetypes or choose more than one. Remember, however, that audiences won't see your mentor in all of his (or her) complexity. They'll want to understand your brand as a single, identifiable character. Archetypes need not express *everything* about your brand. They simply represent the first elements of the personality that audiences will learn about and connect with.

THE PIONEER

Our imaginations are stirred by the idea of boarding a ship heading for terra incognita. We all secretly wish to dive into the deepest unknown, the unexplored corners of the Earth and our souls. Most of us dream of these adventures but prefer to stay safely at home. Not you.

You revel in leaping beyond usual solutions. Visionary new ideas are your lifeblood, and none are dismissed as too bold. You are *curious, innovative, brave,* and *optimistic about the future.*

> FAMOUS PIONEERS: Sacajawea, Davy Crockett, Ernest Shackleton, Amelia Earhart, Steve Jobs

> PIONEER BRANDS: Levi's, Patagonia, Samsung

KEY VALUES: Richness, Uniqueness, Truth

SHADOW: The independent-minded Pioneer can be blindly devoted to newness and adventure, making this archetype, at his or her worst, too impatient to stick around for long-term value building.

THE REBEL

Without order, there is chaos. But order left unchallenged too long leads to only one end: complacency and tyranny. You know this and seek a creative destruction of the status quo. You are driven by the idealistic vision of a better way. Where you tear down a problem, you also point the way to a solution. You value freedom of action and expression and are *fearless, uncompromising,* and *creative.*

FAMOUS REBELS: Che Guevara, John Wayne, the Rolling Stones, Rosa Parks, Banksy, Ron Paul

REBEL BRANDS: Apple (early days), Occupy Wall Street, Harley-Davidson, Virgin

KEY VALUES: Justice, Uniqueness, Truth

SHADOW: The Rebel is easily mistaken for the Vandal, who drifts away from creative destruction toward nihilistic disorder.

THE MAGICIAN

We are all born believing in miracles. When reason tells a child she has reached the limits of what can be done, she utters magic words, believing she can transform the world. As adults, many still cling to a belief in transcendence even as their magic words are silenced.

But you see no reason to settle for what others say can be done. You are *creative, irreverent,* and *energetic.*

You believe that imagination and play can move mountains. You revel in surprising and delighting those around you. And while you seek to share the gifts of your magic, you prefer to keep its secrets for yourself.

FAMOUS MAGICIANS: Merlin, Johannes Gutenberg, Thomas Edison, Nikola Tesla, Michael Jordan

MAGICIAN BRANDS: Pixar, Make a Wish Foundation, TOMS Shoes

KEY VALUES: Playfulness, Perfection, Beauty

SHADOW: Around Magicians hangs the air of mystery; to some, that mystery may smell of fraud.

THE JESTER

Even staring deeply into the mirror, we may find it too painful to truly see our own follies. Yet, ignorant of our own weaknesses, we are doomed to be overwhelmed by them. You provide us the only way to peer behind our masks, as people and as a society, through the safety of humor.

You disguise yourself in the cloak of innocence, making us believe that laughter is witless fun. But you know it is not. You are deeply *intelligent,* seeing reality more clearly than others and then finding a way to show it in the most unexpected ways. You are *playful* but decry nonsense. You are also extremely *brave,* unafraid to hold a mirror up to the powerful.

FAMOUS JESTERS: Coyote (the Native American trickster), Bugs Bunny, Mark Twain, Jon Stewart

JESTER BRANDS: Ben & Jerry's, the Yes Men, GEICO, the Muppets

KEY VALUES: Playfulness, Justice, Simplicity

SHADOW: Jesters must always resist the temptation to fall into frivolity, turning the beauty of life and its possibilities into an endless joke.

THE CAPTAIN

It is the rare hero who can accept the call to adventure when it is only a whisper in a dream. But when called forth by a bold and decisive leader, heroes seem to appear everywhere. As the Captain, it falls to you to bring out heroic action and steadfastly guide those who choose to follow.

Your greatest strength comes from the trust you inspire, and that is derived from your clarity of vision and an ability to make yourself understood. You are *idealistic, confident, tireless,* and *brave.* And while the door is open to you to revel in glory and power, you do not lose sight of your true goal—to empower those around you to become leaders themselves.

FAMOUS CAPTAINS: Odysseus, Abraham Lincoln, Martin Luther King, Wangari Maathai, Oprah

CAPTAIN BRANDS: Obama for America, Nike, LiveStrong, Newt 2012

KEY VALUES: Wholeness, Perfection, Truth

SHADOW: Captains must resist the constant temptation to hold tightly to power and issue orders rather than inspiration; if they don't, they quickly become tyrants.

THE DEFENDER

That which is most beautiful, precious and irreplaceable is often most vulnerable. Beneath your armor of resoluteness, you are driven by a deep love for those people, things, and principles that cannot protect themselves.

You leave it to others to stake out the future. Your job is to defend that which is sacred but may be lost. You are *strong, sensitive, selfless,* and *resolute.* You are often seen quietly scanning the horizon until your sense of justice is violated, at which point you spring into single-minded action.

FAMOUS DEFENDERS: John Muir, Jane Goodall, Ronald Reagan, the Tea Party

DEFENDER BRANDS: Greenpeace, the Republican Party, the Boy Scouts/Girl Scouts

KEY VALUES: Justice, Perfection, Wholeness

SHADOW: Defenders are indispensible to any society, but they are often the last to acccpt needed change many have fallen by the wayside when they fail to recognize the need to loosen their grip on the past.

THE MUSE

Observe a person's life from afar and you will likely find repetition, pattern, even drudgery. Yet each life is punctuated by moments of inspired action, when the spirit is lifted from its day-to-day slumber. These moments bring meaning to our existence. You draw these moments out in others, inspiring through your example of beauty, creativity, and love.

You have a deep faith in those around you and believe humans were born to transcend. Your strategy is to quietly lead by example. You are

humble, imaginative, creative, and *optimistic.* You want nothing more than to see others reach their full potential for self-expression.

FAMOUS MUSES: Charles Darwin, Federico García Lorca, Martha Graham, Maya Angelou, Bob Ross

MUSE BRANDS: Lego, IKEA, Etsy, Home Depot, Apple (modern day)

KEY VALUES: Beauty, Richness, Uniqueness

SHADOW: The gentleness of the Muse is often exactly what's needed, but at times this archetype may drift into passivity when his or her voice and influence is needed most.

When you have made your choice, turn to the chart in the appendix. In the *Mentor Archetype* box, capture the archetype simply by writing its name. In the notes section of this box, write short phrases, either pulled from the archetype descriptions or related ones from your own experience that will cue you to remember what attracted you to the archetype you chose.

In the *Shadow* section of this box, write down a short description of the shadow side of this archetype, especially the elements of the shadow side that feel most true to your brand's own vulnerabilities. This will serve as a constant caution against the most obvious pitfalls your brand will encounter. For instance, if you are marketing an environmental NGO and you've chosen the Defender archetype, you may want to avoid the perception that you oppose any change in our natural environment—since change is inevitable. You might write in this box: "Highlight innovations." This will serve as a note to your team that celebrating positive human interventions in service of conservation will make you seem like a forward-looking Defender rather than a stodgy brand stuck in the past.

Step 2: Bring Your Mentor to Your Hero

Now it's time to introduce your mentor to your hero. Imagine the encounter between them. Where does it happen? What does the mentor say to the hero to *call her to adventure*? What does she say to refuse? (Remember Moses's initial resistance to being called to heroism.) How does the mentor bolster the hero's courage? Write this encounter as a dialog between your two emerging characters.

Here are some examples of successful calls to adventure. Note that the call to adventure in strong storytelling brands is often expressed as the tagline.

THE CALL TO ADVENTURE IN THE REAL WORLD

> Think Different (Apple)
>
> Just Do It (Nike)
>
> Yes We Can (Obama)
>
> Live Below Your Means (VW)
>
> Go Forth (Levi's)

Note the benefit conferred on these storytelling brands that comes from having a compelling call to adventure. They use the call to create some of the most compelling taglines of all time. Compare these to "The Choice of a New Generation." This comparison alone should make the advantage of a storytelling brand clear.

The Brand Gift

What is it about your brand that has brought delight to those who touch it? Is it a physical object? A way of speaking? A visual icon? Ask those whose affinity you have earned what image or idea comes to mind when they think of your brand. For some, the brand gift will be obvious and the very essence of their offering. For others, it will be more elusive or may not exist yet at all. Either way, you won't go far without this intangible, emotional wildcard that plants you in the hearts of your audience in an irrational, sometimes magical way.

Here are some tips for getting started:

Your archetype may point the way: The gift of a Muse brand might be something of great visual beauty—perhaps amazing product design. The gift of a Magician brand may be something never before seen—an emphasis on a new technology perhaps. The gift of a Captain brand might be a great strategy—like Obama's Internet approach.

Your existing differentiator may already be your gift: If you've done traditional marketing strategy work already, your primary differentiator or unique selling proposition (USP) might be the perfect brand gift. But just being different—as the USP stresses—doesn't mean you've got something that makes a difficult action seem more likely to succeed as a brand gift should. Before you just slap a new name on an old marketing concept, ask yourself, "Is there empowering magic here?" or is it just logic-based brand positioning? If it's all about logic it may be time to start again.

If you're struggling to capture your brand gift, return to your unfolding hero's journey. Picture your mentor approaching your hero. What does he hand to her? What does he show her? He can't just convince her that this difficult journey is possible—he must make her feel it.

BRAND GIFTS IN THE REAL WORLD

> TOMS SHOES: The One for One program (one shoe donated for each shoe bought)
>
> OCCUPY WALL STREET: The dramatic physical takeover of public space
>
> TARGET: Amazing aesthetics
>
> COCA-COLA: Joy
>
> LIVESTRONG: The yellow bracelet

Capture your brand gift on the chart in the appendix.

The Moral of the Story and the Brand Boon

Imagine it is a decade since the first encounter between your mentor and hero. The adventure has been a success, and her world is a better place. She's a better person. Of course getting to this point wasn't easy; powerful forces opposed her.

Step 1: Write a Letter from Your Hero Remembering the Journey

Write a third and final installment. This one should read like a letter of gratitude from the hero to her mentor. In it, recall the hero's moment of success.

As you write, try to make clear what knowledge, idea, or object she was trying to bring back to her world. What vision was she trying to realize (it can be as grand as reshaping society or as domestic as helping an aging parent reconnect to joy)? This will serve as your *brand boon*. For Obama, it was an America healed. For Volkswagen, it was the permission to get out of the status rat race. For Annie Leonard, it was a new way to relate to our stuff.

Ask yourself what trials your hero survived and what individuals or internal forces opposed her? Often her enemies will be the reflections of who she might have become if she had failed to take this adventure.

Step 2: Find the Moral of the Story

What does the three-part narrative that you've now constructed attempt to tell us about how the world works? Express the core lesson in a sentence and write it down as if the hero finally has wisdom of her own to share with the mentor. This is your moral of the story.

Does this lesson stretch you to understand life a little more deeply while still making intuitive sense when you read it aloud? If you moral feels counterintuitive, is it a problem of phrasing or are you trying to say something that flies in the face of shared cultural wisdom? If it's wording, make sure you're speaking in simple terms at ground level. Connect it to people on the human scale, in words they can feel and touch. But if your problem is that your moral contradicts what people intuitively feel to be true, beware—you're in for an uphill battle.

Write your moral of the story into the chart in the appendix.

Here are some examples of successful morals of the story brands have used. Note that you won't necessarily find these written down or promoted anywhere by the brands themselves. They are the unspoken central message that can be observed through a long-term body of consistent communication.

POWERFUL MORALS IN THE REAL WORLD

DOVE REAL BEAUTY: Truth is beauty. And the truth is: everyone is beautiful in her own skin.

PATAGONIA: Life is most enjoyable when you live it fully while doing the least harm.

TEA PARTY: Powerful elites are stealing America. Real people can seize it back.

OCCUPY WALL STREET: Powerful corporations are stealing the world. Real people can seize it back.

If you've completed all of these exercises, you will have before you a draft of a complete story strategy. In the next chapters, we'll look at how that strategy spawns actual stories you will tell and live.

CHAPTER SEVEN

Be Interesting

Freaks, Cheats, and Familiars

"I wouldn't watch that," Louis sighed as I closed the picture of the bloody, debeaked chicken. Another video concept went to its grave. Too unpleasant, too horrifying, too preachy, too shocking—it seemed that no matter how we presented the facts, nobody would want to know where their meat comes from.

We had chosen to take this project on precisely because it was so challenging. After decades of trying to stir up outrage about factory farming, nobody had been able to package a message capable of breaking through. Armed with a tiny outreach list and no distribution budget, we were trying desperately to be interesting to a huge audience while explaining a topic that until now hadn't been interesting at all.

But it had been three months of work and we had nothing to show for it.

"This feels too abstract," I said, staring out at the endless concrete surrounding our downtown San Francisco office. "We need to write this on a farm."

Winning the attention of our caveman brains: freaks, cheats, and familiars

"There's a community garden a couple of blocks away we could sneak into," Louis suggested. It was better than nothing so we decided to set up shop there.

Looking for a thread as we walked, we reminded ourselves of what had inspired us to select this project in the first place. I read off the brief: "Factory farming is at the center of so many issues people care about. Human health, workers rights, compassionate treatment of animals, family farms, environmental integrity—are all advanced when the abuses of factory farming are stopped."

As we arrived in the lush garden, I was suddenly reminded of the bucolic images featured on the typical mass-produced food label. Blue sky, greenery, sun. This garden looked much like the logo of our story's nemesis, Smithfield, maker of factory-farmed pork products. "These factory farms know they're so bad that they won't even show their face on their packages," Louis worked his way through the thought. "So they show us the opposite—family farms—instead."

Without realizing it, he had totally shifted our focus away from the dead end of stats and horrifying images and directly at the story wars. The factory farm corporations were winning these wars by telling a story about the innocent beauty of their farms. It's a compelling myth that takes us back to our romanticized agrarian past. The other side, our side, was just slamming people with images of horror.

"Right, that's like something else we've seen before," I said of the lying labels. "What is it?"

Instinctively, we knew that if we could counter the enemy's story with one of our own, using ideas and images people were already well acquainted with, we might cut through their resistance and make them see that our message was worthy of attention. We could join their conversation, meeting them on their turf rather trying to scare them onto ours by waving bloody chickens at them.

I had begun searching for *familiars*—one of the three pillars of storytelling success in our short-attention-span, thumbnail-obsessed digitoral era. I would later come to understand that by mastering these three pillars, marketers can be interesting to the primal brain structures of our audiences. They are the perfect tools for turning a story strategy into actual stories people will notice and want to share.

Back in the garden, our familiar came to us in a flash of inspiration, a perfect metaphor. A factory farm was like the scene in *The Matrix*, where humans are held in pods, raised to feed their mechanized masters. OK, good image, but the metaphor went further. In the film, the machines construct a fantasy world to keep people docile because the real world is too hard to accept—just like those lying labels.

We could tell that we had something, a familiar cultural reference that might bring us to entirely new tribes beyond the Humane Society crowd—action fans, sci-fi nerds, and pop culture enthusiasts. It was 2003, and the wildly popular *Matrix* trilogy would release its final installment in a few months. We knew we had to be there with our movie.

The *Matrix* metaphor also provided us readymade *cheats*—characters in a story who challenge social norms. When someone breaks the rules, we perk up and wonder, What will happen to him? Will he be punished? Will he succeed and rewrite the rules? Natural selection has crafted our brains not just to favor stories with conflict but stories with the kind of conflict that puts characters in opposition to the rules of mainstream society. Of course, that's what *The Matrix* is all about: rebels challenging a society run by soulless machines.

So we would tell a story, as *The Matrix* did, of detestable cultural norms (in *The Matrix*, human enslavement to machines; in our movie, the injustices of industrial food production) and the cheats, or rebels, who defy them. Compelling cheats would be our stars.

"What if the main character was a bull? We'll call him *Moopheus*," Louis said, not looking up from his sketchbook.

With that, our final pillar, *freaks*, fell perfectly into place. Freaks are characters who play off the human brain's preference for focusing on other humans, but not just any other humans. We are drawn to focus our attention on the most *unusual* humans in our environment. Trench-coated animals would fill that role. Before long,

Moopheus and his protégé, Leo the pig, would become Internet legends.

We spent the next couple weeks creating the world of our video. Nothing seemed to get in our way, except the title. I don't know how to explain this, but our *Matrix* spoof about animal products just resisted being named.

Finally, one night, my mind wandering at a bluegrass concert, I was smashed in the face with the obvious. "Louis!" I said as soon as he took my call. "I've got the name—*The Meatrix*."

"That's pretty good," was all he said in reply.

The story of Leo and Moopheus would become the most successful online advocacy video in the history of the Internet. To date, it's been viewed over 20 million times and has been dubbed in more than forty languages. Bloggers made it one of the ten most discussed topics on the Web one week, and fans convinced CNN and NPR to run in-depth segments on the phenomenon. The movie ends with Moopheus offering the viewer the chance to "take the red pill" and find sustainable animal products. It led to hundreds of thousands of sustainable food guide downloads for our client.

By encoding our story with freaks, cheats, and familiars we had turned a fringe activist cause into a mainstream marketing legend. Today, almost a decade later, I finally understand how we did it. We followed our instincts into a new formula for stories based on ancient preferences of the human brain.

A New Definition of *Story*

Why do we need a new formula for stories that work? As we add the outer layer, the actual stories that grow out of our story strategy, why can't we just turn to the old model of character, conflict, and plot that most storytelling manuals teach? The answer is that the digitoral era is far more demanding than our recent broadcast past. Attention spans are shorter. Audiences are disaggregated and stories are told by multiple tellers. Competition is fiercer. And marketers' stories get battered and tested far more intensely. Either they inspire participation and evangelism by audiences or they wither. If we're not speaking directly to the most receptive nerve centers of our audience's brains, our messages might not get noticed at all on the overcrowded digitoral battlefield.

This is the challenge facing not only social purpose messages such as those in *The Meatrix,* but every story told in every imaginable media.

Consider the path taken by a typical story that goes viral these days. In 2010, the most watched video on *all* of YouTube was the *Bed Intruder* video. It attracted more than 50 million demanded views in less than a year. Advertisers spent billions on carefully crafted ads for the Web in 2010, and not one was as frequently requested and passed around as *Bed Intruder,* a story ripped from a local TV news broadcast, posted to YouTube, then remixed into a hip-hop song. In days past, the news clip would have instantly been forgotten, at best inadvertently captured on a few VHS tapes. In the digitoral era, it became the raw material for one of the dominant stories of the year.

Bed Intruder turns a real-life crime in a housing project into an unsettling, comic, hip-hop song available to everyone. And it's not the kind of thing a broadcast gatekeeper would ever have let pass. The tirade by Antoine Dodson, warning that his sister's would-be rapist was on the loose, is undeniably compelling, but also deeply disturbing to many who watch it: "He's climbing in your windows, he's snatching your people up, trying to rape 'em, so you all need to hide your kids, hide your wife, and hide your husband 'cause they're raping everybody out here." Dodson caught the attention of the makers of the Gregory Brothers, creators of *Auto-Tune the News*, who set the rant to music, distorted Dodson's voice to match the tune, and released the video through their own YouTube channel. As the song exploded into almost instant popularity, the Gregory Brothers and Dodson began to create new revenue streams from it. As an iTunes download, it hit number 3 for the year on the R&B charts and 25 overall. Dodson bought a house with the proceeds.

Ownership of the rant would pass from Dodson to the Gregory Brothers to hundreds of fans—further remixes and spoofs attracted millions more viewers. By spreading the word, posting the video themselves, and tweaking the content to appeal to their own social networks, literally millions of fans participated in the song's success. Clearly the makers of *Bed Intruder* had found a way to be interesting where millions of other attempts had failed.

Dig into the *Bed Intruder* story one level deeper, and we discover that ripping off and repurposing content, even extremely edgy content, is not just idle fun with the possibility for accidental, explosive results. It's a multimillion-dollar marketing strategy. *Auto-Tune the News* is part of a Goldman Sachs–funded venture called Next New Networks. Relying heavily on material from independent producers, spread virally and voluntarily by fans, NNN shows had attracted over 1 *billion* views by June 2010.

Bed Intruder is not an explicit marketing effort—though as we'll see, the lessons from its story of success can apply to brands and causes just as easily.

YouTube's most popular online commercial message in 2010 was *The Man Your Man Could Smell Like*—also a remix, respond, re-everything machine.

"Hello, ladies, look at your man," purrs a half-naked, impossibly handsome guy who is just about to step into the shower. "Now back to me. Now back at your man. Now back to me. Sadly, he isn't me, but if he stopped using ladies' scented body wash and switched to Old Spice, he could smell like he's me."

Compared with *Bed Intruder,* this ad more closely resembles a traditional broadcast spot, and once it established online breakthrough success, it did eventually run on TV. Its broadcast-worthiness, however, didn't prevent it from quickly falling into the hands of the crowd. In fact, it was designed to do just that.

Within twenty-four hours of its posting, delighted fans pushed the video out to almost 6 million of their friends. Riding the wave, Old Spice asked these fans to use Twitter to send in questions to which the ad's star would later respond in short video segments. This digitoral-genius strategy allowed the creators to grab the attention of wholly new networks by hitchhiking on the Twitter feeds of everyone from your college roommate to Twitter celebs like Ashton Kutcher and Jessica Biel, who, like the public, found the ad irresistibly interesting. Hundreds of spoofs were quickly made independently as well. Far from seeing this as copyright infringement, the creators sat back and watched the buzz build and sales of Old Spice Body Wash rise 107 percent in the first month of the campaign. The top ten spoofs of the campaign, unsolicited and unsupervised by the brand, brought in over 12 million views themselves. Together the ad makers and the community combined to build tremendous brand value for Old Spice before the marketers ever paid a dime to broadcast it.

Freaks, Cheats, and Familiars

Yes, these story triumphs took advantage of character, conflict, and plot—the traditionally understood elements of story. But how could we possibly reproduce the stunning successes of *The Meatrix, Bed Intruder,* and *The Man Your Man Could Smell Like* using only such general and conventional elements? John Powers would have demanded much more and so will your audiences.

To meet that demand, I propose we go back to our deepest roots, the earliest days of our oral tradition, exploring the commandment Be Interesting in a time machine. What we'll look for in our travels are clues to the resonance of *Bed Intruder* and *The Man Your Man Could Smell Like.* In the Basic Training at the end of this chapter, we'll explore practical ways to apply what's learned in planning your own breakthrough stories.

A side note before we begin: Our search here focuses on viral Internet video, which has become a dominant digitoral art form. But the lessons to be learned here are not limited to this medium— they form the basis of effective storytelling for all types of marketing in our post-broadcast age.

Let's begin our journey *way* back in time with a visit to Adam. This guy lived about seventy thousand years ago on the savannah of East Africa. If you're reading this book, Adam is in your family tree. We find his unique genetic marker passed on the Y chromosome from every father to every child born today.

Adam's social world is much simpler than ours, of course. His is not an interconnected world of 7 billion people. He knows of no more than a few hundred souls. He lives the life of a hunter-gatherer in a clan of about ninety extended family members. A small, flat social network dominates his experience.

There is general agreement among scientists that our brain structures have not evolved much since Adam's day in the sun. Here's how we know: Adam's lifetime coincided roughly with the moment that humans left the small territory in Africa they had long inhabited and began to disperse around the globe. At that time, ours was a relatively homogeneous gene pool. Today, that pool remains strikingly homogenous. Take any three humans from anywhere in the world and compare their genetic makeup. Despite variation in visible traits that seem overwhelmingly important to us, like skin color, height, or hairiness, you'll find less difference between these three humans than between three chimpanzees taken from the species' small territory in Africa. There's only one way to explain this continued similarity in the face of the widely varying environments we now inhabit: since Adam, we simply haven't changed much at all.

If our genetics haven't changed a lot, neither have the brains we're born with because our genes hold the blueprint for the brain's structure. We're still working with Adam's neural architecture. If we brought Adam back to the future in our time machine, provided we picked him up at birth, he'd grow up to fit in perfectly with us modern humans.

Having the same brain as Adam also means that, despite our totally different upbringings, we share many of the same ways of sensing the world around us. In his persuasive book *On the Origin of Stories,* which traces the rise of storytelling through an evolutionary lens, Brian Boyd explains that genetics deeply influence how certain types of information in our environment grab attention. An organism's world, or its search field, offers so much input that if the organism were to focus equally on every piece of sensory data offered to it, it would be totally overwhelmed, following an infinitely large number of search paths.

Evolution, writes evolutionary scholar Henry Plotkin, solves this problem by "gain[ing] knowledge of the world across countless generations of organisms, it conserves it selectively relative to criteria of need, and that collective knowledge is then held within the gene pool of species. Such collective knowledge is doled out to individuals, *who come into the world with innate ideas and predispositions to learn only certain things in specific ways.*" (italics mine)

In other words, whether you're hunting on the savannah or choosing between millions of videos on YouTube, your brain is programmed to ignore almost everything and home in only on what is most important or interesting. Otherwise you'd be pointing your spear at every tree and rock or, just as annoyingly, you'd be lost in an infinite trail of video links, hoping in vain to find something worthwhile. Fortunately, as we'll see, our genes are programmed to cut through almost all of the nonsense and direct our attention directly to nonsense we'll find interesting, like *The Man Your Man Could Smell Like*.

With an understanding of the discriminating nature of our genes, we can begin to construct the basis for stories that grab our attention and stay in our memory. This is a very different, but complementary, approach to building resonance based on myth structure. Where Powers's first commandment, Tell the Truth, is about deeply connecting with audience's values and identities, Be Interesting is all about getting noticed by them in the first place. In *Bed Intruder* and *The Man Your Man Could Smell Like,* I've chosen two case studies that isolate the power of Be Interesting from the resonance building of Tell the Truth. These are *not* empowerment stories that leverage the power of myth—far from it. They're pointless nonsense that still found a path to at least temporary breakthrough success. Because they lacked much truth, they aren't lasting iconic victories, but they are undeniably interesting.

But Adam's getting tired of all this theory. He's walking away. Let's follow him and see what he finds interesting. What's his mind scanning for in his search field? The answer is freaks, cheats, and familiars.

While we follow a few steps behind Adam, pull out your mobile device and watch *Bed Intruder* and *The Man Your Man Could Smell Like*. Ask yourself why these videos were such digitoral hits and jot down a few one-word explanations for the success of these pieces. Sure they're funny, but push your explanations to go deeper. We'll soon see that Adam's brain provides enormous insight into why your brain responded the way it did.

Freaks

Here we go. Something is catching Adam's eye—another human being. So much of Adam's brain is devoted to identifying other humans that within 170 milliseconds he realizes that the face he's spotted is not one that he recognizes and to Adam this is a major red flag.

The widely accepted *social intelligence hypothesis* tells us that the greatest evolutionary pressure for social animals comes from our need to interpret the identity, status, and intentions of other humans and to use the information we get to our best advantage. This is what nature has designed us to do.

The fact that the stranger is human makes her interesting. The fact that she breaks Adam's idea of a normal human puts her on the fast track through his brain to the front and center of his attention. Jerome Bruner, a giant in the field of cognitive psychology, says the very structure of our brains favors attention to the weird: "Our central nervous system seems to have evolved in a way that specializes our senses to deal differently with expected and with unexpected versions of the world . . . The more unexpected the information, the more processing time it is given."

In the largely anonymous landscape of our modern life, we have come to take unknown faces for granted. Our social intelligence is not always on red alert because the presence of strangers is no longer, in itself, a threat or opportunity. On the other hand, a stranger who looks unlike *any* other human we've ever seen will set off alarm bells and we have to force ourselves not to stare.

For Adam, this woman, though she may be average in her own tribe, is a *freak*. She does not fit into his definition of normal and that demands his focused attention as a matter of life and death.

The beginnings of Adam's encounter illustrate two things about Adam's brain. First, that nothing is as interesting to a human being as another human being. Second, one of the most interesting types of human beings is a *novel* human being—a freak.

So Adam's brain is scanning for clues about what to do. Most of his attention is on the strange woman's face, but then, he glances down at her body and notices that she's wearing a shell bead necklace. This is unusual too, and it triggers a memory of a story he's heard often around the campfire. What his brain finds interesting in the plane of reality, it also finds interesting in the plane of imagination. So the stories Adam tells and hears are full of all kinds of freaks—giants, pygmies, forces of nature in human form, and animals that can speak. He has heard a story about the Shell People too, a tribe that, in legend, once sheltered an ancestor of his.

It is no coincidence that Adam has heard this story. Stories, in fact, are designed for just this type of situation. Brian Boyd argues that one key function of storytelling is to make us more expert in social situations, to prepare us for an unusual encounter just like this one. Stories speed up our ability to understand and respond to complex scenarios. Of course, we've all experienced a novel moment just like Adam's in which we don't know the right way to act. Often we'll turn to a story we've heard, true or fictional, that provides us with a lesson—a moral—that we can apply and act on.

People love stories about people, especially people who instantly stand out from the crowd. The lesson here is that to grab attention, we must bring our ideas on everything from climate change solutions to better ballpoint pens out of the abstractions of facts and claims and into the realm of expectation-breaking characters. Audiences will pay attention because they want to see, or hear, what these freaks will do next.

Antoine Dodson of *Bed Intruder* and Isaiah Mustafa of *The Man Your Man Could Smell Like* are freaks. If you found either of these characters displayed in a single frame as a tiny thumbnail on a website, you'd be compelled to click. This alone is a major advantage provided to freaks in our quick search age. Dodson, with a handkerchief sloppily tied to his head, frizzy hair, scraggly beard, and sticklike arms poking through a tank top, is instantly worth our attention. Our brain wants to put him into the neat category of TV-news crime victim, but his head wagging and totally unconvincing expressions of menace defy all expectations of how a typical person might react to an intruder. We've never seen anybody behave this way in this situation. Spend a moment watching and listening to Antoine Dodson and you will never forget him. We are immediately drawn into the story of *Bed Intruder* because its star won't let us look away.

It's hard to look away from Isaiah Mustafa too. With his statue-worthy pectorals and resonant deep voice, Mustafa is one kind of freak marketers have always loved—the perfect-looking man. This catches our attention, but it's not until Mustafa breaks all expectations of the advertising sex symbol that we're riveted. With a shower running full blast in the background and Mustafa's opening lines, we recognize that Mustafa is going to be laughing with us at his own beauty. This ad is someone worth watching both for its star's physical perfection and, because unlike every other perfect man, he's willing to joke about it.

Our brain registers both of these characters as something new. Freaks inspire big emotion, whether it is fear, curiosity, attraction, or humorous delight. In these two examples, our social brain focuses in right away and we are laughing within a few seconds.

If, as you watched these films, you jotted down words like wild, bizarre, unforgettable, or drop-dead gorgeous, you were likely responding, in part, to the freaks on your screen.

Familiars

Back on the savannah, Adam is still considering the intriguing stranger he has just encountered. But now, remembering the legend of the Shell People, he lets his guard down a little, and rather than run to his tribe with an urgent warning, he decides that he will try to communicate.

He proceeds carefully. He wants to reach out but does not go through the elaborate greeting common among his tribe, which he knows the stranger will not understand. Instead, he smiles.

A smile is a universal human social sign, and Adam is not surprised that the woman understands and smiles back. She then puts her hand to her throat and gives a small cough as she frowns and moans slightly. Then she smiles again. Adam instantly understands, she's thirsty! But more importantly, he learns to his delight that they can communicate.

In this interaction, the strangers have found a way to remain as the most important things in each other's search fields by meeting each other on common ground. Had Adam gone through an elaborate greeting ritual specific to his own tribe or had the woman chosen to start jabbering in her own language, they might have frightened each other, or at the very least frustrated attempts to communicate.

Now Adam's social brain is engaging even more deeply. His attention had initially been grabbed because the woman was a *freak* but had she been so freakish that communication was impossible, his attention would have turned away from a positive interaction with her. Thanks to some simple communication markers, however, the woman has now taken on characteristics of a *familiar.*

If marketing guru Seth Godin had been in our time machine, he might want to remind us that our modern world can be seen as a return to tribalism in which people gather around shared interests. These tribes form strong bonds no matter how niche or geographically far flung they are. They also form networks of trust through recommendations and sharing of information they care about. This is essentially what a Facebook wall is or how a social bookmarking service like Digg works. These tools help tribes create a language of familiarity with each other that becomes their members' main sorting strategy, the best way to navigate the flood of information of the digitoral era.

As marketers, we are much like the thirsty stranger in Adam's story—we're not yet members of the tribe, but our success depends on communicating with it. If we're lucky, we'll be novel enough to capture a tribe member's attention. But to hold his attention and eventually have him bring us back to his kin, we must make ourselves instantly *familiar* by speaking a language that he can understand. We must meet him not where *we're* coming from but where *he's* already at.

People speak so many different languages of familiarity that in the broadcast era, marketers had to use a strategy that approximated Adam's smile, speaking a language universal enough that a very broadly defined demographic could respond to it. Today, as people have been empowered to choose what media they take in, the smile is no longer the only, or necessarily the best, strategy. Marketers can now encode messages to be familiar to a single specific tribe.

Doesn't speaking the language of one tribe exclude all others? Here we need to see how the tribe metaphor is imperfect. It would be hard to imagine a single individual seamlessly sharing membership in twenty literal tribes. But in the digitoral era, we can be foodies, underground Reggae fans, baseball enthusiasts, and political junkies all at once. As marketers, when we craft stories to resonate deeply with one tribe, we are more likely to turn that tribe's members into evangelists for our message. A targeted message will first be ushered through the tribe it was designed for, and then those tribe members will use it to reach out to other tribes in which they also claim membership. As a tribe member, I can—using the power of personal recommendation—share a great foodie story I've come across with my baseball tribe. In doing so, I am expressing my passion and also personally vouching for a message that will direct a hot-dog-scarfing Mets fan to the delights of fresh, sustainable food. In this way the encoding of *familiars* into a story doesn't so much limit a message's reach as provide a spark that can catapult it to success.

This strategy of building deep familiarity markers into a message is what I call *arming the choir*. Most of us resist the strategy.

We get so afraid of "preaching to the choir" that we forget that through the web of tribes they belong to, our choir members are our best conduits to the wider public. We fail to meet our audiences where they are and wind up meeting nobody. Adam's stranger deftly avoided the tempting strategy of shouting, "I'm thirsty!" in a foreign tongue. Marketers, on the other hand, often fall right into that trap.

Bed Intruder is a perfect example of how *familiars* form the second building block of an interesting story. By the time the Gregory Brothers discovered Dodson's news segment, it was already picking up viral steam, powered by its strong use of freaks (and, as we'll see in a moment, cheats). By inserting cameos of themselves into the story and introducing a hip-hop aesthetic, the Gregory Brothers helped the movie to meet several tribes on their own turf. The remixed version of *Bed Intruder* quickly became an inside joke to the millions of political humor fans who watch *Auto-Tune the News.* It also became familiar, and thus cool enough to share, to the fans of mainstream hip-hop, who recognized the piece as a parody of rapper T-Pain and his widely imitated auto-tune sound. Recognizing that this was a story designed for them, these tribes began to spread it among themselves and then quickly to other tribes of which they were members. Instead of relegating Antoine Dodson to a hip-hop or political parody niche, these familiarity markers lit up the brains of readymade evangelists, who turned the message's momentum into an avalanche. "This story is not just communicating," these fans said. "It's communicating with *us*. Let's spread it."

The Man Your Man Could Smell Like also owes its success to familiars but, as something closer to a broadcast piece, it is less laser-focused on specific tribes. Anyone can relate to how Adam drew a sense of delight from the fact that he and the stranger shared a common life experience and a way to express it. This is the same delight we get from a parody, in which we instantly recognize that its creators share a cultural reference point with us. A parody is an inside joke between strangers with whom we suddenly feel kinship. It's a powerful strategy for creating familiars.

Mustafa seems to be addressing "ladies" with the piece—"Hello ladies, look at your man . . . " In fact, he's addressing anyone exhausted by the overblown claims of consumer product advertising that for years have treated people like fools. *The Man Your Man Could Smell Like* is a perfectly executed parody of just such an ad. According to its creators: "We're not saying this body wash will make your man smell into a romantic millionaire jet fighter pilot, but we are insinuating it."

Mustafa constantly changes locations throughout the ad: "You're on a boat with the man your man could smell like. What's in your hand? Back at me. I have it. It's an oyster with two tickets to that thing you love. Look again. The tickets are now diamonds. Anything is possible when your man smells like Old Spice and not a lady."

Without the familiar, shared language of beauty product ads, Mustafa would still be a freak, but a creepy one. "Who *is* this guy and what is he trying to say?" we'd wonder. But Mustafa becomes a familiar freak, and a beloved one at that, when we realize we are both inside the same inside joke. We both know that Old Spice won't deliver any of these laughable features, but we could care less, we're too busy bonding.

By adopting the strategy of familiars, the makers of both of these pieces added a second brain-stimulating, attention-grabbing element to their stories. "Not only is this novel," our brain says, "I can relate to this."

Looking back at your notes, if you wrote down words like *hip, current, pop culture,* or *parody,* you may be responding to the familiars before you.

Cheats

Adam and—I can't resist—let's call her Eve, are now becoming comfortable with each other. Adam feels sympathy for Eve and hands over his antelope-skin canteen filled with fresh water.

Even before he lets go of the bag, though, he starts thinking about those beautiful shell beads. He can't help but wonder if this woman will give him one in return. His brain, in fact, is evolved to wonder.

Natural selection provides us with a tricky problem in explaining the development of social creatures. There is, no doubt, an advantage conferred on animals that hunt in a team. Packs or tribes that cooperate with each other are more likely to survive and pass on their genes. In order to hunt together, however, tribe members must all trust that they will share in the kill. This is where it gets complicated, because we'd expect that those who grab as much of the meat for themselves, excluding others, would get the most nutrition, becoming the most robust and fit to reproduce. So while evolution might favor a tribe that learns cooperation, evolution's favoritism for individual members who hoard or *cheat* should make cooperation impossible.

Natural selection has solved this problem by favoring tribes where elaborate emotions and social systems have evolved to punish cheaters, build trust, and allow cooperation to thrive—in other words, to build altruism. Uniquely armed with complex language, humans have mastered this art far better than any other animal.

One way that our brains have evolved to make altruism possible, with all the benefits of social behavior it provides, is by automatically paying close attention to situations where established norms are either being upheld or violated. We want to be sure that if we behave altruistically, our partner will too—otherwise we're evolutionary suckers.

Let's go back to the action to see how this plays out. Eve takes a long swig, then returns the antelope skin. She gives him a smile of gratitude. Now Eve bows her head, smiles again, and walks away. What, no gift in return? Wait, she's a *cheat*! Adam stares in disbelief as Eve strolls off into the distance, never to be seen again.

We'll never know why Eve didn't reciprocate. Perhaps she just happens to be antisocial or maybe in her tribe, the smile was adequate reciprocation. Eve's motivation is of no concern to Adam, though. He's simply angry.

This negative exchange will not just be an unpleasant memory for Adam, it will likely become the basis for a riveting story to share with his tribemates. He may even embellish it to provide extra suspense and drama, perhaps adding a satisfying punishment for Eve to provide resolution—as she walked away, he heard her singing to herself, pleased with the uneven exchange, and this attracted a hungry crocodile. Anthropologists believe that simple real-life events like this one formed the basis of embellished folk tales that have lasted for millennia.

Brian Boyd says such stories have been absolutely critical in human development. Before we had rigid power structures to enforce altruism—like police who arrested you if you didn't pay for your cab—we told stories that reinforced social expectations, and reassured us that those who don't meet them would be penalized. Some scholars go so far as to say that stories to reinforce altruism explain belief in God. Having a higher power to send cheats to the fiery depths is itself a story that reminds us that cheating is a bad strategy even when nobody's looking.

Adam will feel compelled to tell the story of the exchange with Eve. Just as the prior legend of the Shell People's gentleness prepared Adam for a productive encounter, the legend of their poor grasp of reciprocation will prepare future tribe members to be wary of any altruistic exchange.

Here's where Adam's story of indignation gives us a deeper understanding of the resonant stories than the old model of conflict between characters. Conflict doesn't need to be simply about good guys fighting bad guys or one character standing in the way of another's goals. The kind of conflict that really rivets us is the story of *cheats,* people who are in opposition to established norms of behavior. The story is resolved when they are either punished for their behavior or evade punishment, perhaps paving the way for new norms. If the social norms that are being cheated are norms we admire—kindness, reciprocity, creativity—the cheat becomes the villain. We hope to see her punished. Some familiar and timeless examples of this story include Sisyphus, destined to roll a rock up a hill for eternity because he was a poor host (he killed his guests); Ebenezer Scrooge, punished for his lack of generosity (though ultimately redeemed); and Icarus, who plunged to his death, a victim of his own disobedience to his father and his lack of humility before the gods.

In our modern society, where norms are constantly in question and often appear no longer functional, the mirror image of these stories has also emerged, and they're just as powerful. When the norms being resisted are ones we detest—soulless conformity, unjust hierarchy, abuse—the cheat becomes a rebel, and we listen to the story hoping she will overthrow these unjust norms. This formula explains the enduring nature of stories such as *The Wizard of Oz*, in which a young girl reveals the illusory power of a ruler; Robin Hood, in which social inequity is cunningly subverted; and *Pretty Woman*, in which social class constraints on marriage are torn down. Whether they be villains or rebels, in the digitoral age of short attention spans, homing right in on cheats lets us cut directly to the chase, attracting maximum audience attention.

The viral videos we're analyzing are no exception. *Bed Intruder* seems to be successful because those viewers who saw past its exploitation of tragedy found it hilarious. We've seen already that the video's freaks and familiars are major contributors to this. But what raises the emotional stakes and seals the deal is Dodson's totally unexpected reaction to a situation we find extremely compelling. Someone has just tried to assault Dodson's sister in her own bedroom. This is horrible. We are prepared to feel righteous indignation and anger toward the villain, a cheat who has violated a social norm we almost universally uphold—a woman's right to safety. In his comically absurd way, Dodson establishes himself as the sympathetic hero as he seeks justice: "You don't have to come and confess. We're lookin' for you. We gon' find you." It's a story we're programmed to be hooked by.

If Dodson were just yelling at his mom for forgetting to buy milk, he never would have been on the news in the first place. The news, in fact, is almost wholly focused on finding cheats and high-lighting their stories. It was the criminal cheat that made the story compelling and emotional and primed us to witness anger, indignation, and maybe even violence. Instead we get something totally different: Dodson's clownish rant. Millions burst out laughing and forwarded it to their friends.

The Man Your Man Could Smell Like is also funny because of a cheat—"your man." The central joke is that your man is using women's scented body wash. He smells like a lady! This creates an irresistibly amusing little morality tale in which someone who cheats a norm—men should smell like men—risks punishment in the form of losing his woman to someone who smells like he should. Just as Mustafa parodies the handsome pitchman, he perfectly parodies the classic tale of the hero who punishes the cheat, and we instantly respond to the joke. Without it, there's no story and no breakout success.

If you wrote words like *outrageous, uncomfortable,* or *conflict* as you watched these videos, you may have been responding to the *cheats* baked in.

So Adam didn't get what he wanted out of the exchange with Eve. But he did get the elements he needed to tell a great story, and so did we. *Freaks, cheats,* and *familiars* are indispensible tools—and now your tools—for building stories that work. The best thing about them is that they can be applied to any brand or cause. As *The Meatrix* taught me after months of frustration, these story markers can catapult even the most unpalatable information to resonant success when they hit just right. They're the best way to be interesting.

In the Basic Training that follows, we'll put freaks, cheats, and familiars to work alongside your story strategy. The exercises will walk you through a step-by-step process for creating three types of stories your brand needs to tell—*genesis, symbolic,* and *documentary.*

BASIC TRAINING

Generating Your Stories

It's time to start creating breakthrough stories. If you aim to build a complete brand epic, there are three types of stories you'll need to craft.

Genesis stories are about how your organization or company was founded. Of course, where and how your brand began may have nothing to do with where it is now. And the path between the two points may be so meandering and complex that it seems hardly worth recalling. But in the language of story, the information surrounding the birth of a character tells us nearly everything we need to know about who he is. And more grandly, the genesis myth of any religion contains the pattern through which the whole universe is birthed. Genesis stories matter. Get audiences to connect with and applaud your genesis story and you will gain their sympathy and support.

Symbolic stories use fictional characters, symbols, or contrived situations to illustrate a deeper truth. The audience knows that the characters on the screen or page are acting, but they don't care. As we've seen, literal truth is not the measure of a great story. What audiences really want is a chance to learn about how the world is ordered and how they can respond to it. Symbolic stories work—they are the basis of most ad campaigns from the Marlboro Man to *The Meatrix*.

Documentary stories show real-life events in service of a message. The most basic media savvy tells us that documentary stories can be as message-based and prescriptive to audiences as symbolic stories we create from scratch. In the era when everyone's got a camera in his pocket, audiences will expect you to tell real stories of your brand in action. Diverse efforts, everything from a Michael Moore movie to the Pepsi Challenge to Swift Boat Veterans for Truth, fall into this category.

In the broadcast era, brands would spend millions of dollars to deploy their communications, usually investing in one of these types of stories at a time. In the digitoral era, with radically increased audience sophistication and expectations and outreach costs approaching zero, brands must deftly tell all three story types. Deploy stories rich in freaks, cheats, and familiars, and you'll get the attention you deserve. Do all this with a consistent voice, driven by values and oriented around a compelling moral of the story, and you're on your way to winning the story wars. The step-by-step approach laid out here will help you on your way. Now, does a step-by-step approach suggest that you should create your stories in a purely mechanistic way? Of course not. Storytelling is a fundamentally artistic craft. There is no secret code. And these exercises will not write a story for you—the action is still firmly in your hands. Following these guidelines, however, will give you the maximum benefit of the insights in this book thus far, get you unstuck along the way and raise the likelihood of resonance and consistency in your messages.

Set the Stage

Step 1:
Choose Your Story Type

Start by deciding on the type of story you'd like to craft—genesis, symbolic, or documentary.

Step 2:
Cast Your Protagonist as a Familiar

In this Basic Training, we'll use the word *protagonist* to mean the star of the story you're about to create. I use the word to differentiate this character from your *brand hero*—the audience member you are trying to move to action. Most of the time, your stories can't star the actual people you are trying to influence. But your protagonist stands in as a character your brand hero can identify with and root for. To make that happen, your protagonist should have several markers of your brand hero's tribe. In other words, she should be a familiar. Here are some ways to do that.

- Your protagonist may declare that the world is broken in the same way your brand hero would: In the 1980s, Wendy's accomplished this sensationally when an old lady asked the question on the mind of everyone who ate at fast-food restaurants of declining quality—"Where's the beef?"

- Details of your protagonist's life should humanize her and allow your brand hero to imagine walking in her shoes: Studies show that donors are more likely to give to those in need when provided details that make it possible to relate to the recipients—what did he dream of being when he grew up? What was his life like before he fell on hard times? What popular culture interests such as music, food, or religious belief does he share with your hero?

- If we meet your story's protagonist at the beginning of her hero's journey, she may have the same reluctance and doubts your brand hero would. If, on the other hand, she is already on the other side of her hero's journey—that is, she is a hero herself—it should be clear that she was once an ordinary person: Audiences still revel in hearing about Steve Jobs's failures that punctuated his successes. They make us believe that despite our own failures, we can find such success too.

GENESIS STORIES

Your protagonist should be an individual or small group of individuals who set out, likely without a map or specific plan, to find a better way to do something. Genesis protagonists tend to be passionate, dogged, and risk-taking, but rarely are they superhuman. The more down-to-earth they seem, the more familiar they will feel to your audience.

SYMBOLIC STORIES

You have the opportunity to conjure your symbolic protagonist from thin air. Resist the temptation, however, of making your protagonist a stereotyped reflection of your brand hero. Instead, rely on the tips above to encode as many markers of the familiar as possible. Symbolic stories also give us the opportunity to parody deeply familiar elements of pop culture. Making your protagonist or her world familiar to audiences by referencing other well-known characters or situations is a powerful tool. It's not a replacement, however, for making that character relatable using the techniques described above.

DOCUMENTARY STORIES

As you show your brand in action in the real world, it's essential to show how it enhances the lives of individuals. Your job is to identify protagonists who are empowered through your brand. You're in control of who you put front and center. Take the time to find the personalities that will allow for maximum identification.

WRITE IT DOWN: What are some of the qualities, tastes and life experiences that make your protagonist(s) a familiar?

Step 3:
Cast Your Protagonist as a Freak

Next, you will add to the sketch of your protagonist by identifying what makes her not exactly what you'd expect.

Creating identification will push you in the direction of a protagonist who feels comfortable and recognizable to your hero. Now it's time to find the attributes that will grab attention by doing the opposite—breaking expectations.

GENESIS STORIES

Great genesis stories often feature unlikely, unusual, and boundary-breaking individuals who are naive enough to ask, "Why not?" Einstein was a patent-office worker who cracked some of science's greatest mysteries. The founders of Gap were just a frustrated couple who couldn't find a pair of jeans that fit right. Bill Gates was a teenage nerd with a dream.

SYMBOLIC AND DOCUMENTARY STORIES

Your story will be far more compelling if your protagonist surprises the audience. The freakishness of your protagonist might be internal—that is, her personality or social status may be a misfit for her situation. Characters with social status or a mindset that makes them unlikely heroes dominate folktales, religious stories, and compelling history. Cinderella was a lowly maid. Jesus was born in a manger. Both Bill Clinton and Ronald Reagan were raised in poor and broken homes.

Your protagonist's freakishness might also be external, something anyone can see on first glance: Beauty's beast hides a prince. Harry Potter, a child, saves the world. Forrest Gump teaches life's complex lessons.

WRITE IT DOWN: What makes your protagonist a freak?

Step 4:
Cast Your Protagonist as a Cheat

The most compelling protagonists assault cultural norms that are no longer working—and our time of myth gap is full of these broken norms.

GENESIS STORIES

The founding of a new brand or organization is, in many ways, an act of rebellion against the status quo. Your genesis story should not be a simple tale of filling a market niche or offering a new technical solution. If you can honestly cast your brand's beginning as a rebellious contribution to a more altruistic world, you will massively increase your resonance: America's founding fathers created a new nation in resistance to tyranny and privilege. The Nobel Prize–winning founder of the Grameen Bank, Muhammad Yunus, inspired a microfinance revolution when he decided that the entrenched charity model of development was failing the poor. Wikipedia founder Jimmy Wales created the world's largest knowledge base in resistance to a proprietary, elitist model of knowledge building.

SYMBOLIC AND DOCUMENTARY STORIES

We've explored who your protagonist *is*. What she *does* is to challenge norms that are no longer working. Your protagonist isn't just the recipient of your brand's largesse but an active participant in resisting a stifling or counterproductive element of society. Recall how breakthrough brands like Nike, Dove, VW, Apple, *The Story of Stuff*, the Tea Party, and Occupy Wall Street highlight real and fictional characters acting in energized opposition to their broken worlds.

WRITE IT DOWN: What broken societal norms is your protagonist challenging? What does she do to resist those norms?

Step 5:
Identify Your Nemesis

Here, a second character or set of characters will be identified—the nemesis who opposes your protagonist.

If your protagonist is a cheat, she will no doubt offend the powers that be. After all, a good cheat always threatens to topple the status quo. The forces that oppose her will become your story's nemeses. Not all brands or causes need to demonize the opposition, though clearly some do to great effect. Still, it's important to name the people, attitudes, or forces that stand in your protagonist's way; this will allow the stakes and drama of your genesis story to instantly rise.

If your brand or cause was founded in opposition to broken traditions, what were they and who represents them? The cheerleaders of business as usual? Stodgy competitors? Self-serving defenders of injustice? Apple named IBM and then Microsoft. VW named status-mongering car companies. Ben & Jerry's named phony "European" brands like Häagen Daz. The Tea Party and Occupy Wall Street directed unbridled anger by naming big government and corporations respectively.

WRITE IT DOWN: Name the characters or forces that stand in your protagonist's way.

Your stage is now set. The two most important characters have been identified, as has the conflict between them. Many more characters may appear along the way, but the backbone of your story is now laid out before you.

Orient to Your Unique Voice

Now you're ready to start putting your characters and conflict into action. But knowing the content of your story does not necessarily mean you've decided how you will tell it. In this step, we will make that decision.

Step 6:
Find Your Tone and Character

Determining the right voice here is key. Will you use humor? A strong sense of urgency? Aesthetic beauty? To make this decision, look to the archetype you've chosen for your brand mentor. Each archetype points to a particular storytelling tone. The Jester, for instance, is rarely earnest, while the Defender won't often be found cracking jokes. Storytelling consistency requires that you understand the dominant storytelling voice of your brand mentor and stick to it. It's not that the Defender never laughs, but if you're inclined to emphasize humor in every communication, it may be time to look for a new archetype to embody. The chart depicted in figure 7-1 plots the archetypes on two axes: playful to serious and inspirational to directive.

Playful archetypes tend to rely on humor, whimsy, and unexpected juxtaposition in their storytelling. They love irony and parody. Serious archetypes are more comfortable with a direct appeal that stirs simpler emotions like pride, optimism, and outrage. Directive archetypes are more prescriptive, ready to map out a clear path for those they mentor. Inspirational archetypes prefer to set their audiences in motion by empowering them to find their own journeys.

This chart, like the archetypes themselves, is only a guideline. There are examples of archetypes that break these rules in all kinds of classic stories. Your goal should not be to place your brand voice on this chart exactly where your archetype lies, but where you believe your brand authentically lives. You may also find clues to your voice suggested by your brand gift. A brand whose gift is joy, for instance, might modify its Captain archetype to be both authoritative but also

FIGURE 7-1

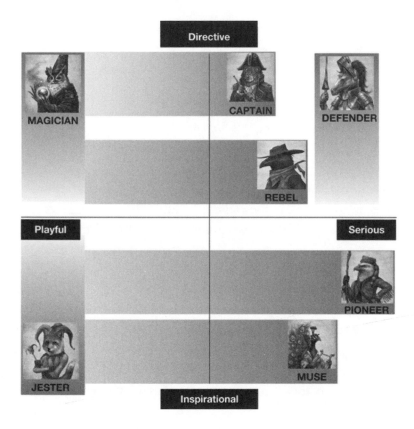

celebratory and optimistic. The voice you choose will remain at the core of all of your communications, so it must allow you to speak comfortably. If your voice places you on the opposite corner of the chart from where your archetype sits, you may ask yourself if your brand and archetype are truly a match.

Review your chosen archetype description in the chart in the appendix. Now think about how you plan to make that archetype uniquely yours.

WRITE IT DOWN: Note three to four adjectives that describe the specific voice you've chosen to take on. Words may include: nurturing, wacky, calming, knowledgeable, edgy, and so on.

Craft Your Story

Now you're ready to start writing, drawing, or storyboarding your story. It's best to quickly read the Trials that follow to know how your story will be tested. Then come back and start executing with Step 7.

Step 7:
Draft Your Story

You've got your heroes, your nemeses, your moral (from the previous Basic Training), and your voice. Whether you are writing a speech, designing a poster, shooting a viral video or a thirty-second ad, the artistic journey is now yours to take. When I begin my own writing journey, I like to study my inputs once (story strategy, protagonist sketch, etc.) then put them aside, knowing they are accessible without my conscious focus. Next, allowing the creative side of my mind to take over, I picture several landscapes or sets where my characters might dwell—I go right to the visual and physical. I then start imagining actions and dialogue within that space. Some of these spaces immediately dissolve—they're nonsense. Others become excellent sets for compelling stories. With the spaces that work, I write the outline of the action. Then I stop, check against my inputs to see if I am hitting on my strategic and tone commitments. Finally, I return, adding to the sequence of events and refining. This is, of course, only one of hundreds of processes writers use. The trick is to notice the processes that tend to work for you, name them, and repeat them. (For additional writing tips and interactive worksheets for generating stories, visit WinningtheStoryWars.com.)

Sketch out a concept for the story you plan to tell and, if appropriate, a rough script. You won't want to polish it to perfection at this point because your story faces trials ahead that may fundamentally reshape it.

Test Your Story

Once you have an idea laid out for your story, you'll want to test it. Are you using your story wars training to achieve consistency, or are you falling into the temptations of the broadcast era's five deadly sins?

THE TRIAL OF VANITY

SIN: Is your story all about how great your brand is?

SUCCESS: Or is it about how great your audience members can be?

THE TRIAL OF AUTHORITY

SIN: Are you relying on abstract data or technical expertise to make a connection? Are ideas the only stars of your story? Are you appealing only to your audience's rational side?

SUCCESS: Or have you created emotionally appealing characters whose actions and experiences reveal a deep truth about the world and make your facts more believable?

THE TRIAL OF INSINCERITY

SIN: Are you saying only what you think your brand hero wants to hear?

SUCCESS: Or are you expressing the moral of the story at the heart of your brand—an insight that resonates with audiences but pushes them to think in ways they may not have before?

THE TRIAL OF PUFFERY

SIN: Are you ordering your audiences to get moving using some detached "voice of God"?

SUCCESS: Or are you speaking in the unique and very human voice inspired by your brand mentor's archetype? Are you offering audiences your unique brand gift that makes action feel desirable and exciting?

THE TRIAL OF GIMMICKRY

SIN: Are you trying to make a quick emotional connection by putting all your eggs in the basket of nonsensical humor or high-intensity emotion?

SUCCESS: Or are you building emotional affinity around shared values—layering humor and emotional intensity on top of this solid foundation?

Step 8:
Refine

Where you are falling into sin, reorient toward success by refining your story. Keep your one-page story strategy by your side to check your work but use it loosely enough to empower, not limit, your imagination.

CHAPTER EIGHT

Live the Truth

Pushing past the journalists and shouting rabble outside his office, Tony Hayward begins to wonder if he has been silently transported to a perverse and personal hell. He appears to be in St. James Square on an average, overcast morning. He appears to be stepping into the same building he enters every weekday. This appears to be his life, except for one terrifying detail: every television, every phone, every mouth around him has been enlisted as an instrument of his torment, spewing an endless flow of angry questions—questions no reasonable person could possibly answer.

"Mr. Hayward, how long until the well will be capped?"

"Mr. Hayward, will this spill be worse than the *Valdez*?"

"Mr. Hayward, will BP declare bankruptcy?"

If becoming the most hated man in the world just meant death threats and stones thrown by protestors, he could handle it. But it's the questions that are beginning to drive him mad. He wishes he could simply ignore them. But he is condemned to give answers,

The final climb to authentic breakthrough: Live the Truth

knowing the only reward if he survives with his sanity intact will be one final question:

"Mr. Hayward, when will you resign?"

Bleak.

He gets off at the sixth floor and steps into a conference room, nervously eyeing the executives who have gathered there, half-expecting them to turn on him too. One of the attendees will later describe an icy stare coming from his boss's once open, boyish face.

"You're getting paranoid, Tony," he thinks to himself. "You know these people. This is your team."

He relaxes for a moment, and BP's embattled CEO allows himself the luxury of asking a question of his own.

"What the hell did we do to deserve this?"

Nobody dares to answer, but someone does scribble the question down and later will pass it off to a reporter. It is printed and reprinted millions of times over. In the months that follow, Tony Hayward, who runs what investigators would call the world's most reckless and aggressive oil company, will be asked hundreds of times how he could have asked such a stupid question.

In fact, Hayward's question wasn't nearly as stupid as it may appear. Instead, it offers an important insight into the psychology of a man and a company that had fallen victim to its own deceptive empowerment marketing strategy. By *telling the truth* about the dangers of humanity's dependence on oil and enlisting people to fight it, BP had risen to tremendous heights as *the* green energy brand. It had also set itself up for a tremendous fall—and not only because the 2010 *Deepwater Horizon* oil spill destroyed billions of dollars of green brand equity. Less appreciated, but perhaps more importantly, BP's false green brand likely played a significant role in *causing* the spill itself—blinding its executives to the outrageous liabilities in the firm's ultra-risky exploration strategy, making them believe that they were the "good guys," regardless of mountains of evidence to the contrary. The disaster makes a perfect cautionary tale for Power's third and final commandment, Live the Truth: "Stick to the truth, and that means rectifying whatever is wrong in the merchant's business. If the truth isn't tellable, fix it so it is."

Ignore these words at your peril.

In this final stage of our exploration of the story wars, we'll examine the absolute necessity—and some simple how-to's—of living out the values-based stories your brand tells. Authenticity, especially in our current age of transparency, is no longer optional. It belongs at the heart of your story strategy whether you're marketing a cause or a product.

Greenwash and Groupthink:
The Tragic Fall of *Beyond Petroleum*

By 1997, the audacious John Browne had fixed on the idea that he would create the world's largest oil company—by exploration, acquisition, and branding. The British Petroleum CEO believed, many thought insanely, that customers could be taught to identify with a brand of gasoline. Browne knew that if this feat could be pulled off, it would give him an enormous competitive advantage as he acquired smaller companies, supercharged their sales with his brand, and rolled them up into an empire.

The inspiration for an iconic oil brand first occurred to Browne while he was serving on the board of Intel. He had been deeply impressed that a company that manufactured an essentially invisible product—a microchip—could become one of the world's most recognizable brand names thanks to the clever "Intel Inside" campaign. "People don't ask whether BP is inside," he told *Harvard Business Review*. "Maybe someday they will."

But the irrepressible executive had a tremendous uphill climb ahead of him. The public was reporting that they hated oil companies, and pumped their gasoline only grudgingly. Since the 1989 *Exxon Valdez* disaster, anyone involved with the petroleum industry was seen as a villain. And with rising concern about climate change, the situation was only deteriorating. A major industry survey at the time found that motor fuels made up the absolute worst-performing category in terms of brand affinity.

Browne was ready to do something radical, and in 1997 he made an appearance at Stanford University, surrounded by solar panels, declaring that the evidence was irrefutable—there is a direct link between manmade greenhouse gases and climate change. Something must be done, now. Later that year, Browne dramatically withdrew British Petroleum from the Global Climate Coalition, an oil interest group devoted to questioning the science of climate change.

All this was worthy of tremendous international attention and acclaim. Browne had just reversed a major oil company's story strategy, rolling out new values (including Truth), new heroes (consumers who care), and a whole new moral of the story (we must work together to find alternatives). It was a tectonic shift in the story wars—an oil company no longer resisting, but joining, the fight against climate change.

By 2000, changes to British Petroleum's brand would be unmistakable and sweeping. The name was changed to BP and the new tagline, "Beyond Petroleum," would serve as the firm's de facto long-form name. The BP shield was replaced with a helios, a symbol of the sun that doubled as a flower. Browne would follow the rebrand with promises of multibillion-dollar investments in alternative energy and a pledge to cut his own company's emissions drastically.

The new look was all sunshine and optimism, and the ads that accompanied it followed a classic and hardhitting empowerment marketing approach—so not surprisingly, they worked spectacularly. BP was not asking audiences to believe they could consume their way out of the oil problem. That would have been seen as obvious greenwashing. Instead, BP's creative team at Ogilvy & Mather decided to tell a deeper truth. The ad campaigns would call on audiences to engage in a conversation and a partnership with the brand in making tough choices and ultimately in creating solutions. The messages were far from feel-good, but they were tremendously inspiring.

"It wasn't in the spirit of 'Don't worry your pretty little heads: We'll get you the oil that you need,'" recalled Ogilvy's North American chairman John Seifert of BP's "On the Street" campaign. These celebrated ads featured everyday people grappling with the tough problem of oil dependence.

The ads followed all the rules we've observed so far for empowerment marketing success. They stepped into the myth gap, offering a new story for a society realizing that old visions of progress and explanations of how to get there no longer made sense. And they emphasized the importance of honesty, calling people to think deeply and act selflessly.

"Think about your children," a woman in one ad snarls when asked what she would say to an oil executive. "They're breathing the air I'm breathing, that you're breathing, and it's bad . . . If you have alternatives, invest the money in alternatives. You'll still make money. It won't make you a Communist. It'll just make you a better human being."

Audiences and critics were wowed.

The new look and the authentic-seeming conversations that accompanied BP's image refresh would make Browne's vision of a lovable oil brand come true—beyond even his lofty dreams. BP quickly rocketed to number one in the motor fuels category for brand loyalty and soon launched out of that group to become one of the world's most beloved brands in *all* categories.

Browne himself would become the celebrated "green oilman," and even more dramatically he was dubbed "the Sun King" by the business press. As he worked feverishly to consolidate smaller companies into BP—buying Amoco and Arco in quick succession—the halo around BP's chief continued to expand. He had already been knighted in 1998 following his Stanford speech, and in 2001, he was appointed to the House of Lords with the title of Baron Browne of Madingley. The world was buying BP's version of the truth.

Investors were buying it too. A 2007 *BusinessWeek* article argued that the company's excellent risk rating, which was better than rival ExxonMobil's, could be traced to BP's commitment to alternative energy. This was an amazing coup, because over the previous five years BP had been slapped with 760 safety violations to ExxonMobil's *one*. The story BP was telling was just too good to be undermined by facts on the ground. But the facts had long been grim.

While dramatically telling the truth about the problems with fossil fuels, BP was living a lie—there was nothing "beyond petroleum" about the oil giant's operations. For years, Browne had been spending more on green advertising than on alternative energy research, and even his long-term multibillion-dollar commitment to clean energy was smaller than BP's single-year spend on oil exploration. By 2010 BP's investment in hydrogen, wind, solar, and biofuels amounted to just 6 percent of its overall capital expenditures.

In 2010, looking back on BP's operations, the *Wall Street Journal* would note that the company's business strategy had long been "predicated on being a leader at the industry's frontiers—drilling the world's deepest wells in the Gulf of Mexico, scouring for oil in the Arctic, squeezing natural gas from the rocks of Oman." Not exactly *beyond* petroleum. As the Baron travelled around the world receiving awards and accolades for his green commitments, he was also driving up profits by cutting costs—laying off thousands of employees, many of them engineers whose job it was to ensure that BP's aggressive projects wouldn't lead to disaster for workers and the environment.

The results of Browne's hard-driving approach would be dramatic and tragic—and until the ultimate disaster of the largest spill in American history, they would be amazingly hidden beneath the brand's feel-good image. In 2005, a fire at a BP refinery in Texas killed 15 workers and injured 170 others. The government would find that the deaths were no freak accident but the result of grossly negligent corporate behavior. BP would be slapped with the largest fine in OSHA history. In 2006, a ruptured BP pipeline spewed more than 200,000 gallons of crude oil onto the Alaska tundra—the worst onshore spill in Alaskan history. A congressional investigation found that negligence and cost-cutting played a major role in this fiasco too.

These disasters and the many hundreds of documented near-disasters made it clear to many BP employees that for Browne, caution and safety were simply not high priorities. He enthusiastically focused on only three things: aggressive oil exploration, cost-cutting, and green branding.

Even in light of damning government reports, internal investigations, and warnings from other oil companies of impending disaster, Browne would remain at the helm of BP. It was only in May 2007, after an embarrassing personal and legal scandal, that the Sun King stepped down and his protégé, Tony Hayward, a twenty-seven-year BP veteran, took over.

Hayward touted himself as a reformer. And he seemed to believe it. But after almost three decades and a long stint in Browne's inner circle, he was a company man through and through. While he talked confidently of BP's radical shift to a focus on safety, he was in reality deeply steeped in BP's tradition of say a lot, do a little.

One former BP safety engineer summed up the superficiality of the company's safety approach, saying that executives were "focused so heavily on the easy part of safety, holding the hand rails, spending hours discussing the merits of reverse parking and the dangers of not having a lid on a coffee cup, but were less enthusiastic about the hard stuff, investing in and maintaining their complex facilities." It's because, he said, when it comes to oil, "they just go after it with a ferocity that's mind-numbing and terrifying."

Hayward, like Browne, was all for safety when it was easy, but when it conflicted with maximum oil output, safety always seemed to take a back seat. That's why by 2010, under Hayward's regime, BP had become the world leader in "ultradeep" offshore drilling while remaining at the top of the list when it came to safety violations. All the while its website proudly proclaimed: "'Beyond petroleum' sums up our brand in the most succinct and focused way possible. It's both what we stand for and a practical description of what we do."

So it came as no surprise to industry observers and many BP employees that on April 20, 2010, a megadisaster finally occurred. The explosion of the *Deepwater Horizon* oil platform would kill eleven workers and release more than 5 million barrels of oil into the Gulf of Mexico over five months. The spill took just four days to surpass the scale of the infamous *Exxon Valdez*. Numerous investigations would place the blame for the explosion on BP's cutting of costs, inattention to safety, and overly aggressive attitude toward extracting oil from difficult-to-reach reserves.

So how could Hayward have asked, "What the hell did we do to deserve this?" He posed this question honestly, not for the sake of PR, but in the privacy of his own office. Here was a man with more access to the facts of BP's reckless behavior than perhaps anyone on Earth. He had presided over one of the world's most deceptive brands. He came in with a reformer's mandate, yet he had utterly failed to shift the company away from its reckless behavior.

In truth, Hayward was only the latest tragic figure to ask this apparently ridiculous question. It's one that has been posed, just as strangely, throughout history by misguided leaders who have isolated themselves within a reality of their own making, surrounding themselves with others who come to see the world just as they do—however distorted that vision may be. We can just as easily imagine John F. Kennedy asking this question of his advisors after the Bay of Pigs debacle, or Richard Nixon asking it after Watergate or George W. Bush after no WMDs were found in Iraq. The question must have rattled off the skyscrapers on Wall Street for months after insane lending practices began bringing legendary institutions to their knees. This phenomenon is called *groupthink,* and it tends to run rampant in organizations that refuse to *live the truth* proclaimed in the stories they tell.

Psychologist Irving Janis developed the groupthink model in the early 1970s, partly to explain how disastrous decisions like these so often get made by otherwise intelligent members of a decision-making group. When certain conditions are present, Janis discovered, groups quickly reach consensus decisions with amazing disregard for obvious warning signs that they are on the wrong track. Extremely cohesive groups, oriented around a strong leader, will ignore or punish dissenting opinions. Before long they stop being aware that dissent exists at all. At this point, the realities of the outside world start to become less important than the illusory reality created by the insiders themselves. Victims of groupthink tend to be overly optimistic that desired results will come their way and dangerously enthusiastic about risk-taking because they believe they cannot fail. What looks like evil or stupid behavior from the outside looks totally reasonable and justified when seen from within.

As John Browne rose to the zenith of his global esteem, groupthink descended upon BP's core leadership team like a thick fog. Red flags about safety concerns flew up everywhere in the form of external and internal investigations and even massive government fines. Browne and his men, including Hayward, optimistically responded with superficial fixes, believing these measures could address deeper safety issues while keeping oil flowing at maximum rates. Whistleblowers tried desperately to get executives to maintain safety equipment, and top talent resigned in protest when they did not. Executives consistently ignored such dissent. When Hayward took over, the leadership team spent countless hours discussing plans to reorient its approach to safety even as they increased the riskiness of the projects they undertook. From the inside, it all looked perfectly normal.

Why did BP's leaders fall so completely under the spell of groupthink? Blame it, in large part, on the success of Beyond Petroleum and Ogilvy's brilliant ad campaign.

Irving Janis identified eight key symptoms that both indicate the conditions of groupthink and cause defective decision making as a result. At the top of this list, just under symptom 1—illusions of invulnerability—he placed "Unquestioned belief in the morality of the group." A sense of moral rightness, Janis argued, blinds group members to the consequences of their actions. *Being* the good guys, it turns out, makes what you actually *do* seem irrelevant—even when what you do puts yourself and others at grave risk.

It is beyond question that Browne's inspired Beyond Petroleum campaign cast BP convincingly as global good guys. Customers believed it and they made BP the most highly rated gasoline brand. Investors believed it and gave the company implausibly high risk ratings. The Queen of England believed it. And most tragically, so did John Browne and Tony Hayward. Mesmerized by their own saintliness, BP's leaders felt free to engage in far riskier adventures than other, less-pious oil companies would ever dare attempt— remember that publicly reviled ExxonMobil earned only one safety violation in the time it took for BP to rack up 760.

BP's powerful empowerment marketing strategy created a valuable community of customers, but it also created an overly cohesive leadership team, blind to its own faults. Lives, livelihoods, and ecosystems would come crashing down as a result. So would one of the most valuable brand images of the twenty-first century. Hayward was shocked, and that's likely because he was just as fooled by Beyond Petroleum as anyone else.

While few of us have the power to generate profits or tragedy on the scale of BP, every marketer can learn from the oil giant's giant error. Creating a story strategy based on higher values that have little or nothing to do with the operational values of your brand puts you on a razor's edge. As the strategy begins to succeed, as so many empowerment marketing strategies do, the reality depicted in the stories you tell becomes more real to you than the realities of the world your brand actually inhabits. Convinced of its higher morality, your team becomes so enamored of the story, however untrue, that focus on the fundamentals of running a business wavers. Risks rise while thoughtful analysis falters. And one of the worst victims of greenwashing, surprisingly, becomes the greenwashed brand itself.

Pepsi's Reflop

The Pepsi Refresh Project is, as I write, the most successful social media marketing effort in history. But its success, much like BP's, hides the fact that it is built on blindness to the realities on the ground.

Refresh began when, in 2010, PepsiCo canceled its Super Bowl TV advertising in favor of a people-powered charity campaign. That year, the soft-drink maker offered $20 million in small grants to nonprofits—its customers would decide where that money would go. The campaign was built on the idea that people should have a chance to express their values and Pepsi would listen. Together the brand and its fans would partner to "Refresh Everything." It's hard to imagine a better example of moving audiences from consumer to citizen.

So did it work? Well, the campaign brought in 80 million votes in its launch year and 3.5 million Facebook fans. Pepsi was connecting to an enormous group of people who cared. And according to Pepsi research, a full third of the public now recognizes the campaign. But there was an insidious problem hidden behind these amazing numbers.

With an obesity epidemic emerging as the health crisis of the decade, soft drinks are beginning to look like petroleum did in the 1990s. People involved in the work of nonprofits are more likely than most to be aware of social concerns like this one. A *Wall Street Journal* article pointed out that many of the applicants and voters drawn in by the first season of the campaign don't drink soda at all—like Don Evans, who serves Vancouver's homeless. He's grateful for the $25,000 grant he won from Pepsi and said without it, his clients wouldn't have a place to keep their belongings. But he told the *Journal* he doesn't drink soda and has no plans to serve it. And not everyone is as gentle as Evans. Many Refresh voters aggressively objected to what they perceived as Pepsi's hypocrisy. So many negative comments were submitted in the "Health" and "Environment" categories that they had to be abandoned altogether in the campaign's second year. The soda maker said the conversation in these categories didn't reflect the "lighthearted nature" of the brand. Unfortunately for Pepsi, the business of refreshing society isn't always lighthearted fun.

Pepsi can rearrange the categories and stifle the commentary, but that won't erase the fact that the first year of the campaign was, in the words of one beverage industry analyst, "an absolute failure." In 2010, the year of PepsiCo's legendary social media triumph, the number of Pepsi cases sold dropped 4.8 percent. Even more embarrassingly, regular Pepsi fell behind Diet Coke in sales for the first time ever.

Pepsi may ultimately learn to iron out some of the Refresh Project's disconnect between marketing success and sales, but as long as it is unable to effectively and authentically integrate its products and services into its vision of refreshing the world, the marketing triumph will be illusory. And that's a big part of the reason why the single most successful social media campaign in history is in fact, to this point, a failure. Twenty million dollars in donations against billions in sales does not constitute living the truth. A much deeper connection between your values and actions is needed and demanded by your audiences.

———————————

As Pepsi or BP can tell you, stepping up with an empowerment marketing approach can be dangerous and complex.

Fortunately, we are not all doomed to repeat these mistakes. Your story strategy can drive you to actually live out the values at its core and the digitoral era has brought armies of potential allies who can help you do just that. They are the newest major force in the story wars—the *agents of authenticity*—and they are everywhere.

Agents of Authenticity: From Enemies to Allies

The agents of authenticity are lab technicians analyzing Barbie's packaging. What they're looking for is evidence of wood from Sumatran rainforests buried in the cardboard's DNA. When they find that the toy, so beloved by girls everywhere, is responsible for the deaths of baby tigers (also beloved by girls everywhere), they pass the information on to the Greenpeace media team. Greenpeace turns the revelation into a viral video story in which Ken hears Barbie's been trashing the planet and dumps her.

A few hundred thousand angry letters later, and Mattel, the world's largest toy maker, is trying to plead ignorance while simultaneously announcing a new packaging policy. News of the campaign will eventually go mainstream but not right away. That only happens after it's picked up from Greenpeace's own publishing platform, from YouTube, and from the local news channels that covered a handful of protestors outside corporate headquarters. Today's agents of authenticity are forensic experts and masters of social media.

Agents of authenticity appear in the form of undercover journalists from *Don't Panic* magazine come to offer a deal to the director of corporate partnerships at Conservation International. The journalists share CI's stated goal of environmental protection. But they've been looking at the nonprofit's partner list—Chevron, Monsanto, Shell, *BP*—and they've begun to wonder if CI is willing to partner with *any* corporation that offers it financial support. So they've set a trap, claiming to be marketing executives from the world's largest arms dealer—Lockheed Martin. They meet the CI rep at a restaurant and, with a hidden recorder running, make their pitch. The phony execs say Lockheed has taken a hit in the press as a result of the "collateral damage" their bombs are causing in Iraq. But all the negative attention is not fair—after all, they recycle in their offices and reuse old munitions from the battlefield to make new weapons.

"How involved would you be in helping us dampen and satisfy the needs that the hungry media has?" one of them asks.

"We'd be working as a team on it," the CI director responds. They set up a plan for Lockheed to adopt an endangered Middle Eastern vulture as a mascot. CI agrees to put together a communications plan for them. Will there be audits into the company's actual practices? No, that's not part of the partnership for which the arms dealers will write a hefty check.

CI claims the video made from this conversation is unfair. It misses some details, obscures the nuance. Still, it seems clear that a top-level CI employee values corporate partnership above actual corporate responsibility and that CI's seal of approval may be available to anyone willing to pay the fee.

Don't Panic's undercover video lit up thousands of environmental blogs and news sites and caused a major embarrassment for CI across its community of potential partners and supporters. The agents of authenticity are highly creative, and they're not afraid to take on their own nominal allies.

But most agents of authenticity aren't activists. They're parents using mobile apps like GoodGuide to get health information that can't be found on product labels. When one finds out her favorite brand of no-tears baby shampoo contains neurotoxins, she tweets, alerting her social network and the brand itself to the deep irony that an "ultragentle" product causes brain damage. One is a traveler who has been mistreated by the counter rep of an airline built on a story all about care for its customers. He has a personal publishing platform that reaches fifteen hundred people who deeply trust his opinion. For fifteen hundred travelers—and after his stinging posts go viral, 150,000—the next chapter brings an unexpected, and unwelcome, twist to the airline's story.

Agents of authenticity are donors who can now track where their dollars really go, voters who can find out where a candidate's dollars really come from, and customers who can talk to each other about their entire experience dealing with a brand. They're increasingly comfortable with Yelp, Twitter, Facebook "likes," and Amazon reviews. If they're under fifty, they're more likely to get their news online than through broadcast. More often than not, that online news contains a social layer, attaching the comments and recommendations of their friends to every piece of information they receive. The world of conversations that matter is becoming transparent, and the price of admission to that world is authenticity.

No matter how carefully you craft your story strategy, it is your audience, many of them agents of authenticity, who will write its most important chapters. To anyone who owns or manages a brand, including a personal brand, today's audiences appear to be far more frightening than the passive media consumers of the broadcast era. That is, they're frightening until you understand a simple truth: they don't hate you. In fact, chances are, if they're calling you to authenticity it's because they want to *love* you. They've connected with your core values. They've been inspired by your marketing. And they want nothing more than to see you live the truth you're telling.

Case in point: Greenpeace's real target in the Barbie campaign was Sinar Mas, the largely invisible paper-products company that is deforesting Sumatra. But companies like these can be difficult to influence: "The leadership of Sinar Mas doesn't care about a few folks around the globe calling them out," says Rolf Skar, a Greenpeace organizer who helped craft the Barbie campaign. "So we trace their products up to brands who have customers that do care. They have real brand liabilities. Mattel's not the most evil company in the world. But the values they're trying to communicate to consumers are in such blatant contrast to what's going on that it makes it pretty easy to tell a story about what they're doing and get people interested in acting."

Customers love Mattel's brand story of childhood fun and innocence and they want it to be true. When it turns out that the company's actions put this story in doubt, that information becomes worth sharing in the community of parents and kids who care about these products the most. Mattel has suddenly become a cheat and therefore storyworthy. Greenpeace knows this and though its campaigners will probably never love Mattel, they are counting on the desire of millions to love the brand and see it live its truth.

The *Don't Panic* journalists and all the environmental bloggers who picked up the sting story don't want to see Conservation International fail. They deeply want to see the giant NGO succeed in protecting the environment, the purpose it was founded to achieve. But when a brand like CI loses its way, the agents act.

Nike was never the only or worst offender in the use of sweatshops; it was just the brand that customers most wanted to love, thanks to its empowerment marketing successes. Human rights campaigners knew this and successfully made Nike synonymous with sweat labor. Their aim was to get the sneaker legend to live up to its story. Same with the successful viral campaign to get toxic chemicals out of Apple products. Customers want Apple to be as clean and revolutionary as the image presented in its stories. People *want* to love these brands. And if these brands live the truth, they will. If you plan to build an iconic brand around iconic stories, you should expect to face this same need for authenticity. This is just as true for a locally revered brand as it is for a brand that is iconic on a global stage. At any scale, people are passionate about the truth behind brands they love.

Even for those ready to live the truth, however, achieving authenticity is far from easy. Just look at Mattel. It was exposed for a hypocrisy buried deep in its supply chain. And liabilities like these can be hidden anywhere. Try to address your brand's missteps all at once and you'll quickly see you're on a fool's errand. So where to begin?

Building Your Authenticity Team

Here's yet another place where a well-defined story strategy proves to be an invaluable tool. Brands built on clearly expressed core values have declared the truth they plan to live. So they know where the agents of authenticity are likely to focus their scrutiny in their relentless search for hypocrisy. And they know where to start working toward living the truth.

The process begins by inviting the agents of authenticity to be your allies. Open your doors and let them say to your face what they'll be tweeting and blogging about anyway. The most effective way to do this is by building an authenticity team, starting with outsiders who embody each of your core brand values in their purest form.

If you've built a story strategy around uniqueness—the expression of personal gifts; creativity, and nonconformity—you may identify an influential educator who's pioneered new ways to bring out individual expression in students. This person may be a renowned university professor or someone working quietly in your neighborhood school. Either way, you're looking for someone who is unwavering in his commitment to uniqueness and extremely articulate about his belief in that value. On the other hand, if the justice value sits at the heart of your brand—living by high moral values, overthrowing tyranny—you may engage with an on-the-ground political organizer who has shown unusual courage in the pursuit of her cause.

The people you will seek are often NGO leaders, journalists, artists, and influential bloggers. You may even find them on Twitter, pointing out your authenticity gaps, cleverly disguised as the bane of your existence. These agents are likely not loyal to your organization but they are fiercely loyal to their own values. When approached with the request to help your brand live the values they so cherish, many will enthusiastically accept the challenge.

Allies can also be found closer to home. If you've chosen values that fit your organization's character, there will no doubt be people on your team who are already living and promoting these values. No matter where they fall on your organizational chart, these internal agents of authenticity can also be invited to join your authenticity team.

Identifying Opportunities to Live the Truth

The first work of the authenticity team is to figure out where opportunities to live the truth lie—and these opportunities should be both *reactive* and *proactive*. Take BP, for instance. Had its leadership team consistently made room in the decision-making process for internal or external agents of authenticity, the spell of groupthink that overtook them might have been broken. They would have been better equipped to identify the mismatch between their marketing and their operations and in doing so would have become aware of their greatest corporate liabilities—at a savings of countless billions of dollars.

The reactive work, then, is to examine your operations, partnerships, products, and services, looking for obvious betrayals of your core values. This process is a powerful focusing tool. Simply trying to make your organization a "better citizen" is a hopelessly broad mandate. Surgically removing instances of hypocrisy in the face of your declared values is a challenging but ultimately approachable task.

The identification of proactive opportunities to live the truth can be even more rewarding because your actions here provide true buzzworthiness to the stories your brand will tell. This process begins when you turn the relationship between your brand and its values on its head—instead of seeing values as vehicles to push your brand, think of your brand as a vehicle to promote values.

This is exactly what Blake Mycoskie did, making his company one of the hottest story-based brands of the last ten years. TOMS Shoes went almost overnight from a tiny startup to a major national player.

Mycoskie built the brand around his inspiring personal story that began with a trip to Argentina and an encounter with children who lacked even a single pair of shoes. Looking for a creative way to get this basic necessity to his new friends, he chose the not-so-obvious route of founding his own shoe company. He figured that if he donated a pair of shoes to someone in need for every pair he sold to a wealthy hipster, he could change the world. Today, it's impossible to encounter the TOMS brand without learning immediately about Mycoskie's values and story expressed in the One for One program. "I realized the importance of having a story today is what really separates companies," he told *Fast Company*. "People don't just wear our shoes, they tell our story."

By founding a company as a vehicle for his values, Mycoskie wrote an epic, still unfolding story in which not only he, but his customers, play the role of heroes. This is complete story wars success and it has made TOMS the subject of sustained viral buzz.

Not every brand has the luxury of actually being founded on serendipity and passion like TOMS, but storyworthiness can be manufactured by creating proactive opportunities to live your values. But be forewarned, this work will fail if it leads only to a generalized commitment to do good. Great stories come from a highly creative and focused commitment to bring your values to life.

Here's what success in this arena looks like: Patagonia translated its core values into operating principles, one of which is to influence other businesses to protect the environment. To live this commitment, Patagonia's leadership team focused in and got creative, launching 1% for the Planet, a separately branded program that commits businesses to donate 1 percent of revenues to environmental organizations. So far over a thousand brands have signed on, raising tens of millions of dollars for causes. Not satisfied to stop there, Patagonia seized an opportunity to mentor Walmart to get into the sustainable cotton and organics market. As a result, organic clothes began to get commoditized and Patagonia, in turn, came up with an even deeper way to live its truth and differentiate the story of its products. It started the Common Threads program, which takes back worn-out polyester clothes and recycles them into new premium apparel, reducing energy use by 75 percent. The brand is now rolling out a customer pledge that includes this commitment, previously unimaginable coming from a retailer: "We make useful gear that lasts a long time. You don't buy what you don't need." Once *this* revolutionary approach inspires other brands to commit to more sustainable practices, Patagonia will move on again. Each of these steps is designed specifically to link back to the company's core values, creating a consistent and clear story of the brand's evolution for Patagonia's millions of loyal customers.

Finding opportunities to proactively live your truth is quickly becoming mandatory because the effectiveness of bland, unspecific appeals to customer virtue is losing currency. This is likely a result of the bad name given to green marketing by brands like BP over the last decade. A survey by Underwriters Laboratories found that 95 percent of all green claims made in 2010 were guilty of one or more of the "seven sins of greenwashing" that the surveyors identified. Not surprisingly, nearly two-thirds of Americans no longer trust sustainability-related marketing claims. Green marketing is on its way to the exit, and authenticity-story-based marketing—declaring clear values that your audiences share and finding creative ways to manifest them in the real world—is poised to take its place.

Paul Hawken, one of today's most prescient sustainability visionaries, sees this as an epochal shift: "If there's any deficit we have right now, it's for meaning," he explained when I asked him about the future of marketing. "If green is your strategy, I wish you well. But if your marketing narrative is a way to reconstruct the social bonds that have been broken, it can create an ecosystem that gives people a sense of belonging to something larger." This is such a powerful approach, Hawken believes, that "eventually, you'll see green not marketed as green at all."

Proactively living your values is the only path beyond meaningless do-good marketing claims. And there are opportunities to proactively live the truth in the brand's relationships with all stakeholders—customers, employees, competitors and the communities in which you operate.

Collect the Stories of Your Journey

Perfect alignment of your organization's values and actions may be a destination you will never fully attain, but the moment you set out on that path, you begin generating compelling content perfectly aligned with your story strategy.

Sharing this content requires a strong stomach for transparency—announcing where you're going means admitting where you are. But take heart, the hero's journey always begins in an imperfect world with an unlikely hero. That's what makes your journey to authenticity a compelling story and not just another feel-good advertising campaign. Transparency turns your marketing into an honest conversation and makes your story worthy of buzz.

The first opportunity to tell a compelling story appears as soon as an authenticity team is created. Brands that create these teams invite unlikely outsiders into their inner sanctums. These outside leaders often make powerful starring characters in the stories you will tell. Like characters in myth, they are the embodiment of values—that's why they were chosen to begin with. And as unlikely guests within your tribe, they are *freaks,* demanding attention by defying expectations. By transparently documenting the explorations of the team, gathering stories of the conflicts and challenges that emerge and making these stories public, your journey to live the truth becomes a powerful marketing tool.

Of course, the members of your authenticity team won't stick around if they're just superficial mascots for your brand. To effectively tell your story, these team members must be allowed to speak in unfiltered terms about their experiences and challenges with your journey to authenticity. This total transparency can be difficult, and brands that feel the need to censor every communiqué from behind their walls will ultimately fail in their attempt to tell these stories.

Next, as you move from the design to implementation phase, story elements begin to materialize all around you. Documenting the ways in which your brand has become a vehicle to promote higher-level values makes your story believable and engaging.

NikeBetterWorld.com is an expertly executed example of a brand explaining its authenticity journey in terms that are perfectly aligned with its core values and story strategy. The brand, so famously built on the competitive pursuit of perfection through hard work and struggle, shows point by point how it lives its perfection value in the real world. It's designed a running shoe specifically for Native American feet to help that community fight diabetes through exercise. The N7 fund gives the shoes away for free. Nike is a founding partner of the Homeless World Cup, in which desperately poor but heroically determined people from around the world compete on the soccer pitch as a doorway to a better life. Its engineers have figured out a way to make professional soccer jerseys from plastic bottles, saving 13 million containers from landfills every year. And as Nike's competitive spirit has led it to sustainability leadership, it offers its patents to other companies to help them along on their journey. NikeBetterWorld stands in stark contrast to the vague social responsibility promises of many of its competitors. Noticeably absent on NikeBetterWorld, however, is a statement on the brand's commitment to fair labor practices. Several long-term campaigns continue to press Nike to leave its sweatshop past behind and until this happens, the company will remain in conflict with its clearly stated value of perfection—and it will continue to miss an obvious opportunity to live the truth.

If your authenticity team has generated actionable and tangible opportunities to more deeply live your truth—whether reactively or proactively—real people, creatures, and places will be positively impacted. The faces and narratives behind these impacts become the invaluable basis for documentary stories told across your communications platforms. Your story wars success depends on the constant collection and telling of these authentic stories of progress toward the goal of values deeply lived.

As these raw story materials begin coming in, your story strategy again becomes critical. What happens in the real world won't be compelling or useful in your marketing until you apply techniques that turn people, facts, and events into compelling stories. But you now have the strategies you need to do this. Your stories of authenticity will become powerful marketing tools when they are told in a way that aligns with your values and moral of the story; when they reflect the tone of your brand mentor, and when they emphasize freaks, cheats, and familiars. None of the true stories you will collect should be presented without your story strategy close at hand.

Telling the story of your journey to authenticity is, without a doubt, a creative challenge, but it is also a tremendous opportunity. If a tiny fraction of the billions of dollars and millions of hours that brands spend on meaningless, easily ignored advertising were diverted to this practice of storytelling, the media landscape would be far more crowded with meaningful stories and compelling brands. As it is, the opportunity for breakthrough is wide open, because only a select few brands and causes have learned to tell these stories well. This opportunity is now yours.

You've probably noticed that Powers's third commandment, Live the Truth, is the most demanding of all. It requires buy-in at all levels of the organization and especially from top leaders who don't usually see themselves as responsible for marketing. But in an age of transparency, the walls between those running an organization and those telling its stories are toppling quickly. Organizations that retain these walls will find themselves ill-equipped on the battlefield of the story wars. In organizations where these walls do come down, marketers have a chance to step into a starring role in the unfolding story of their brands and our culture at large. Perhaps it's an unlikely place for our profession to find itself. After all, we started life off pushing patent medicines, cigarettes, and cynical manipulation. But then again, aren't the heroes of our best stories always the least likely ones?

Epilogue

In 2007, my wife and I traveled to the Middle East. At the time, Chelsea was pregnant with our first child, and I often caught my mind drifting into the future. As we wandered through the land of Abraham, I kept returning to the thought that this child of ours might live to see the end of the twenty-first century, a time horizon I had never before considered. While our daughter Mira was, for the moment, so comfortingly close to us, I knew that she was destined to live in a world beyond our reach and even our imagination. The thought was both exhilarating and terrifying.

As we made our way through Israel and Jordan, where the stories of the ancient past are a constant and living companion to modern life, I realized that this anxious parental uncertainty about the future is not unique to my generation. Nuclear weapons, rapid technological innovation, and climate change are only our particularly modern agents of uncertainty. Our ancestors have left us with their own tales of deluges, migrations, and conflicts that made their future equally unknowable. I began to see these old stories through the eyes of an expectant parent from long ago. And I suddenly knew that we have always regarded our unborn children with a combined sense of wonder and fear. What world will rise to meet her? How can I prepare her for the unknown?

These questions can never be answered rationally, and that's one reason that stories are told in the first place. They provide just enough explanation and meaning to help us face, and even to dare to help design, the unknowable future our children will inhabit.

Toward the end of our trip, we spent the night at a camp in the Negev, where our host told us the desert's local legends—legends that have spread, in the form of Old Testament stories, across continents and millennia to shape so much of today's world.

The sun rose early the next morning, and while the camp slept, I scrambled up a small rise to look out over the landscape. I could see for miles but couldn't locate a single tree, shade spot, or source of water. The sun had only begun its ascent but I could tell it would be a hot, unforgiving day. I tried to imagine myself surviving here, clawing life from a land so reluctant to give it. The competition for the Negev's scarce resources would have been fierce. My life would have been a constant struggle against my neighbors and my god, either of whom could end my existence at any moment.

For the people of the Old Testament, living here would have been a struggle through scarcity almost unimaginable today for many of us. The stories they have left us with were crafted to provide explanation and meaning within that unforgiving desert reality. And these stories were indispensable, providing the rules for life that made survival possible and existence purposeful.

But their reality is not ours. Today, at least in the West, humanity faces the challenges not of scarcity but of overabundance—too many people, too many options, too much stuff, and too much waste. Where scarcity does exist, it is a failure of our own ethics and imagination. As Gandhi pointed out about our modern world: "The Earth provides enough to satisfy every man's need but not every man's greed."

No longer at the mercy of our gods and nature, we need new myths and new understandings of our old ones to guide us through this equally perilous landscape of abundance. If we do not, and consumption remains our highest purpose, we may find our future looks a lot like life in the ancient Negev. But we have the means to design the future we want; what's most needed are the stories that will engage millions of people to want to get there.

Within those ancient desert stories are words of immense wisdom that should not be—and probably never will be—forgotten. But if we cede the making of myth to that long-ago epoch, we also cede the most powerful tool we have to craft our destiny. Thanks to the technology we now have to spread stories and ideas, we can rewrite our stories on a time scale never before possible. The old desert stories took several thousand years to make their way around the globe. New stories can accomplish that feat in a single day. And while no single story or storyteller will singlehandedly deliver the new myths we need, a steady shift in our media landscape away from stories of blind consumerism to ones of engaged citizenship will allow us to lay the foundations of a far better future.

These were my emerging thoughts as I climbed down from that barren overlook and headed back toward the camp. As I got closer, I heard my host working in the tent kitchen and felt enormous appreciation for the hot tea and hearty breakfast I knew would be waiting for me. And I felt an equally enormous appreciation for the fact that I am a marketer—a modern mythmaker with the power to shape the future with new explanation, meaning, story, and ritual. I couldn't imagine a more meaningful life's work.

Jonah Sachs's

Story Strategy Map

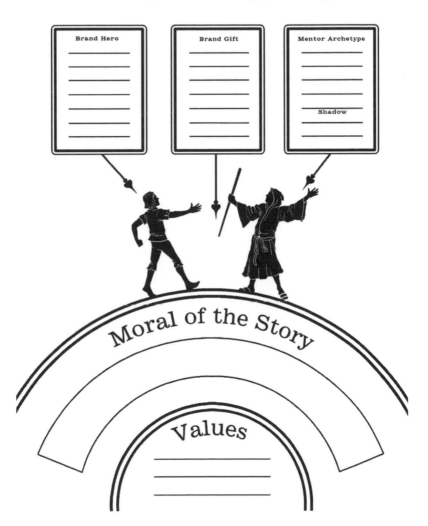

FURTHER READING

Atkin, Douglas. *The Culting of Brands: When Customers Become True Believers*. New York: Portfolio, 2004.

Bierlein, J. F. *Parallel Myths*. New York: Ballantine Books, 1994.

Campbell, Joseph. *The Hero with a Thousand Faces*. Princeton, NJ: Princeton University Press, 1968.

Campbell, Joseph, and Bill D. Moyers. *The Power of Myth*. New York: Doubleday, 1988.

Curtis, Adam (director). *The Century of the Self* (documentary film). London: BBC Four, 2002.

Fox, Stephen R. *The Mirror Makers: A History of American Advertising and Its Creators*. Champaign, IL: University of Illinois Press, 1997.

Goble, Frank G. *The Third Force: The Psychology of Abraham Maslow*. New York: Grossman, 1970.

Godin, Seth. 2005. *All Marketers Are Liars: The Power of Telling Authentic Stories in a Low-Trust World*. New York: Portfolio, 2005.

Heath, Chip, and Dan Heath. *Switch: How to Change Things When Change Is Hard*. New York: Broadway Books, 2010.

Holt, Douglas B. *How Brands Become Icons: The Principles of Cultural Branding*. Boston: Harvard Business School Press, 2004.

Kirsch, Jonathan. *Moses: A Life*. New York: Ballantine Books, 1998.

Mark, Margaret, and Carol S. Pearson. *The Hero and the Outlaw: Building Extraordinary Brands Through the Power of Archetypes*. New York: McGraw-Hill, 2001.

Ogilvy, David. *Ogilvy on Advertising*. New York: Crown, 1983.

Quinn, Daniel. *Ishmael*. New York: Bantam/Turner Book, 1995.

Reinsborough, Patrick, and Doyle Canning. *RE:Imagining Change: How to Use Story-Based Strategy to Win Campaigns, Build Movements, and Change the World*. Oakland, CA: PM Press, 2010.

Sivulka, Juliann. *Soap, Sex, and Cigarettes: A Cultural History of American Advertising*. Belmont, CA: Wadsworth Publishing Company, 1998.

Spector, Barry. *Madness at the Gates of the City: The Myth of American Innocence*. Berkeley, CA: Regent Press, 2010.

Steffy, Loren C. *Drowning in Oil: BP and the Reckless Pursuit of Profit*. New York: McGraw-Hill Professional, 2011.

Vincent, Laurence. *Legendary Brands: Unleashing the Power of Storytelling to Create a Winning Marketing Strategy*. Chicago: Dearborn Trade Publications, 2002.

NOTES

Chapter One

14. *Brad Jakeman, the former advertising chief:* Danielle Sacks, "The Future of Advertising," *Fast Company,* November 17, 2010; http://www.fastcompany.com/magazine/151/mayhem-on-madison-avenue.html?page=0%2C0.

14. *The average tenure for today's chief marketing officer:* Ibid.

16. *In 1990, for a handsome and predictable fee:* http://en.wikipedia.org/wiki/Cheers#Ratings.

17. *Ideas in the oral tradition:* Charles Darwin, *On the Origin of Species, 1859;* the whole of the quotation reads: "It is interesting to contemplate an entangled bank, clothed with many plants of many kinds, with birds singing on the bushes, with various insects flitting about, and with worms crawling through the damp earth, and to reflect that these elaborately constructed forms, so different from each other, and dependent on each other in so complex a manner, have all been produced by laws acting around us . . . Thus, from the war of nature, from famine and death, the most exalted object which we are capable of conceiving, namely, the production of the higher animals, directly follows. There is grandeur in this view of life, with its several powers, having been originally breathed into a few forms or into one; and that, whilst this planet has gone cycling on according to the fixed law of gravity, from so simple a beginning endless forms most beautiful and most wonderful have been, and are being, evolved."

17. *It's a useful concept in helping:* Richard Dawkins, *The Selfish Gene,* 30th anniversary ed. (New York: Oxford University Press, 2006).

21. *"Is that sulfur I smell?":* Glenn Beck, "Dangers of Environmental Extremism," October 18, 2010; http://www.foxnews.com/story/0,2933,601962,00.html.

22. *"I'm a brand":* "Brand it Like Beck," *Forbes.com,* June 4, 2009; http://video.forbes.com/fvn/celebrity-09/brand-it-like-beck.

26. *"If we decide to all look out for each other":* Author interview with Annie Leonard, September 2010.

27. *"One of these two positions will eventually win out":* Glenn Beck and Joe Kerry, *Glenn Beck's Common Sense: The Case Against an Out-of-Control Government, Inspired by Thomas Paine* (New York: Mercury Radio Arts/Threshold Editions, 2009), 65.

Chapter Two

37. *"And so there's a Republican narrative":* Francesca Polletta, *It Was Like a Fever: Storytelling in Protest and Politics* (Chicago: University of Chicago Press, 2006), vii.

41. *"that was naive on both of our parts":* Elizabeth Kolbert, "The Catastrophist," *The New Yorker,* June 29, 2009; http://www.newyorker.com/reporting/2009/06/29/090629fa_fact_kolbert.

43. *McDonald's suffered the deep ridicule:* http://consumerist.com/2007/03/top-10-worst-marketing-gaffes-flops-and-disasters.html.

44. *'Don't even bring up kids here':* Author interview with Nate Stanton, September 2010.

Chapter Three

55. *For weeks, he had been living off:* The account of Robert Oppenheimer's experience testing the atomic bomb is drawn largely from Richard Rhodes, *The Making of the Atomic Bomb* (New York: Simon & Schuster, 1995.)

58. *In the words of Isidor Rabi:* Rhodes, *The Making of the Atomic Bomb.*

58. *And Albert Einstein urgently warned:* Ibid.

59. *British anthropologist Bronislaw Malinowski said:* Frances Harwood, "Myth, Memory and the Oral Tradition: Cicero in the Trobriands," *American Anthropologist* 78, no. 4 (1976): 785.

59. *This sacred, imaginative realm:* Myth scholar J. F. Bierlein explains that myth "describes the reality beyond our five senses. It fills the gap between the images of the unconscious and the language of conscious logic."

59. *In fact, Joseph Campbell called myths:* "Lecture I.1.5, The Vitality of Myth," Joseph Campbell Foundation; http://www.jcf.org/new/index.php?categoryid=104&p9999_action=displaylecturedetails&p9999_svl=I15.

64. *Myth, he said, "is what is believed always":* Carl Jung, *Collected Works of Carl Jung, Vol. 5,* (New York: Pantheon Books, 1953), xxiv.

71. *moving the "Indians" away from the "fort":* Richard Slotkin, *Gunfighter Nation: Myth of the Frontier in the Twentieth Century* (New York: Maxwell MacMillan International, 1992), 3.

71. *launched modern environmentalism: Silent Spring and the Birth of the Modern Environmental Movement* (New York: Paley Center for the Media, 2009); http://www.paleycenter.org/away-we-go-green-silent-spring/.

72. *"People start pollution":* Martin V. Melosi, *Garbage in the Cities: Refuse, Reform and the Environment* (Pittsburgh: University of Pittsburgh Press, 2005), 226.

72. *seventy cans of trash are made upstream:* John Young and Aaron Sachs, "The Next Efficiency Revolution: Creating a Sustainable Materials Economy," Worldwatch Institute, 1994, 13.

76. *"what the American people think of capitalism":* http://news.yahoo.com/blogs/ticket/republicans-being-taught-talk-occupy-wall-street-133707949.html.

Chapter Four

80. *Not the kind of thing you can plan for:* Holly Matson, "In Poor Fashion? Kenneth Cole Missteps in its Spring Collection's Online Launch," *Bolin Marketing,* February 7, 2011; http://bolindigital.com/in-poor-fashion-kenneth-cole-missteps-in-its-spring-collection's-online-launch.

84. *1 million marketing messages in our lifetime:* Norman Herr, Internet resources to accompany *The Sourcebook for Teaching Science* (San Francisco: Jossey-Bass, 2008); http://www.csun.edu/science/health/docs/tv&health.html.

85. *all myths are about:* Joseph Campbell and Bill D. Moyers, *The Power of Myth* (New York: Doubleday, 1988), 41.

86. *participation at the polls consistently falling:* "National Voter Turnout in Federal Elections: 1960–2010," InfoPlease; http://www.infoplease.com/ipa/A0781453.html. See also http://elections.gmu.edu/Turnout_2010G.html.

86. *the child uninitiated by myth:* Campbell and Moyers, *The Power of Myth,* 152.

87. *"nothing is so completely at variance with human nature":* Sigmund Freud, *Civilization and its Discontents,* trans. and ed., James Strachey (New York: W.W. Norton, 1961), 58.

87. *"forging the greatest society ever":* Adam Curtis, *The Century of the Self,* (London: BBC Four, 2002).

88. *undifferentiated parts of a writhing mass:* Stephen R. Fox, *The Mirror Makers: A History of American Advertising and its Creators* (Chicago: University of Illinois Press, 1997), 98.

91. *"advertising by fear":* Fox, *The Mirror Makers,* 98.

93. *Lyndon Johnson's 1964 "Daisy" campaign spot:* "Top 100 Advertising Campaigns," AdAge.com; http://adage.com/century/campaigns.html.

96. *if everyone consumed like an American:* "Humanity Now Demanding 1.4 Earths," Global Footprint Network, November 30, 2009; http://www.footprintnetwork. org/it/index.php/blog/af/humanity_now_using_the_resources_of_1.4_planets/.

96. *indicators of individual happiness stayed flat:* Mark Anielski, *The Economics of Happiness: Building Genuine Wealth* (Gabriola Island, BC: New Society Publishers, 2007), 40–41.

97. *As Robert Kennedy said:* "Remarks of Robert F. Kennedy at the University of Kansas, March 18, 1968," John F. Kennedy Presidential Library and Museum; http://www.jfklibrary.org/Research/Ready-Reference/RFK-Speeches/Remarks-of-Robert-F-Kennedy-at-the-University-of-Kansas-March-18-1968.aspx.

97. *"The only myth that is going to be worth thinking about":* Campbell and Moyers, *The Power of Myth,* 41.

98. *People who emphasize extrinsic values:* Jon Alexander, Tom Crompton, Guy Shrubsole, "Think of Me as Evil?," Public Interest Research Centre and WWF-UK, 23–35.

Interlude

103. *John Powers paused:* The story of John Powers is taken largely from Stephen R. Fox, *The Mirror Makers: A History of American Advertising and its Creators* (Chicago: University of Illinois Press, 1997).

107. *Powers's three commandments:* Fox, *The Mirror Makers,* 28.

Chapter Five

114. *"It's not a coincidence":* http://www.huffingtonpost.com/arianna-huffington/companies-and-causes-soci_b_845657.html.

116. *a typical Cadillac ad from 1959:* Heon Stevenson, *American Automobile Advertising, 1930–1989: An Illustrated History* (Jefferson, NC: McFarland, 2008), 100.

117. *VW celebrated joyful modesty:* As the 1970s rolled around and the campaign aged, VW failed to heed the true lessons of its own success. Its marketers were too focused on the story's cover, instead of the core. They kept the off-beat approach but lost track of its positive values. By the time Zsa Zsa Gabor became the glamour-exuding spokeswoman for the new luxury Beetle, the automaker had entered a long period of cultural irrelevancy.

119. *Sigrid Sutter, quoting Keats:* "Dove's Campaign for Real Beauty," Media Awareness Network; http://www.media-awareness.ca/english/resources/educational/teachable_moments/campaignrealbeauty.cfm.

120. *mythic structure in movies:* Christopher Vogler, *The Writer's Journey: Mythic Structure for Writers,* 3rd ed. (Studio City, CA: Michael Wiese Productions, 2007), 30.

121. *"tools for those kinds of people":* Walter Isaacson, *Steve Jobs* (New York: Simon & Schuster, 2011).

122. *tearstains on the hundreds of messages:* Much of the material in this section is drawn from Ellen McGirt, "The Brand Called Obama—2008 Presidential Campaign—Barack Obama and Business/Fast Company," *Fast Company,* April 2008; http://www.fastcompany.com/magazine/124/the-brand-called-obama.html.

124. *raised over $500 million online alone:* http://voices.washingtonpost.com/44/2008/11/obama-raised-half-a-billion-on.html.

124. *"it won't resonate in the online world":* Ellen McGirt, "The Brand Called Obama—2008 Presidential Campaign—Barack Obama and Business/Fast Company," *Fast Company,* April 2008; http://www.fastcompany.com/magazine/124/the-brand-called-obama.html. See also Michael Grunwald, "How Obama Is Using the Science of Change," *Time,* April 2, 2009; http://www.time.com/time/printout/0,8816,1889153,00.html.

128. *"capable of something grander than war and prejudice and hatred":* "Overcoming Evil: An Interview with Abraham Maslow, Founder of Humanistic Psychology," *Psychology Today,* 1968.

128. *"a cripple psychology and a cripple philosophy":* Frank G. Goble, *The Third Force: The Psychology of Abraham Maslow* (New York: Grossman, 1968), 25.

129. *"a far goal toward which all men strive":* Goble, *The Third Force,* 110.

133. *society continually stimulates insecurity at the lower levels:* Ibid.

135. *the foundations for an empowerment marketing story strategy:* There is breakthrough value in Maslow's Hierarchy, but keep in mind that Maslow's model, like Freud's, is only a myth—a story about human nature that provides explanation and meaning. We may never find scientific proof that one is more literally true than the other. And Maslow's intense emphasis on individuality at the top of the pyramid shows limits to the universality of some of the needs he identified—not every culture, after all, strives toward individuality. As societies and the circumstances they find themselves in shift, so too do their highest ideals and their specific views of transcendence. There is nothing to be gained by taking Maslow's hierarchy as orthodoxy. Values have been added and removed from this list by countless psychologists, and I recommend you feel free to do the same. But if you choose to be

guided by this far more optimistic myth about humanity, you can create your strategy's center from a far wider range of values and take your first steps toward story wars success.

137. *"sharing our core values with our customers":* Author interview with Rick Ridgeway, June 2011.

138. *an ice cream empire out of nothing:* Information in this section comes from my personal conversations with founder Ben Cohen and from Ben Cohen and Jerry Greenfield, *Ben & Jerry's Double-Dip: How to Run a Values-Led Business and Make Money, Too* (New York: Simon & Schuster, 1998).

Chapter Six

145. *he slipped out of bed:* Much of the account of Moses's life comes Jonathan Kirsch, *Moses: A Life.* (New York: Ballantine Books, 1998).

146. *"something I always wanted to say":* Joseph Campbell and Bill D. Moyers, *The Power of Myth* (New York: Doubleday, 1988), 71.

150. *real heroes are more often pulled:* In some hero's journey stories, tragic events destroy our hero's old world and compel action of some sort. Even in these circumstances, the hero is constantly tempted with options to refuse the difficult path that leads to living out her values.

153. *"Mentors also strengthen the hero's mind":* Christopher Vogler, *The Writer's Journey: Mythic Structure for Writers,* 3rd ed. (Studio City, CA: Michael Wiese Productions, 2007), 120.

153. *an important lesson for marketers:* Because Exodus is such a foundational story of three of the world's major religions, a tremendous number of layers, meanings, and contradictions have been revealed within it. It is even believed to have three sources of authorship with completely different agendas. Especially befuddling, at times, is the relationship between Moses and God. Thanks to some particularly troubling passages, God may even appear to be Moses's nemesis—he tries to kill Moses without explanation as he begins his quest and intentionally hardens Pharaoh to every demand Moses makes. Yet, despite some of the complexities, the hero's journey pattern shines powerfully through this story. My short retelling of it is not meant to be exhaustive but to highlight the elements of this pattern.

155. *his character as a human being:* Statistics from http://www.freerepublic.com/focus/f-news/956032/posts.

156. *leads directly to markedly better financial performance:* Relying on Young & Rubicam's brand Asset Valuator, which surveyed over 120,000 respondents, the authors cited were able to determine whether audiences clearly associated each brand studied with an archetype or if they held a more muddled view. Looking at trends from 1993 to 1999, they found that the MVA (a measure of total market value) of brands that clearly stuck to a single archetype in people's minds rose 97 percent more than muddled brands over the same period. Margaret Mark and Carol S. Pearson, *The Hero and the Outlaw: Building Extraordinary Brands Through the Power of Archetypes* (New York: McGraw-Hill, 2001).

169. *a more in-depth view of your brand hero:* Basic Trainings seeks to simplify the process of creating a brand strategy so that it can be tried out in one or two sittings by a single person or small team. Of course in the bigger picture, there is still need for research, collaboration across the organization, and testing. Without this deeper work to validate and evolve your strategy, it will not likely be ready for the

real world. However, these simple steps, supported by research and testing, can form the basis of a lasting, breakthrough strategy. As the saying goes: "A minute to learn, a lifetime to master."

170. *the first elements of the personality:* My understanding of archetypes in branding has been deepened greatly by Mark's *The Hero and the Outlaw,* which will serve readers who wish to go deeper into this discussion. While some of the discussion is drawn from insights in this classic text, much material here is unique to the empowerment marketing model.

Chapter Seven

187. *sales of Old Spice Body Wash rise 107 percent:* David Griner, "Hey Old Spice Haters, Sales Are Up 107%," *AdWeek,* July 27, 2010; http://www.adweek.com/adfreak/hey-old-spice-haters-sales-are-107-12422.

188. *less difference between these three humans:* Brian Boyd, *On the Origin of Stories: Evolution, Cognition, and Fiction* (Cambridge, MA: Belknap Press of Harvard University Press, 2009), 21.

188. *An organism's world:* Boyd, *On the Origin of Stories,* 39.

189. *"innate ideas and predispositions to learn only certain things":* Boyd, *On the Origin of Stories,* 40.

190. *"The more unexpected the information":* Kendall F. Haven, *Story Proof: The Science Behind the Startling Power of Story* (Westport, CT: Libraries Unlimited, 2007), 51.

191. *more expert in social situations:* Boyd, *On the Origin of Stories,* 49.

193. *a return to tribalism: Ted Talks: Seth Godin on the Tribes We Lead,* filmed February 2009, posted May 2009; http://www.youtube.com/watch?v=uQGYr9bnktw&feature=player_embedded.

Chapter Eight

215. *"People don't ask whether BP is inside":* Steven E. Prokesch, "Unleashing the Power of Learning: An Interview with British Petroleum's John Browne," *Harvard Business Review,* September–October 1997.

218. *"squeezing natural gas from the rocks of Oman":* Guy Chazan, "BP's Worsening Spill Crisis Undermines CEO's Reforms," *Wall Street Journal,* May 3, 2010; http://online.wsj.com/article/SB10001424052748704093204575215981090535738.html.

219. *"a ferocity that's mind-numbing and terrifying":* Oberon Houston, "Oberon Houston: Beyond Petroleum—Events in the Gulf of Mexico Affect Us All Comment," *Conservative Home,* June 3, 2010; http://conservativehome.blogs.com/platform/2010/06/oberon-houston-.html.

220. *reasonable and justified when seen from within:* Irving L. Janis, *Groupthink: Psychological Studies from Policy Decisions and Fiascoes,* 2nd ed. (Boston: Houghton Mifflin, 1983), 174–197.

221. *A sense of moral rightness:* Ibid.

223. *no plans to serve it:* Valerie Bauerlein, "Pepsi Hits 'Refresh' on Donor Projects," *Wall Street Journal,* January 30, 2011; http://online.wsj.com/article/SB10001424052748704832704576114171399171138.html.

223. *"an absolute failure":* Ibid.

225. *with a hidden recorder running:* Chris Lang, "Conservation International: 'Are They Any More than a Green PR Company?' " *redd-monitor.org,* May 12, 2011; http://www.redd-monitor.org/2011/05/12/conservation-international-"are-they-any-more-than-a-green-pr-company"/.

227. *"pretty easy to tell a story":* Author interview with Rolf Skar, July 2011.

230. *"People don't just wear our shoes":* Ariel Schwartz, "Toms Shoes CEO Blake Mycoskie on Social Entrepreneurship, Telling Stories, and His New Book," *fastcompany.com,* September 6, 2011; http://www.fastcoexist.com/1678486/toms-shoes-ceo-blake-mycoskie-on-social-entrepreneurship-telling-stories-and-his-new-book.

231. *"seven sins of greenwashing":* Terrachoice, "The Sins of Greenwashing, Home and Family Edition, 2010: A Report on the Environmental Claims Made in the North American Consumer Market," 2010; http://sinsofgreenwashing.org/findings/greenwashing-report-2010/.

231. *"green not marketed as green at all":* Author interview with Paul Hawken, May 2011.

233. *a statement on the brand's commitment to fair labor practices:* www.nikebetterworld.com.

INDEX

ACKNOWLEDGMENTS

The path that led me to *Winning the Story Wars* began decades ago in elementary school, where I first met Louis Fox. Through his relentless insistence on creative play, I discovered my own calling to imagine new worlds and tell stories.

The idea to write a book documenting what I've learned since would never have occurred to me had it not been for the vision of three extraordinary women: Joy Tutela, my talented and relentless agent at the David Black agency; my business partner McArthur Krishna, who convinced me to take the time away from my work to write; and Ellen Neuborne, who first helped me craft my ideas into the outline of a coherent and compelling story. They are the heralds who called me to an adventure I tried repeatedly to refuse.

The process of actually writing the book spanned eighteen months, during which I was constantly reminded by my expert coach, Nan Satter, and my editor at Harvard Business Review Press, Jeff Kehoe, that I indeed could cross the finish line. Nan was steadfast that I not just talk about stories but tell them—and that probably saved the book. Jeff's enthusiasm for the material and belief in the project got me through times of deep doubt, and I will always be grateful for his support. During that time I relied heavily on my insightful research assistants, Kristina Kearns and Luke Thomas, with further research support from my sage elders, Nigel Hodge and Allan Sachs.

Many of the ideas in *Winning the Story Wars* are my interpretation of the wisdom of so many mentors. First and foremost is Annie Leonard, the most clear-minded and generous person I know. Paul Geduldig inspired me to work with the Moses story when I attended his hero's journey–themed Seder. My high school science teacher, Jonathan Heiles, first introduced me to the practice of storytelling as an art and gifted me many hours of fascinating tales. My understanding of cultural studies owes much to the brilliant Wesleyan University professors Richard Slotkin, Henry Abelove, and Joel Pfister. My love of stories was inherited from my father, Allan Sachs, an extremely talented teller of children's tales, who kept me endlessly entertained with the fantastic adventures of his youth, and my mother, Nancy Kantor-Hodge, who never let a day go by without reading to me.

For the artistry that brought my world of the story wars to life, I'll be forever in debt to Drew Beam and his magic ability to conceive of and paint anything.

There are dozens more people who sped me along my way and kept me on track when I wandered, and while I won't be able to thank all of them here, I'd like to acknowledge the generosity, feedback, and support of Leann Alameda, Eric Assadourian, Meredith and Dan Beam, Colin Beaven, Alexina Carr, Mary Corey, Ruben DeLuna, Dorothy Deng, Ari Derfel, Susan Sobel Finkelpearl, Jared Finkelstein, Margot Fraser, Susan Fredrickson, Jay Golden, Witch Harriet, Amy Hartzler, Annie Hughes, Ben Jackson, Steven Larsen, Linda Lawton, Elizabeth Lesser, John Lithgow, Marianne Manilov, Michael Margolis, Charles Melcher, Deb Nelson, Erica Priggen, Ellen Roche, Mark Rovner, Emily Sachs, Neil Sachs, Rolf Skar, Eric Smith, Nate Stanton, Russ and Nancy Suniewick, Barbara Talbott, and Mary Yeager.

Finally, I wish to thank my wife, Chelsea, whose love, faith, and encouragement have made not just this project, but everything, possible.

ABOUT THE AUTHOR

JONAH SACHS is an internationally recognized storyteller, designer, and entrepreneur. As the cofounder of Free Range Studios, Jonah has helped the representatives of hundreds of social brands and causes break through the media din with campaigns built on proven storytelling strategies. His work on legendary viral videos such as *The Meatrix* and *The Story of Stuff* series has brought key social issues to the attention of more than sixty million viewers. His interactive work has been honored with "Best Of" awards three times at the standard-setting South by Southwest Interactive Festival.

Jonah lives in Oakland, California, with his wife Chelsea, their daughter Mira, and son Orion.

ABOUT THE ILLUSTRATOR

DREW BEAM'S professional career started when, at the age of fourteen, he designed T-shirts for Apple's launch of the first Power-Book. After earning his BFA at Rhode Island School of Design (RISD), Drew built a successful career creating visuals and innovation strategies for dozens of *Fortune* 500 companies. Drew has been called a Renaissance man by clients and colleagues alike because he can often be found working on paintings, designs, or music; acting, directing videos, illustrating books, or doing brand consulting. His illustrations have been published by Time Warner Books, Penguin

Books, and *Rolling Stone* magazine, to name just a few. Today he serves as the Innovation Director at Free Range Studios.

Drew lives in San Francisco, California. When he's not working, he's sculpting, writing music, frolicking with his dog Stuart Donovan, mushing his cat Mothra, and giggling about life with Amy, his fiancée.